# THE
# GENERATION
# MYTH

# THE GENERATION MYTH

## WHY WHEN YOU'RE BORN MATTERS LESS THAN YOU THINK

# BOBBY DUFFY

BASIC BOOKS

New York

Basic Books
Hachette Book Group
1290 Avenue of the Americas, New York, NY 10104
www.basicbooks.com

Printed in the United States of America

First US Edition: October 2021

Published by Basic Books, an imprint of Perseus Books, LLC, a subsidiary of Hachette Book Group, Inc. The Basic Books name and logo is a trademark of the Hachette Book Group.

The Hachette Speakers Bureau provides a wide range of authors for speaking events. To find out more, go to www.hachettespeakersbureau.com or call (866) 376-6591.

The publisher is not responsible for websites (or their content) that are not owned by the publisher.

Print book interior design by Amy Quinn.

Library of Congress Cataloging-in-Publication Data
Names: Duffy, Bobby, author.
Title: The generation myth : why when you're born matters less than you think / Bobby Duffy.
Description: First edition. | New York, NY : Basic Books, [2021] | Includes bibliographical references and index.
Identifiers: LCCN 2021015650 | ISBN 9781541620315 (hardcover) | ISBN 9781541620308 (ebook)
Subjects: LCSH: Generations. | Knowledge, Sociology of. | Ignorance (Theory of knowledge)
Classification: LCC HM711 .D84 2021 | DDC 121—dc23
LC record available at https://lccn.loc.gov/2021015650

ISBNs: 9781541620315 (hardcover); 9781541620308 (ebook)

LSC-C

Printing 1, 2021

*For Jimmy, Birdie, Bobby, Mary, Jim, Anne, Jim,
Louise, Bridget, and Martha—four generations of my
family who will see two hundred years of history*

# CONTENTS

# THE QUESTION OF OUR GENERATION

We are teetering on the brink of a generational war. Wherever you look, generational betrayals and battles are poisoning relations between old and young. Older generations have stolen younger generations' future, while the young are killing traditions that older generations hold dear. Emerging generations of "social justice warriors" find themselves facing a "war on woke." Baby Boomers are selfish sociopaths, while Millennials are narcissistic snowflakes.

This, at least, is the endlessly repeated story. But is any of it true?

I began the research that would inspire this book with the intention of separating generational myths from the reality. We seem to intuitively grasp that this idea helps us understand something important about who we are and where we are headed; however, much of the discourse on the topic is based on stereotypes and lazy thinking, making it useless or dangerous. My argument is that although it is possible to learn something invaluable about ourselves by studying generational dynamics, we will not learn these lessons from a mixture of manufactured conflicts and tiresome clichés. Instead, we need to carefully unpack the forces that shape us as individuals and societies; the generation we were born into is merely one important part of the story, alongside the extraordinary influence of individual life cycles and the impact of historical events.

More systematic generational thinking, and the long-term perspective it encourages, will show that the real problem isn't warfare between generations but a growing separation between young and old. It will show us that the resentments people may have for other generations have more to do with growing economic, housing, and health inequalities. It will explain how and why our culture is changing, on key issues from race to gender identity. And it will help us understand how support for political parties is shifting and whether democracy is really dying. It can tell us a great deal about many of the biggest issues humanity faces, from climate change to mental health.

Ultimately, it will show that the social progress we've come to expect as an inevitable feature of new generations taking over is far from certain. It is the product of collective intergenerational will, a dedication to protecting the opportunities that mean the future can be better for our children and grandchildren—a future that looks increasingly under threat.

□ ■ □

The COVID-19 pandemic has only increased the urgency of this type of generational perspective, not least because the virus itself and the measures that have been introduced to control it have affected different generations in radically different ways.

Most obviously, the immediate health threat is hugely dependent on your age. If you were born at the start of the Second World War or earlier, there was a one in twenty chance you would die if you caught the virus. At the other end of the age spectrum, the probability of dying was vanishingly low, doubling with every eight years of age, a generational example of the gruesome exponential curves we've learned to dread during the pandemic.[1]

This massive disparity led to a spate of commentary fretting that the young would flout the measures to control the virus ("a generational war is brewing over coronavirus," claimed the *Wall Street Journal*).[2] For a brief moment, some called the virus a "Boomer remover," but the term was distasteful to all but a tiny minority and it quickly fizzled out.[3] What really surprised people was the level of solidarity between generations. The overall picture, across countries and age groups, was of incredible compliance with extraordinary measures imposed mainly to protect older generations.

This solidarity from younger generations came despite the fact that the economic and education consequences of the lockdown were clearly going to have a greater negative effect on them. In the UK, for example, young people are two and a half times as likely to work in sectors that were most affected by the social distancing measures, such as hospitality.[4] But much more than this direct impact, economists have also talked about the "scarring" these types of exceptional shocks leave on an economy, where progress can be lost for good, both for countries and individuals. Although we can't yet know what the scale of this loss will be, we can be sure that the young will suffer more than the old, because the wounds are deeper in the early stages of your life and career, and you live with the scars for longer.[5] This is an incredible misfortune for younger generations who have already been disproportionately affected by the 2008 financial crisis, previously considered our era-defining economic event. This enormous global recession had already stalled or reversed generational economic progress for young people in many Western countries.

A disease that disproportionately affects the old plus protective measures that disproportionately affect the young seem almost designed to fracture intergenerational ties. But we are surprised at the real outcome only because we have been so conditioned to view generations as opposed factions in a global culture war.

Take climate change, another issue of global concern. At the end of 2019, Greta Thunberg was named *Time* magazine's Person of the Year. Just sixteen years old, she was the youngest-ever recipient of the award. The magazine called her a "standard bearer in a generational battle, an avatar of youth activists across the globe." Her young peers, they suggested, looked to her example in their fights for everything from gun control in the United States to democratic representation in Hong Kong and greater economic equality in Chile.

*Time*'s recognition of Thunberg's achievements was certainly warranted, but is the suggestion that she is at the front line of a war between old and young correct? It is true that she triggers a lot of ire from a particular type of older (and mostly male) critics. There was Donald Trump, of course, with his suggestion that she needed to work on her "anger management problem." And the television personality Piers Morgan, who mocked her for claiming that her childhood had been stolen, while also crossing the Atlantic on a racing yacht. But, as we'll see, the data on how people really feel about climate change don't reflect a simple age-based battle. The demographics of climate campaigners, for example, stretch from one end of the life cycle to the other, from Thunberg and thousands of other young activists at one end, via Roger Hallam and Gail Bradbrook, the founders of Extinction Rebellion (aged forty-five and forty-eight), to the author and climate campaigner Bill McKibben (sixty), the former US vice president Al Gore (seventy-two), and David Attenborough (ninety-three).

Concerns about climate change, growing inequality, stalling economic progress, and polarizing politics relate to how *all generations* see the future. These issues are therefore fundamentally generational, because they are connected to our desire to see our children, and their children, do better than we did. Our confidence in generational progress was already failing before the pandemic, particularly in many Western economies, and this is a key reason people of all ages are more likely to question whether our economic and political systems are working.

Although no simplistic "war" rages between age groups, this sense of stalled progress and future threat is nonetheless stronger in young people. Age has become one of the most prominent political dividing lines in a number of countries, and it seems likely that the pandemic may accelerate these trends. Tumultuous times historically awaken generational awareness. One of the fathers of generational thinking, the Hungarian sociologist Karl Mannheim, outlined a compelling vision of why it matters, drawing on the upheaval of his own lifetime, in the first half of the twentieth century. For Mannheim, generations are not just a group of people born at the same time; they have a social identity formed by common, and often traumatic, experiences.[6] His insight was that major events have a stronger effect on those who come of age during them, because we tend to form our value systems and behaviors during late childhood and early adulthood. When generations are shaped by disparate contexts and life prospects, the connection between them becomes strained.

As Mannheim understood, periods of rapid technological and social change also increase both the importance and the difficulty of maintaining intergenerational connections. We need to be careful when assessing claims that our own times are changing more quickly than previous eras, as every generation tends to think the same, but the speed of adoption of and the reach achieved by some modern technologies have had a qualitatively different impact. While it took decades for the inventions of previous industrial revolutions to be widely adopted, the process took just thirteen years for the central technology of modern life: the smartphone.[7] According to the German sociologist Hartmut Rosa, a "circle of acceleration" has developed, where "technical acceleration tends to increase the pace of social change, which in turn unavoidably increases the experienced pace of life, which then induces an ongoing demand for technical acceleration in the hopes of saving time."[8] Regardless of whether our era is experiencing a "Great Acceleration," these technological changes contribute to a growing disconnection between age groups. Today's generations live increasingly separate lives in distinct physical and digital spaces, allowing deeper misperceptions and stereotypes to breed.

Faltering economic progress, threats that may prove existential for coming generations, and a pace of change that splinters the connection between young and old—each of these trends makes generational analysis vitally important in understanding our futures.

A generational perspective also encourages us to take a longer-term view. The ability to envisage a distant future and work toward it is one of the defining characteristics of humanity, but in evolutionary terms it is a relatively new skill. We are more often most concerned with the immediate, vaguely worried about the medium term, and entirely oblivious about the long term. This is an immense gamble in the face of existential threats like climate change, and it means that we often miss the opportunity to actively shape a better future.

However, the generational analysis in this book is not focused solely on these massive social, economic, and technological challenges. It will also help us to understand the evolution of our attitudes, beliefs, and behaviors across all aspects of life. For example, even apparently minor choices, such as whether to own and drive a car, have shifted significantly in recent decades. Is this because young people today have a different attitude toward fossil fuels, less money to spend, a more urban lifestyle, or because they are growing up more slowly? Understanding why these changes are emerging is necessary to help us plan for our likely futures.

My aim is not to prove that everything can be explained by generational differences or that they are always the most important divisions in society. Indeed, a significant part of this book is dedicated to debunking generational myths that distract us from the real trends. My goal is to find out whether and how societies are really changing, and what that might mean for the future.

## OUR LIVES IN LINES

Most people recognize that our current crop of generations runs from Generation Z, the youngest adult generation, to Millennials, Generation X, Baby Boomers, and, finally, the oldest living generation, those who were born before the end of the Second World War. Yet we don't necessarily know what these divisions actually mean. Our primary way of understanding generations, through superficial and poor-quality punditry, manufactures a multitude of generational differences. Although these fake differences may individually seem trivial and sometimes even funny, there are so many that they can infect the opinions and actions of even sensible sceptics. Assertions that all Millennials are either narcissistic, materialistic, or civic minded (depending on whom you listen to) don't help anyone. Each is part of a multimillion-dollar "generation industry" that encourages researchers to reduce vast swathes of the population to a handful of characteristics and behaviors.

Another equally unhelpful strand of generational thinking regards generations as repeated waves of archetypes that react predictably to the previous one. This long-term view of generations, developed by US authors William Strauss and Neil Howe, suggests every generation falls into one of four types—idealist, reactive, civic, and adaptive—that exhibit common characteristics. They claim that these generations have appeared in the same order throughout US history, in an eighty-year cycle of crisis and renewal, and that this in turn has driven the dominant social conditions in any era. Their account is fascinating and compelling, but it reinforces our assumptions of irreconcilable differences across generations, and it represents a dubious reading of history that's closer to astrology than academic study. Their generational analysis was embraced by the likes of Al Gore and the Republican strategist Steve Bannon (though to divergent political ends) and can feel prophetic now—not least because they predicted that an era of crisis would engulf the mid-2000s to the mid-2020s. It would be foolhardy to bet that the COVID-19 era we are living through will not later be regarded as a historically recognizable crisis. But the fact that the pandemic was instigated by a novel coronavirus that originated in the Wuhan district of China only highlights the absurdity of claiming that this crisis is the result of a particular constellation of generational types and the four-generation cycle of catastrophe that Strauss and Howe claimed to have identified.

We have simultaneously gone in two bad directions. One strand of thinking, inspired by Strauss and Howe, zooms out by a million miles and assures us that generations fall into a repeating cycle of types before offering something that resembles a horoscope. The other approach claims that frothy, exaggerated differences in generational characteristics are in fact real, shifting tides.

In contrast, true generational thinking can be a powerful tool that helps us understand the changes and challenges of our day. This starts by recognizing an underappreciated fact: there are just three explanations for how *all* attitudes, beliefs, and behaviors change over time—period, life-cycle, and cohort effects. By studying how these three effects individually and collectively shape us, we can develop a powerful new understanding of how and why societies are changing, and a much greater ability to predict what comes next on the biggest issues of our times.

**Period effects:** The attitudes, beliefs, and behaviors of a society can change in a consistent way across all age groups. These period effects often occur in response to a major event that affects everyone, whether directly or indirectly,

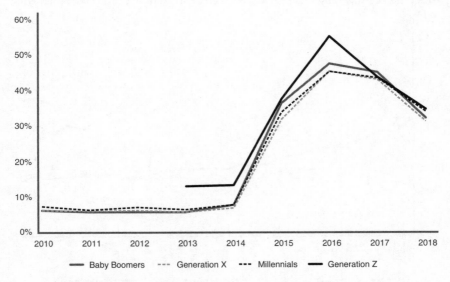

Figure 0.1: Percentage of French adults who say terrorism is one of the most worrying issues in their country. Source: Ipsos, What Worries the World survey. Around one thousand interviews per month (2010–2018).

like a pandemic, war, or economic crisis, and they often look like the pattern we see in Figure 0.1. This example measures concern about terrorism in France. Few people in any generation were worried about terrorism before 2015 and 2016, when there was a severe spike in concern following a series of attacks in which more than two hundred people were killed. Every generation of adults surveyed responded to this series of tragic events in the same way.

**Life-cycle effects:** People also change as they age or as a result of major life events such as leaving home, having children, or retiring. Figure 0.2 tracks the proportion of each generation in England classified as being a "healthy weight" as they get older. You can follow your own generational line and see that, on average, people get fatter as they get older (as I'm all too aware). Each generation slowly drifts downward, a result of too many calories and not enough exercise for their falling metabolism until, in middle age, only around a quarter of people are still at a healthy weight.

**Cohort effects:** A generation can also have different attitudes, beliefs, and behaviors because they were socialized in different conditions from those of other generations, and thus they remain distinct from other cohorts even as they age. Figure 0.3 shows the proportion of US adults who say they attend a religious service at least weekly. The oldest generation are much more likely to attend regular religious service, with clear steps down, until we reach what

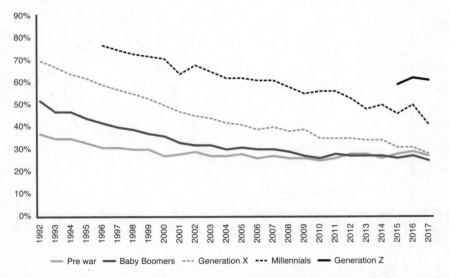

Figure 0.2: Percentage of adults with a healthy weight in England. Source: Health Survey for England (1992–2017).

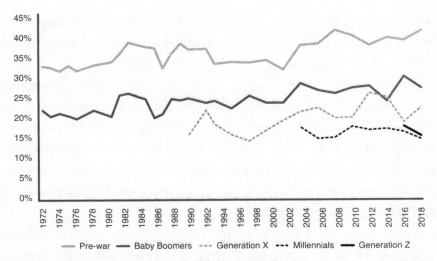

Figure 0.3: Percentage of adults in United States attending religious services at least weekly. Source: US General Social Survey (1974–2018).

looks like rock bottom with Millennials and Gen Z. And this pattern of generational gaps has not changed much, all the way back to 1975, showing how important when you were born is in shaping your relationship with religion.

Every change we see in societal attitudes, beliefs, and behaviors can be explained by one or, more often, a combination of these three effects. And here we can state more precisely the basic problem with the generational "analysis" in most commentary: explaining all of a person's attitudes and behaviors according to when they were born relies solely on identifying cohort effects—and misses out on two-thirds of our understanding of societal change. This approach is far more compelling and useful than the sensationalist claims that often pass as generational thinking. Once you realize that *all* societal change is explained by a combination of these three effects, you have a framework for a deeper understanding of where we are now and what is likely to come next. You may find yourself asking "is this a cohort, period, or life-cycle effect?" about any societal change—and that simple question will help you identify what's really important.

Throughout the book, we'll identify similar trends by looking at charts like these using "synthetic cohort analysis." It has a fancy-sounding name, but it is entirely intuitive. All we do is define groups according to when they were born and track their average progress as they get older. Of course, most of the patterns we'll see are not as clear-cut as in the examples above, and it is not possible to entirely separate the three effects in any case.[9] They nearly always interact, but understanding that interaction is incredibly valuable in itself.

To examine how we are changing, I have analyzed some of the biggest surveys conducted in the world over the past fifty years. I've assembled a data set of more than three million interviews from these surveys, linked to help separate the myths of generational difference from the reality. This allows us to get closer to the underlying changes occurring in societies around the world. I've also drawn on a series of new survey questions specially commissioned through the global research firm Ipsos.

Before we dig in, we must recognize some of the common misperceptions that get in the way of identifying actual change. In particular, we are often fed analysis that confuses age with generation and stereotypes both the old and the young.

## OUR GENERATIONAL DELUSIONS

Older people have always had a problem with the young. According to the Cambridge scholar Kenneth John Freeman, Socrates indicted young people for a whole host of things, including their

> luxury, bad manners, contempt for authority, disrespect for elders and a love for chatter in place of exercise. . . . Children began to be the tyrants, not the slaves of their households. They no longer rose from their seats when an elder entered the room; they contradicted their parents, chattered before company, gobbled up the dainties at table and committed various offences against Hellenic tastes, such as crossing their legs.[10]

Bizarre complaints about the young didn't start or stop in ancient Greece. In 1624 Thomas Barnes, a minister at a London church, complained that "the youth were never so sawcie, yea never more savagely sawcie." In 1771, nearly 250 years before "snowflake" became an attack on the young, a reader's letter to *Town and Country* magazine moaned that youth were "a race of effeminate, self-admiring, emaciated fribbles." And in 1843, the seventh Earl of Shaftesbury lamented in the House of Commons that "young ladies" in the market town of Bilston had taken to "drive coal-carts, ride astride upon horses, drink, swear, fight, smoke, whistle, sing, and care for nobody."[11] Nineteenth-century Bilston sounds like an amazing place for a night out.

Young people have also always been seen as being susceptible to the latest fads and fashions, willing to discard traditional values in favor of dangerous new entertainments and technologies. In 1906—nearly a century before violent video games—the *Dawson Daily News* in Yukon, in the northwest of Canada roared, "BOYS ARE RUINED. Dime Novels Cause Lads to Murder."[12] Going back a little further to 1859, an article in *Scientific American* warned that the new craze for *chess* caused "pernicious excitement" among children of a "very inferior temperament."[13]

These repeated waves of moral panic provide a historical context to apocryphal fears about how Millennials' habits are supposedly "killing" everything from wine corks to wedding rings and the Olympics to serendipity.[14] In just a few short years, Millennial-bashing became an established cliché to be mocked in satirical social media posts; @NewCallieAnn tweeted, "I cut my finger slicing open an avocado and now I can't fix my topknot."[15]

Our relentless criticism of Millennials, and increasingly Gen Z too, is a result of a set of human biases that have nothing to do with the essential character of these generations. Generally, people think the past was better than it really was because they forget the bad bits—in these cases, the dodgy behavior of their own youth. We call this bias "rosy retrospection." We also struggle to keep pace with how social norms change over time, and older people look at the young through the frame of the values that held sway when they were young themselves. Societal values, beliefs, and attitudes shift over time, but our individual ideas of what is right or acceptable are "sticky," which makes emerging attitudes and behaviors seem strange and unsettling.

Older generations fare no better than younger ones in the public imagination. Psychologists have found that many Western cultures categorize older people according to seven basic stereotypes, more than half of which are negative: "curmudgeon/shrew," "severely impaired," "despondent," "recluse," "perfect grandparent," "golden ager," and "John Wayne conservative."[16] In entertainment or advertisements, older people are almost always depicted this way, whether they are skydiving silver foxes or frail, frightened grannies holding on tightly to their stair lifts as they slowly head to bed at 8 p.m. And that's when they appear at all—people over sixty are hugely underrepresented in the media, compared with their large share of the world's population and their even greater share of its wealth.

You would think that smart ad executives would have caught on to the shifting demographics a long time ago, given the number of news analysis pieces that have been written on the subject. In fact, one *Time* cover story noted that some ad agencies were setting up special units to study and reflect older adults as a growing consumer force: "There was a time when advertisers behaved as though no one past middle age ever bought anything more durable than panty hose. No more."[17] That story ran in 1988—thirty-three years ago—yet surprisingly little has changed since then. The former CEO of a major retailer recently confessed that his company had twelve customer segments for people under fifty-five but lumped everyone older into one segment.[18]

The main generation of older people today, the Baby Boomers, are also subject to attacks. "OK, Boomer," Gen Z's sarcastic collective eye roll, has taken a firm hold and was even used as a put-down by one young MP during a debate about climate change in the New Zealand parliament.[19] Boomers may not get quite as much opprobrium as Millennials, but what they do receive is weighty. Forget the examples of products and traditions that Millennials have supposedly killed off; there are frequent claims that Baby Boomers have ruined *everything*.[20] A modern test of what people really think of you is to type your name into Google and see what autocompletes. Boomers don't come out well; they are "the problem," "selfish," "self-centered," and "the worst generation."

Between today's young and old generations is Generation X. This is where I fit in—and yes, I recognize the irony that my obsession with generations is in stark contrast with the scant attention paid my own. As one fellow Gen Xer tweeted, "I am neither a millennial nor a boomer. I come from a generation so irrelevant that people can't even be bothered to hate us."[21]

It all started so well. My generation got its name from Douglas Coupland's hip 1991 novel *Generation X*, which followed the supposed "slacker" lifestyle of the twentysomethings of the day. Coupland took his title from a 1990 book on the American class system by the cultural critic Paul Fussell. As he dissected layer after layer of class—from "top out-of-sight" to "mid-proletarian" to "bottom out-of-sight"—Fussell described how some young people were

trying to free themselves entirely from this rigid system: "Impelled by inso-
lence, intelligence, irony and spirit, X people have escaped out the back doors
of those theaters of class which enclose others."[22] Insolent, intelligent, ironic,
and spirited—my generation is definitely the coolest.

However, Generation X has received virtually no attention since those
heady days. As one writer put it, they're the "smaller 'middle child' generation,"
squashed between Baby Boomers and Millennials, the two demographic and
cultural heavyweights.[23] Out of the limelight, Gen X has produced a sub-
genre of generational commentary that resembles photobombing a family
get-together you haven't been invited to. Some of it claims that Gen X can
save the world (or "keep everything from sucking"), while other elements of
it tip into embarrassing youth bashing: "The Millennials have taken a rep-
utational beating in the last few years, some of it gratuitous, most of it justified. They are needy nellies who can't take a joke."[24] This seems somewhat
beneath a generation that takes its name from a novel in which the narrator
observes, "The car was the color of butter and bore a bumper sticker saying
WE'RE SPENDING OUR CHILDREN'S INHERITANCE, a message
that I suppose irked Dag, who was bored and cranky after eight hours working his McJob."[25] The forgotten middle child has forgotten what it felt like to
be young.

Where do you fit in this generational procession? Table 0.1 outlines the
most widely accepted definitions. In the United States, the Pre-war generation is sometimes split into the "Greatest Generation," those born prior to
1928, and the "Silent Generation," those born between 1928 and 1945. I have
grouped them together throughout this book, partly because these labels are
generally not used outside the United States but mostly because the Greatest
Generation now make up a minute portion of the population.

| Pre-War | Baby Boomer | Generation X | Millennials | Generation Z |
|---|---|---|---|---|
| Born before 1945 | Born 1945–65 | Born 1966–79 | Born 1980–95 | Born 1996–2010? Born after 1997? Born after 2000? |
| **In 2021** | | | | |
| Age 77+ | Age 56 to 76 | Age 42 to 55 | Age 26 to 41 | Age 11 (?) to 25 |

Table 0.1: Generational birth years.

There isn't complete agreement on where one generation ends and another starts, particularly around the Millennials and Generation Z, where the boundaries are only just emerging. Where you place generational cutoffs is, in any case, to some degree arbitrary. Those at the edges of each group will tend to share characteristics with their birth year neighbors, because social change tends to be gradual rather than sudden. Not to devalue generational thinking— as we will see, there *are* distinctive characteristics that we can identify using these classifications. The basic point is that many other social divisions—like class and ethnicity—also simplify the underlying realities, yet each still tells us useful things about the makeup of and attitudes within society.

Some researchers are already imposing an end point on Generation Z and starting to call the group that will come next "Generation Alpha." We won't be looking at this youngest generation in this book—because it's ludicrous to do so when the oldest are around ten and the youngest haven't even been born.

This desperate attempt to label a generation that consists of young children and those who have yet to be conceived demonstrates our obsession with coining names for generations. The US Census Bureau almost certainly came up with the term "Baby Boomers," while Douglas Coupland undoubtedly popularized "Generation X." William Strauss and Neil Howe are credited with coining the term "Millennials," while "Generation Z" follows the first name given to the Millennials, "Generation Y." But this summary hides countless failed attempts. "Generation Me," "Generation We," "the Net Generation," "Next Boomers," "Centennials," "iGen," and even "Generation K" (after Katniss Everdeen, the protagonist of The Hunger Games series of novels and films) were all tried out at one point or another.

As we may have expected, the media is already using the "COVID Generation" to analyze the predicted effect of the pandemic on the younger generation. Whether it takes hold will become clear only in the coming years, but it certainly has a more powerful claim than names based on characters from forgettable movies. I have no particular interest in the naming of generations—the real value is not the label but what the trends show us about the experiences of different groups in the past, and what they suggest about our future.

## WE *CAN* SEE THE FUTURE

The generational analysis in this book is inevitably future focused, but it does not require any spurious leaps from exaggerated differences or astrological thinking. It is built on three of the few—maybe the only—incontrovertible facts about humans: we are born, we age, and we die. This is seen in each cohort's share of the adult population over time, in Figure 0.4. In 1972, around 80 percent of the adult population in the UK were born before the end of the Second World War; now they make up just 12 percent. It won't be long until they are all but gone, as Gen Z makes its way into adulthood and "replaces" them. There is no way to understand how society as a whole will change in the future without understanding what is really different between the generations.

There are skeptics of using past generational changes to predict the future. In *The Black Swan*, Nassim Nicholas Taleb wrote, "History and societies do not crawl. They make jumps." He argued that we largely do not see these jumps coming. Change is instead driven by "black swan" events such as the 2008 global financial crisis, which was the focus for Taleb's analysis, and now, even more powerfully, the COVID-19 pandemic. These events are rare, have extreme effects, and seem predictable only in retrospect, despite our tendency to believe subsequently that we knew they were coming.[26]

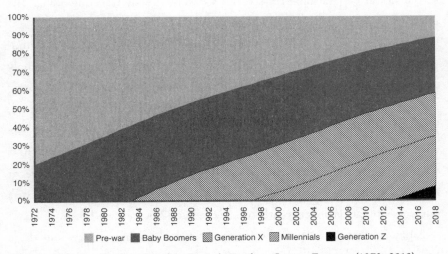

Figure 0.4: Generational profile of the United Kingdom. Source: Eurostat (1972–2019).

To illustrate the deep unpredictability of future outcomes, Taleb cites an example given by the mathematician Michael Berry, who looked at the challenge of predicting the movement of billiard balls on a table. It starts easily enough, but by the ninth impact, the outcome is so finely balanced that you need to account for the gravitational pull of the person standing next to the table, and by the fifty-sixth, the position of every elementary particle in the universe needs to be factored into your calculations. How can we possibly have an accurate understanding of the possible futures in complex human systems, particularly with "black swan" events like the 2008 crisis or the pandemic coming along and upending the table?

My many years of following generational lines has left me less pessimistic about our ability to see the future. Of course, it is possible that we will suddenly stop getting more overweight as we age or that the whole of Generation Z will embrace Christianity en masse, but such things seem unlikely. Taleb recognizes that there are "long quiet stretches" where sudden shocks don't happen, and we will see plenty of those in our charts. But generational analysis is helpful even in understanding the influence of the unexpected: we'll also vividly see the different economic life courses created for younger generations by the 2008 crisis, for example.

This is the crucial point: understanding the impacts of period-effect shocks like the financial crisis and the pandemic is greatly enhanced by a clear view of the slower generational trajectories we were already traveling along. The effect of any crisis is shaped by the context it lands in.

A generational frame helps us understand the influence of major demographic trends too, such as our increasing life expectancy and increasingly aging societies. This is one of the most significant changes that we're seeing today, and it has huge implications for how we should understand the future. In Japan, the median age (the age of the middle person, if you lined up the whole population, from young to old) was forty-six in 2015, and by 2050 it will have increased to fifty-three. This increase of seven years may not seem like a big shift, but it reflects an incredibly aged society; 33 percent of Japan's current population are currently over sixty, but 42 percent will be by 2050.

Japan is often held up as the exemplar of the "graying society," but there are even more dramatic changes coming in other countries. For example, the median age in Brazil was just thirty-one in 2015 but will increase to forty-five by 2050. The proportion over sixty will rocket from just 13 percent in 2015 to 30 percent by 2050. The shifting age balance in our populations is due to not just increasing longevity but the steeply falling birth rates seen around the world. A generational perspective shows that this is not a sudden change but the end of a long trend that will be incredibly difficult to shift.

I examine these generational trends across countries rather than focusing on one because they are increasingly global phenomena. Early twentieth-century thinkers like Mannheim tended to see generations as nationally bounded, because of the importance of shared experience in forming meaningful cohorts. But with the globalization of so many aspects of life, sociologists have recognized that generations could also be globalizing. Businesses and consumer products are now multinational by default, and new communications technologies provide many more ways to share experiences across national boundaries. Even before COVID-19, traumatic events and threats such as the climate emergency, economic crises, and the "war on terror" had a more global perspective. The pandemic has again accelerated this trend, emphasizing our profound global interconnections. At the time of writing, 213 countries or territories had reported cases of the virus; more than this, our response and the economic implications of these measures are much more international than in any previous pandemic.[27]

This is not to say that differences between countries are unimportant. "Country before cohort" will still be a regular message in this book: even now, *where* you are born often remains more important than *when*. The true value of the international study of generations isn't in identifying global generational groups; looking at generations across countries reveals when and why generational difference is important.

In the end, the fundamental reason that now is the right time to take an international look at generations is that, even before the pandemic, the assumption that our children will enjoy a better future had evaporated in a number of more developed nations. For example, more than a decade after the 2008 financial crisis, only 13 percent of people in France expected a better life for young people, while 60 percent expected the future will be worse. The contrast with lower-income nations such as China, Indonesia, and India is stark: two-thirds or more in these countries are confident in a better future for their young people. If people in Western countries—of every generation—maintain this increasingly pessimistic view, it will have profound repercussions. Not only will we risk losing the optimism and dynamism of youth; when people think progress has stopped, they start to question the value of the whole system. We know this is important to people: in the same study, 77 percent of people agreed that every generation *should* have a better standard of living than the one that came before it, with only 15 percent disagreeing.[28]

As far as we can tell, such pessimism about the future for coming generations is a new trend in more developed economies. In both the UK and the United States, we have seen a stunning reversal: the proportion of Brits who think the future will be better for their children halved between 2003 and 2019, and the proportion of Americans who think it's unlikely their kids will have a better future has nearly doubled.[29]

When we see how incomes and wealth have stagnated for recent generations of young people, we can start to understand why.

# CHAPTER 1

# STAGNATION GENERATION

"The Baby Boomers—Can They Ever Live as Well as Their Parents?" This was the anxious question posed by a *Money* magazine headline in March 1983. The implied threat was seriously undermined by the accompanying photo shoot of a real-life couple, which contained glimpses of a luxurious and tastefully decorated (for the time) home. The cover line offered a more direct spoiler: the couple were "Not Yet 30" but had "two strong careers and a prospering business on the side." It's clear that they were hardly the 1980s equivalent of minimum-wage employees toiling in an Amazon warehouse on zero-hours contracts, supplementing their meager earnings by trading on eBay and waiting for drones to take their jobs.

Of course, *Money* magazine had a particular target market—well-off middle managers interested in tables of mortgages and tax-efficient saving schemes. That makes the uncertainty implied in the question all the more striking now, when we know how things turned out. The question "Can they ever live as well as their parents?" reflects the fundamental belief that animates the social contract between generations. As individuals, we have a deep desire for our children to do better than we did, and we've become accustomed to guaranteed generation-on-generation progress across society as a whole.

It's easy to forget that progress was not always a given for Baby Boomers. Several serious economists raised doubts about their financial future. In his 1980 book *Birth and Fortune*, Richard Easterlin argued that being part of a big cohort like the Baby Boomers was bad for your economic success, given the competition for education, resources, and jobs. Being a member of a smaller cohort, like the interwar generation, marked you out as part of the "lucky few," where wages would rise as demand for workers outstripped supply. It seemed a perfectly reasonable assumption to many then, but as David Willetts outlined in his 2010 book *The Pinch*, globalization entirely changed the calculation.

After countries with lower labor costs like China opened up to world trade in the 1990s, the generations following the Boomers had to compete with many more people, which kept wages down. As Willetts put it, "The Boomers gain in two ways. When it comes to political power and all the decisions taken by national governments, they are a big cohort. But when it came to the post-war global labour market they were part of a small cohort: they were a scarce resource that could get away with charging a higher price for their labour."[1]

Downward trends in financial progress in many Western countries came after the Baby Boomers were well established in their careers and more able to weather the storm. And then came the 2008 financial crisis. Before the COVID-19 pandemic, this was *the* generation-defining economic event and the cause of a largely lost decade that hit younger generations particularly hard. There were tentative signs of a recovery in generational progress in the late 2010s, which has made the timing of this latest generation-defining shock even more cruel.

The net effect has been that income growth for younger generations in many countries has ground to a halt or reversed, while the vast majority of gains in wealth that we have seen in the past decade or so have gone to older generations. A generational perspective, separating period, cohort, and life-cycle effects, is vital to determining how these shifting economic conditions have utterly changed the life course of whole cohorts. Not only have your chances of economic success been affected by the accident of when you were born, but they are also increasingly affected by your parents' assets.

## POORER LONGER

The UK-based think tank the Resolution Foundation has analyzed personal income across the United States, the UK, Spain, Italy, Norway, Finland, and Denmark, using data that stretch all the way back to 1969, when the oldest Baby Boomer was twenty-four years old. The study compares average disposable real incomes—that is, adjusted to take inflation into account and after subtracting housing costs—of three 5-year slices of each cohort, to compare generations when they were the same age, in their thirties, forties, and sixties.[2] It's a cascade of ever-decreasing gains for each new generation.

Baby Boomers enjoyed significantly improved incomes in middle age compared with the Pre-war generation, up 26 percent when each were aged forty-five to forty-nine. Gen X started off well compared with the Boomers, but their incomes stalled as they ran into the aftershocks of the 2008 recession, which hit when the oldest were in their early forties, and ended up only 3 percent ahead of Boomers. Most strikingly, Millennials' real disposable income was actually 4 percent down from Gen X's when they were in their early thirties. Progress didn't just stall, it *reversed*—driven by the financial crisis.[3]

These averages hide significant variation across countries. One of the best places to be a Millennial is Norway. There, Millennials aged thirty to thirty-four earned 13 percent *more* than Gen Xers at the same age. Not too bad, you might say (while researching Norwegian work visa requirements). But this still represents a slowdown in economic progress: Gen X earned incomes that were 35 percent more than Baby Boomers at that age range.

More typical is the pattern in the United States. Generation X had 5 percent lower real income at ages forty-five to forty-nine than Boomers did at the same age, and Millennials had an income that was 5 percent less at ages thirty to thirty-four than Gen X.

As demoralizing as things are in the United States, they're nothing compared to the generational disaster that is underway elsewhere. In Italy, Gen X had 11 percent less income than Baby Boomers when each were forty-five to forty-nine years old, while Millennials had 17 percent less income than Gen Xers when they were thirty to thirty-four. This is not so much a ratcheting down as a free fall.

The trends in the UK have not been as dire, but they still represent a shuddering halt to progress, particularly for Millennials. Data from 2018 showed that Gen Xers are slightly ahead of where Baby Boomers were when they were in their mid-forties, but Millennials are slightly behind where Gen X were when they were in their early thirties.[4]

These economic realities are powerfully reflected in how the different generations in Britain *feel*. This is a key question, because if groups feel left behind, they're more likely to question the entire social contract. Since 1983, the British Social Attitudes survey has asked people whether they identify themselves as a high, middle, or low income. And when we look at the proportions of each generation placing themselves in the "low-income" group over the past three and a half decades, in Figure 1.1, we can see dramatic life stories played out in five simple lines.

One sad story stands out. Look at the gap between Millennials and all other generations for the years between 2008 and 2015. It is not normal for this many people in their early to mid-career (the oldest Millennial was thirty-five in 2015) to feel poorer than the rest of the population, including retired generations, for so long.

A large part of the explanation for the relative experience of Millennials is the remarkable fall in the proportion of the oldest living cohort, the Pre-war generation, who count themselves as having a low income over the past couple of decades. The trend is especially unusual given the changing labor market

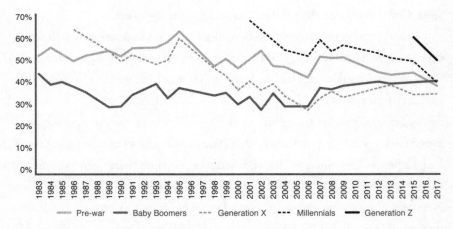

Figure 1.1: Percentage of adults in Britain saying they have a "low income." Source: British Social Attitudes, 1983–2017.

position of this group during this period. In 1983, only 26 percent of this Pre-war generation had retired—but by 2017, when the youngest was seventy-two, nearly all had retired.

Although this may partly be due to decreased expectations (people generally expect to have less in retirement), it also reflects the much stronger pension position for many in this generation compared with the generation before them and compared with working-age people today. The UK Office for National Statistics estimates that the average retiree's disposable real income increased by 16 percent between 2008 and 2018, while it increased by only 3 percent for working households.[5] By 2016, net incomes after housing costs were actually £20 per week *higher* for the retired than they were for working-age people, having been £70 per week *lower* in 2001. That's a huge switch. More than this, the pattern extends down into the poorest ends of each group. The poorest fifth of working-age households are getting by on £2,000 less per year than the poorest fifth of retirees.[6]

The end of the chart promises a hopeful future for younger generations, with a steep drop in the proportion of Millennials who say they have a low income, and Generation Z have entered adulthood much closer to the overall average than Millennials did. They are still the generations that are most likely to feel poor, but the difference is less than in the recent past. However, although it is too early to assess the lasting effect of the COVID-19 pandemic on incomes, signs are that these faint glimmers of optimism will be snuffed out. Analysis across China, South Korea, Japan, Italy, the United States, and the UK shows that in all except South Korea, the young are much more likely than others to have already experienced a drop in income, with the UK seeing one of the biggest relative declines.[7]

## BLAMING THE VICTIM

These types of major shifts in income make the "advice" that regularly targets these younger generations particularly maddening. "Small 'Swaprifices' Could Save Millennials Up to £10.5bn a Year" was one especially toe-curling example of this trend, in a press release from Barclays Bank in 2019.[8] Not only does it confirm that awful attempts at catchy portmanteaus should be a sackable offence—it also typifies the victim blaming of young people for their tough financial circumstances.

The thrust of the "analysis" was a breakdown of how young people spend £3,300 per year on daily treats, going out, and fashion, followed by some finger-wagging about how this group could save "a whopping" amount by making "minor changes to their spending habits."[9] Of course, £3,300 is not a vast amount to cover all those different types of spending in a year, especially when it includes things like "food" and "clothing." Even the frivolous-sounding "daily treats," for example, totaled just £441 a year, or about £1.10 per day.

This is typical of the curious double whammy for younger cohorts today. Not only have they had a much tougher financial time, but they are also criticized for the reduced spending they do manage. It's also a case of us missing the real shift in generational circumstances. In the UK, for example, over-fifties account for around one-third of the population but 47 percent of consumer spending, which has increased by eight percentage points since 2003.[10] In the United States, over-fifties already account for more than 50 percent of spending, and they've been responsible for more spending growth in recent years than any other cohort.[11] The figures are staggering: the American Association of Retired Persons estimates that in the United States, over-fifties spend nearly $8 trillion each year—more than the combined GDP of France and Germany.[12]

A new consumption gap has opened up between younger and older households in many countries. In 1989, twenty-five- to thirty-four-year-olds and fifty-five- to sixty-four-year-olds in the UK both spent about £260 per week on nonhousing consumer goods such as clothing, entertainment, travel, and eating out. By 2014, fifty-five- to sixty-four-year-olds were spending, on average, £50 a week—nearly 20 percent—*more* than twenty-five- to thirty-four-year-olds.

Although this narrative of profligate youth massively misses the point, it remains pervasive. In a global survey of twenty thousand people, the second–most popular adjective to describe Millennials was "materialistic." The stereotype is sticky partly because it is endlessly repeated, for both Millennials and Gen Z. As the author of *Generation Me*, Jean Twenge, put it, "[Millennials'] brand of self-importance also shows up in materialism."[13] In her later book on Gen Z, *iGen*, she wrote, "[Gen Z] are very interested in becoming well-off and less focused on meaning than previous generations."[14]

Those are some sweeping generalizations that you'd need cast-iron data to support. But on each survey measure held up as evidence—whether it's a desire to earn more than their parents, believing that it's important to be well-off financially, or not finding fault with advertising products that people don't need—the major shift actually happened between Baby Boomers and Gen X, and there is nothing particularly new in Millennial and Gen Z attitudes. And there are also plenty of countertrends—for example, recent generations care half as much about what their friends and family have.[15]

These figures don't suggest some emergent generational trend in materialism, newly presenting in Millennials and Gen Z as a distinctive characteristic. Instead, Gen Xers blazed the trail, and younger cohorts have stuck to it. It might be that American Gen Xers were raised in a period of increased consumerism and exposure to advertising that hasn't changed all that much over the past forty years, despite new technologies. Or it could be that these generations came of age during a shaky financial period and carry the scars of that experience. In the United States, income stagnation set in earlier, with Gen Xers rather than Millennials.

It makes sense that money becomes more of a focus when your financial prospects are diminished. Indeed, we see this tendency in behavioral science studies of poverty. These show that a lack of resources induces a "scarcity mindset," where immediate goals take precedence over peripheral goals: "Scarcity orientates the mind automatically and powerfully toward unfulfilled needs."[16] Young people's responses to these US surveys reflect the undeniable fact that financial progress was less certain when they were coming into adulthood.

These blunt characterizations reflect a tendency to pick on younger generations for traits that are created by context. This faulty interpretation of cause and effect is related to another common bias, which social psychologists call the "fundamental attribution error," a term coined by the Stanford University professor Lee Ross. This is the tendency for people to overemphasize personality-based explanations for behaviors that we observe in others, while underemphasizing situational explanations. A driver who cuts us off in traffic is a jerk, for example—but when we do the same thing it's because we're late for a vital appointment. This is often why we blame victims for their own misfortune.

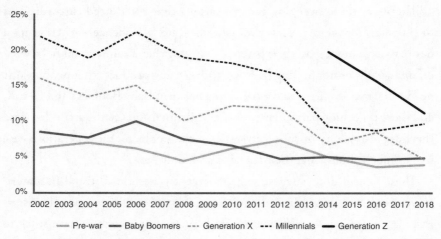

Figure 1.2: Percentage of adults in Germany who say that "It is important to be rich" is true of themselves. Source: European Social Survey, 2002–2018.

There is another important point. The surveys of high school students cited above are a powerful resource, but they cannot pinpoint what is truly generational because they track the same age group over time. We don't know how each successive wave of these kids changed as they aged, and that is why it is also useful to check these trends with generational analysis.

Consider the example in Figure 1.2 from Germany. At just about any point from 2003 to 2012, it could be summed up under the banner headline: "Materialistic Millennials Are Twice as Likely to Say It's Important to Be Rich Than Their Wiser, Better Elders." But that headline could also have been repeated between 2014 and 2016 for Gen Z. Looking generationally, it's clear that focusing on getting rich is primarily a life-cycle effect, a feature of youth that we tend to grow out of.

## THE WEALTH OF GENERATIONS

Achieving these childhood dreams of becoming rich is increasingly about the wealth you have rather than the salary you make. The main economic change of the past few decades, across numerous countries, is how much more quickly wealth has grown than income, largely driven by a housing boom. And because wealth is more unequally distributed than income, including by age, this has resulted in greater concentrations of wealth among older groups. In fact, since 2007, *all* of the extra wealth created in the UK went to people over forty-five, with two-thirds going to those over sixty-five.[17] This feels less fair than income differences, because the amounts are so large and wealth is not as clearly linked in our minds to merit or hard work.

The UK is far from alone in this trend. Credit Suisse, the international investment bank, produces an annual global wealth report, which I always look forward to, in order to ogle the ultra-high-net-worth individuals. The 2017 report included less pleasurable reading for younger generations, however, with a whole chapter dedicated to "the unlucky Millennials."[18]

The report described how the 2008 recession, and subsequent higher levels of unemployment and lower wage growth, hit younger people's savings potential, especially in richer countries. But it wasn't simply that incomes were stagnating—home prices also remained high, as government action supported existing homeowners through interest rate cuts and by pumping money into the system. These factors were coupled in several countries with rising student debt loads, creating a "perfect storm" for stifling wealth accumulation. In contrast, according to the authors, Baby Boomers' "wealth was boosted by a range of factors including large windfalls due to property, pension and share price increases."[19]

Separate analysis in Australia illustrates this increasingly unbalanced distribution of wealth. More than two-thirds of the $2.3 trillion in household wealth generated in Australia in the first half of the 2010s went to those aged fifty-five or older. Those aged sixty-five to seventy-four were on average and in real terms $480,000 wealthier in 2015–2016 than those in the same age group twelve years earlier. In contrast, households headed by thirty-five- to forty-four-year-olds were on average only $120,000 wealthier, and for twenty-five to thirty-four-year-olds, the figure was a measly $40,000.[20] Figure 1.3 shows this incredible wealth curve, where only older cohorts are benefiting significantly.

These gains are not due to the frugal habits of older people, yet that is the view encouraged by a stream of articles on how the young could learn a thing or two about finances from their elders. A *Forbes* piece titled "5 Money Tips Millennials Can Learn from Their Grandparents" included this timeless piece of wisdom from one grandfather: "Eat at a reasonably priced restaurant. . . . It all comes out the same the next day."[21] As the Credit Suisse report suggested, older generations' greater wealth wasn't derived from following

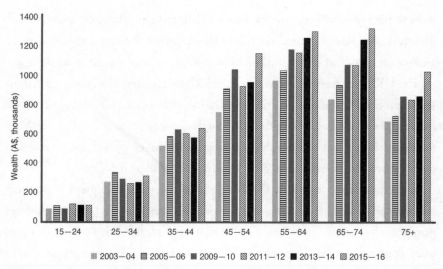

Figure 1.3: Gains in wealth among Australian households, 2003–2016. Source: ABS Survey of Income and Housing.

such nauseating advice but was rather the result of unexpected financial windfalls.[22]

Economists distinguish between "passive" asset gains—where we benefit from the overall performance of the market—and "active" gains, where our savings decisions influence our outcomes. The vast majority of gains across most Western countries are a result of people just sitting back and profiting from repeated waves of property booms and stock market rises.[23]

You might be thinking that the young should suck it up for now and wait for their own "passive gains" of inheritance from their loaded parents. Surely all those assets gathering at the top of the generational hierarchy will soon be flowing down to the youngsters? There is, after all, a lot more wealth out there: the value of estates passed down has more than doubled in the UK in the past twenty years, and it will double again in the next fifteen.[24]

Unfortunately, that will not help hard-pressed middle-age groups through tough times. First, inheritance is shifting to later in life. In the UK, the most common age at which today's twenty- to thirty-five-year-olds will inherit is sixty-one.[25] That's a long wait for cash-strapped Millennials and Gen Zers, and it is increasingly likely to be eaten up by the cost of caring for their longer-living parents.[26]

However, the key point is that these figures for average gains among older cohorts mask a huge amount of variability. Plenty of older people have acquired very little or nothing. My own inheritance so far has been a Seiko watch and a love of whisky, which, though they hold a lot of personal value, aren't going to help me pay off my mortgage. This disparity is one of the big challenges for the future. Dependence on inheritance to accumulate wealth will reinforce inequality, increasing the gaps between the top and bottom for younger cohorts.[27]

This pattern of growing inequality from generation to generation isn't a new one—the rich have been passing on their wealth to their children throughout history. In one study, the economists Gregory Clark and Neil Cummins created a database of 634 rare surnames (including wonderful examples like Bigge, Angerstein, and Nottidge) so that they could track inheritance across five generations in English and Welsh probate records between 1858 and 2012. They tagged each person who died in the first generation as rich or poor based on the value of their estate and watched the wealth flow down to the present day. Even after high inheritance taxes were introduced between the wars, the children of the rich remained rich, to a quite remarkable extent. As Clark and Cummins conclude, "To those who have, more is given."[28] So the pattern may be old, but the increased scale and generational concentration of wealth is new—and brings greater potential to divide.

It is, of course, possible to bring forward some of this transfer in wealth through gifts or loans, and many do, through an increased reliance on the "Bank of Mom and Dad" (BOMAD). In its early days, BOMAD, as typified by a 2004 BBC TV series, was the generational equivalent of an intervention, as parents and experts were drafted to teach feckless youngsters the value of money.[29] Today it is a much bigger business. For example, nearly two-thirds of US Millennials say their parents helped them out "a lot" or "some" when they were just starting out, compared with 36 percent of those parents who say they got this level of financial help at the same stage in life.[30] A study out of the London School of Economics showed that in 2017 some 34 percent of first-time home buyers in England received money from their parents to put toward their deposits. The amount of money contributed is substantial: the

BOMAD gave enough money in 2018 to be ranked tenth among UK mort-gage lenders.[31]

But BOMAD is not a real bank, not least because almost all transfers of wealth are given as gifts rather than loans. As one of the parents surveyed, a sixty-seven-year-old, said, "I think that young people today have it far tougher than my husband and I did. Our son and daughter-in-law have the triple whammy of student debt, horrendously high rents and rocketing house prices. I am just so pleased that we are able to help." Another, a seventy-five-year-old, noted, "Aren't we lucky that we were able to help our children like this? And aren't they?"

They are indeed lucky to have parents who can help, because the average growth in wealth among older generations hides massive variations. In the UK, for example, the top 25 percent of Baby Boomers have an average of around £600,000 in total wealth, while the bottom 25 percent have under £100,000. The increases in wealth for Boomers overall over the past ten years largely come down to acceleration in growth at the top: the top 25 percent gained around £200,000 between 2007 and 2016, while the bottom 25 per-cent barely gained at all.[32] The same pattern was seen in the United States. In 2004, the top 5 percent of American Baby Boomers owned 52 percent of all financial assets within their cohort, a figure that increased to 60 percent in 2016. By contrast, the bottom 50 percent saw their tiny share of wealth decrease, from 3 to 2 percent.[33]

The huge growth and uneven concentration of wealth bakes in the gen-erational transfer of inequality, and this involves much more than just pure cash, as the sociologist Robert D. Putnam powerfully argues in his book *Our Kids*. Advantages have piled up for the kids born to the right parents, all but guaranteeing their own success in life—in stark contrast to those struggling at the bottom. Putnam presents dozens of "scissors graphs" showing the top pulling away from the bottom on all sorts of factors, including obesity, mater-nal employment, single parenthood, financial stress, college graduation, and friendship networks. This increasingly has a geographical dimension, with economic sorting at the neighborhood level, and social sorting within schools, churches, and community groups: "Whether we are rich or poor, our kids are increasingly growing up with kids like them who have parents like us." This represents, Putnam warns, "a kind of incipient class apartheid."[34]

These increasing gaps between rich and poor have consequences not just for the individuals left behind but for how people see the system as a whole. One of the questions in the World Values Survey, the biggest social survey in the world, covering one hundred countries, asks people whether they think wealth can grow so that there is enough for everyone or whether people get rich at the expense of others. In a number of advanced economies, younger generations are the most suspicious about whether wealth really does trickle down. In Germany, for example, nearly two-thirds of the Pre-war generation agreed that "wealth can grow so there is enough for everyone" in 1997. By the mid-2010s only around half of this oldest generation still believed this was the case, and only one-third of Millennials thought the same thing. There are both generational and period effects at work here, with each generation having a gloomier outlook than those born before the end of the war, and a general decline in faith across all generations.

These perceptions are based on economic reality. Through much of the postwar period, "a rising economic tide lifted all boats," according to the sociologist Douglas Massey. And as Robert Putnam puts it, in the early decades of this period, "the dinghies actually rose slightly faster than the yachts." In fact, incomes for the bottom fifth of society in the United States grew a bit more each year, compared to incomes for the top fifth. But then in the 1980s the tides started to turn, first with income gains stalling and then, after the 2008 financial crisis, sometimes reversing.

As sentiment in Germany shows, a majority of the oldest generation are holding on to the view that the system works, *because it used to*, but this belief is fading out with them.

You may wonder, why have we let this happen? A large part of the reason is the continuing rise in individualism across countries, which is a powerful cultural tide that informs many of the trends we'll see throughout this book. For decades, Ron Inglehart, director of the World Values Survey and professor emeritus at the University of Michigan, and his colleagues have tracked the generationally driven shift from "security values" (such as the importance of economic growth and maintaining order) to "self-expression values" (such as valuing freedom of speech and gender equality) across dozens of countries.[35] Others, such as Geert Hofstede and Shalom H. Schwartz, have measured similar factors using different models.[36] Each of these thinkers brought distinct angles to this research, but they all found similar trends—of a slow, evolutionary, and generational shift toward the individualist end of each measure across many countries.

Long-term trends in our politics have also pushed us along the path to individualism. Margaret Thatcher's 1975 Conservative Party conference speech is an excellent example: "We believe [people] should be individuals. We are all unequal. No one, thank heavens, is like anyone else, however much the Socialists may pretend otherwise."[37] Ronald Reagan was a fellow staunch supporter of "rugged individualism." In his famous "A Time for Choosing" speech in 1964, he described his resentment of the tendency in some quarters to refer to the people as "the masses" and asserted that individual freedom was still the best approach to solving the complex problems of the twentieth century.[38] Younger generations today are at the end of this long shift, and they have a particularly strong sense of personal responsibility for how life turns out. They tend to blame themselves.

## THE END OF THE CONTRACT?

I ran a survey on generational differences with the *Guardian* several years ago. It was one of the first international surveys that examined the decline in people's belief that the future was going to be better for young people in the world's richer countries. I wasn't alone in being concerned. So too was Ángel Gurría, secretary-general of the Organisation for Economic Co-operation and Development (OECD). "What would be tragic is if the very trait that we count on the young to infuse into our societies—optimism—were to somehow become permanently scarred," he said in response to the report. "We can't afford that."[39] There is a reason why leaders of global economic organizations are alarmed by generation-on-generation declines and loss of faith in a better future. If things aren't going to get better, what's to stop people from attempting to overturn the system altogether? Our long drift to individualism and increased sense of personal responsibility has forestalled this outcome—but that has a breaking point. And even if we're not heading toward a revolution, this stalled generational progress is behind a lot of the explosive tension in societies today.

So what should we do? A lot of analysis suggests it's simple: take from the old to give to the young. The tone is set by countless stories in the media of "selfish" Baby Boomers looting the economy and the environment in lives of happy abandonment, leaving future generations to fend for themselves. A number of books with titles like *The Theft of a Decade: How the Baby Boomers Stole the Millennials' Economic Future* have been published in recent years. Some of them are well-reasoned analyses that point out the coincidence of many favorable circumstances and political decisions that have caused today's generational divergence. However, their polemical framing suggests that a whole generation is to blame for a trend that they happened to benefit from. One book, *A Generation of Sociopaths: How the Baby Boomers Betrayed America*, scores this cohort against indicators of sociopathy.

Indeed, a number of generational analysts have been predicting a breakdown in the intergenerational contract for some time. For example, in 1992, David Thomson, an academic from New Zealand, asked, "Why should the young adults of the 1990s and beyond feel bound to pay for the welfare state of their predecessors? What bonds, what obligations, what contract requires this of them? Why would they not argue that there now is no contract between generations, because it has been voided by the behaviour of their elders?"[40]

This may seem a compelling argument, but it underplays some clear "bonds" and "obligations" within families and overplays the generational drivers of our motivations. In fact, the vast majority of people don't want to act on grudges against older generations. For example, a question in the American General Social Survey asks whether the government should be responsible for providing a decent standard of living for the old: in 1984, around nine in ten people agreed, with no difference between the generations—and in 2016 the position was *exactly* the same. Indeed, American Millennials and Gen Xers are slightly *more* likely to say that more money should be spent on retirement benefits.[41] This pattern is mirrored in other countries: for example, a majority of each generation in the UK consistently selects benefits for the retired as a priority for any extra government spending.[42]

There are *no* countries where there is strong agreement among any age groups that older people get more than their fair share. For example, in a UK study on how younger people might achieve a better quality of life, all the most popular answers are actions that could benefit everyone: making jobs more secure, supporting economic growth, increased housing, and improved health care. Only tiny minorities select shifting the balance of taxation to the old or reducing welfare benefits for the retired.

Whichever way you look at the evidence, there is little sign of a coming "generational war" based on economic resentment—and there are a number of excellent reasons for this. Most obvious are our family connections, which are driven by both practical and emotional factors: we don't want our parents and grandparents to be penalized, partly because we love them and partly because it may cost us time or money. More generally, we have a strong belief that those who have contributed should receive support—and that older people, having been around for longer, have contributed most.[43]

This lack of generational tension is also related to the fact that we inevitably pass through each age range ourselves. Unlike gender, race, ethnicity, or even social class or income, we *cannot avoid* switching categories ourselves (except through dying). As a result, we see our own futures in the older people ahead of us, and that includes the level and nature of support we'll get from government. Contrary to common misconceptions, the main outcome of taxation and welfare is *lifetime* redistribution—the transfer of money between different periods in someone's life—rather than the redistribution of money between different income groups.[44] And when you see the system in those terms, the idea that younger generations should want to tear up the intergenerational contract makes much less sense. If a generation shifts the balance away from the old, they will likely lose out themselves at a later life stage. Overall, it's no surprise that young people are not ready to go to war with their grandparents.

We cannot dismiss concerns that current young generations will have a poorer economic future than their parents. The social contract between generations is under real strain. However, this is more the result of increasing economic precarity for large proportions of the population while wealth is increasingly concentrated among the few. It is this growing imbalance and the consequent baked-in inequality that are the real issue. And this is where we need to focus in order to regain a sense of optimism for future generations.

# CHAPTER 2

# HOME AFFRONT

In the late 1960s four well-dressed Englishmen were reminiscing about their tough upbringing over a fine bottle of Chateau de Chasselas. They've done well for themselves, each having grown up destitute. You might say they got lucky, entering the workforce during the postwar boom, but they also had that famous Yorkshire grit to draw upon. The state of their childhood housing, for example, was shocking:

**Englishman #1:** *We used to live in a tiny, tumble-down old house, with great holes in the roof.*

**Englishman #2:** *House! You were lucky to have a house! We used to live in one room, twenty-six of us, all there, no furniture, 'alf the floor was missing, and we were all 'uddled together in one corner for fear of falling.*

**Englishman #3:** *Room! You were lucky to have a room! We used to have to live in t' corridor!*

**Englishman #4:** *Corridor! Ah, we used to dream of livin' in a corridor! That would ha' been a palace to us. We used to live in a water tank on a rubbish tip. Ah, every morning we'd be woke up by having a load of rotting fish dumped on us! House? Huh.*

**Englishman #1:** *Well, when I said "house," I mean, 'twere only a hole in ground covered by a couple of foot of torn canvas, but it 'twere house to us.*

**Englishman #2:** *Well, we were evicted from our 'ole in the ground; we 'ad to go and live in the lake.*

**Englishman #3:** *Hey, you were lucky to have a lake! There were over a hundred and fifty of us living in a small shoebox in t' middle o' the road.*

**Englishman #4:** *Cardboard box?*

**Englishman #3:** *Aye.*

**Englishman #4:** *You were lucky.*[1]

As they conclude, if they had tried telling this to the coddled young people of their day, the Baby Boomer generation, "They wouldn't believe you."

I can hear Michael Palin's broad Yorkshire accent from this Monty Python sketch every time I read the comments and tweets on articles about how rough the housing situation is for young people today. For every tale of Millennials and Gen Zers being victim-blamed by landlords for mold in apartments caused by them "breathing at night" or for rat infestations because they're "keeping food in cupboards," there's also a stream of responses from older generations recounting their own miserable housing stories: "Renting has always been shit. Why do you think you lot are so special?"[2]

The keyboard warriors have a point, of course. The reality is that housing was much worse in the relatively recent past, not just because of unscrupulous landlords but also in the provision of the most basic amenities. In 1967, around one in seven American and British households still had no indoor flush toilet, and 22 percent of Brits didn't have hot running water.[3] In 1970, only one-third of British homes had central heating, which typically meant that only one room in the other two-thirds of homes was heated.[4] These living conditions were the childhood experiences of many Baby Boomers, including my parents.

It's not outlandish to expect improvements in living conditions over decades, but headlines like "'Slugs Came Through the Floorboards': What It's Like to Be a Millennial Renting in Britain" miss the story.[5] The real problem is that a combination of skyrocketing housing costs, stricter mortgage lending rules, stagnating incomes, rising debt, and faltering economic growth following both the 2008 financial crisis and the COVID-19 pandemic are delaying when young people leave their parents' homes, swallowing more of their income on housing, and diminishing their prospects of buying their own home. These major shifts in circumstances are changing the life course of a generation. They have all sorts of knock-on effects for the potential of younger cohorts to generate wealth, the nature of their family relationships, their feelings of independence, and the timing of their transition into long-term relationships and parenthood. When you were born really does shape your housing prospects and outcomes in many countries—it's a crucial aspect of an apparent trend toward "delayed adulthood," a slower life course for more recent generations of young people.

Even without these long-term effects, this unstable situation has changed how many young people experience their youth, as the housing horror story of Lindi, a sixty-three-year-old Baby Boomer, shows.[6] In the 1970s, Lindi lived in what she and her partner called "Maison Crap," on the top floor of a London block where, in the derelict floors below, pigeons were the only other tenants. But Lindi, rather than moaning that "kids today don't know how good they have it," recognized the enormous increase in housing costs faced by the current younger generations. When she was in her twenties, she spent around a quarter of her salary on rent, while the average young private renter in London these days spends around half their income on accommodation.[7] "It pains me to see people in their twenties not enjoying life as we were," she said. "A lot of people of my generation were lucky enough to be carefree."[8]

The story of housing, as we will see, has little to do with the feebleness or fecklessness of the young and everything to do with how the financial barriers to property ownership have grown in recent decades. The financial crisis and its aftermath have transformed the housing life cycle of younger generations, illustrating how powerful unmet aspirations can be when we're deflected from what we see as the natural path to progress—and how difficult it will be to meet or manage those expectations.

## LOCKED OUT?

The gaps in wealth accumulation between generations that we saw in Chapter 1 are, to a large degree, explained by the enormous boom in house prices over the past few decades. There is now an unimaginable amount of money stored in peoples' homes—about $200 trillion, or three times as much as all publicly traded shares in the world.[9]

In some countries, house prices have more than tripled between the 1970s and 2019, after taking inflation into account. For instance, prices have increased in real terms by 256 percent in Ireland, 227 percent in the UK, 212 percent in Australia, and 197 percent in Canada. The figures are not as dramatic in the United States, but an increase of 69 percent in real terms has still pushed home ownership beyond affordability for many, particularly in the context of income stagnation. In 1975, it would have taken someone earning the median wage nine years to save up a 20 percent deposit for the median home in the United States; today it would take fourteen years in the country as a whole and up to forty years in expensive cities like San Francisco and Los Angeles.[10] It is even worse in Britain: it took an average family headed by a twenty-seven- to thirty-year-old just three years to save for an average-sized deposit in the 1980s; by 2016 this ballooned to nineteen years, partly owing to increased house prices but also to stricter lending rules.[11]

It's no surprise then that younger generations are increasingly locked out of home ownership. This is especially evident in Britain's experience, illustrated in Figure 2.1. Back in 1984, when the average Baby Boomer was in their late twenties, two-thirds of the generation already owned a home. When Generation Xers were the same average age, in 2001, a slightly lower 59 percent were homeowners. But by 2016, when the average Millennial was in their late twenties, only 37 percent owned their own home. This is a precipitous fall in home ownership in the space of two generations.

We can see all three types of societal change—period, life-cycle, and cohort effects—playing out in the diverging generational lines in this chart. The cohort effect is obvious for Millennials, who started out and have remained at a much lower level of ownership than older generations. But we can also see how ownership life cycles have been utterly reshaped. There had been a clear pattern of ownership rates increasing as we aged, as shown by Gen Xers until the mid-2000s, when they looked set to end up at a similar level of ownership as the Baby Boomers and the Pre-war generation. But then the housing price boom and subsequent credit crunch changed their course entirely. The flatlining in home ownership for Gen Xers since 2008 shows the magnitude of this period effect.

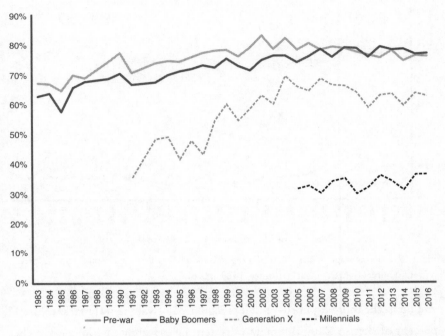

Figure 2.1: Percentage of British adults living independently from parents who own their own home or have bought with a mortgage. Source: British Social Attitudes, 1983–2017.

It's not just Millennials who've had the housing ladder kicked away from them, then. Many more people in this middle-aged cohort are now facing utterly different living arrangements from those they could have expected if they'd been born just a handful of years earlier. For example, the number of flat-shares among Britons aged between thirty-five and forty-four nearly doubled between 2009 and 2014, and tripled for those aged between forty-five and fifty-four.[12] The comedian and actor David Mitchell, who starred in the long-running British sitcom *Peep Show*, called it a day after nine seasons, when he was forty-one, saying, "Two middle-aged men sharing a flat like that, that's too sad. It's got to stop, because we've got older."[13] Tragically, it would have been more on trend to keep it going: its depiction of a maddeningly claustrophobic domestic lifestyle and the despair that comes from surviving on a tight budget ("Butter the toast, eat the toast, shit the toast. God, life's relentless") is becoming an increasingly familiar portrait of middle age.

Apart from awkward flat sharing, the inevitable consequence of decreased home ownership among younger generations has been a huge increase in renting. And in a country with constrained social housing such as Britain, renters

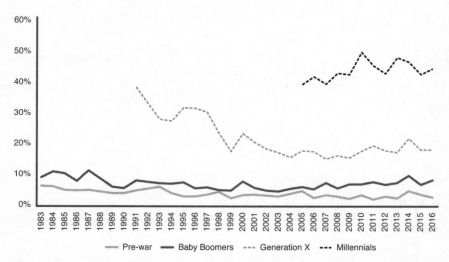

Figure 2.2: Percentage of British adults living independently from parents who are private renters. Source: British Social Attitudes, 1983–2016.

end up in the more expensive and less regulated private rental market. Just 11 percent of British Baby Boomers were renting privately in 1984, when they were an average age of around thirty. This had nearly doubled for Generation X when they were the same average age, in 1999. And within a generation it has doubled once again, with 44 percent of Millennials renting privately in 2016 and no sign of this declining.

The financial implications are truly life altering. Across all types of tenures, housing costs have been increasing for decades. Only 9 percent of the average Pre-war generation's income was spent on housing when they were in their late twenties. That figure is 24 percent for Millennials. But it's worse for private renters, who now spend over a third of their income on rent, with no prospect of this enormous slice of their earnings generating any wealth. Instead, they are boosting the wealth of (mainly older) landlords.

The generational pattern of home ownership in the United States, shown in Figure 2.3, is eerily similar to Britain's. In 2004, for example, 54 percent of Gen Xers owned their own home when they were an average age of thirty, a figure slightly ahead of Baby Boomers at a similar age, in 1986. Home ownership for Gen X continued to rise steeply and looked set to meet Baby Boomer levels, which had leveled off at around 80 percent, right up to the crash. But, as in Britain, Gen X home ownership then decreased and stagnated: now in

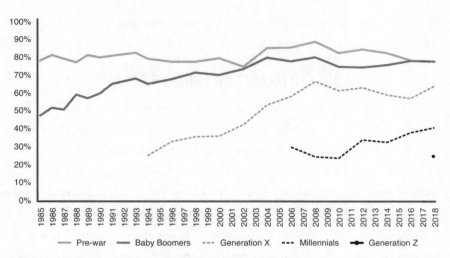

Figure 2.3: Percentage of US adults living independently from parents who own their own home or are buying with a mortgage. Source: General Social Survey, 1985–2018.

their forties and fifties, they are well behind Baby Boomers at the same age. The housing and financial crisis occurred when Millennials were at an early stage in their potential homeowning years, and in 2018 they reached an average age of thirty with just 41 percent owning their home, significantly below Gen X at that age.

Even countries that have a very different housing market are starting to show the signs of generational pressures on home ownership. In Germany, for example, rates of home ownership have traditionally been significantly lower than in most other countries, and owning a home there has tended to come later in life. For example, German Baby Boomers only reached peak home ownership (66 percent) in 2012, when they were an average age of fifty-seven. The explanations for these differences flow from a long series of choices, going back to the rebuilding of the housing stock following the Second World War, including more sensitive regulation of and support for the private rental sector, stricter financing of mortgages, and an absence of the government tax incentives.[14] German society chose to favor renting over owning to a much greater extent than many other countries, and ownership rates and house prices have been more stable as a result.

Up until recently, each successive German generation seemed to follow a very similar path, with Millennials tracking the home ownership trend line of Gen X. But new analysis shows that this is changing: just 12 percent of twenty-five to thirty-four-year-olds now own their home, compared with 23 percent at the end of the 1990s.[15]

## A BROKEN MARKET AND BROKEN DREAMS

The fact that home ownership among the young is declining even in Germany, a country where home price rises have been less extreme than those seen elsewhere, suggests that the trend is about more than the market value of homes. Instead, decades of policy decisions helped older generations to buy homes—and then, when the property bubble burst, there was a push to introduce stricter regulation. For example, older generations in the United States benefited from less restrictive planning regulations and tax relief on mortgage payments, while British Baby Boomers in the 1980s and 1990s were given the "right to buy" council homes at a discount of up to 50 percent of market value and with a 100 percent mortgage guarantee.[16] Though the Right to Buy scheme continues, its terms are far less attractive and accessible. In the wake of the crash, governments helped existing owners avoid foreclosure and then tightened lending rules for newcomers to the market. This happened in other countries, too.[17] Greater difficulty in getting a mortgage and larger deposit requirements are two of the main reasons cited for lower home ownership among the young in Germany, for instance.[18]

In the end, the key drivers are the interaction of these policies with changing economic circumstances; though the generation-shaping breaking point was caused by the 2008 crash, pressures had been building for some time. These included the income stagnation we saw in Chapter 1, in addition to other financial burdens that fell more heavily on recent generations. For example, researchers from the Federal Reserve Bank of New York have found that the increase in education debt explains up to 35 percent of the decline in home ownership for American twenty-eight to thirty-year-olds between 2007 and 2015.[19] Nearly half of US Millennials borrowed money to pay for their education—ten percentage points higher than Gen Xers and more than twenty-five percentage points higher than Baby Boomers—and they also borrowed much larger amounts.[20]

It's the *interaction* between when you were born and other inequalities that affect your chances of owning property. For example, in the United States, the gap in home ownership rates between those who are more and less educated has tripled between 1990 and 2015.[21] A quarter of all Millennial homeowners in the United States had parental help with both their college tuition fees and the deposit on their home, despite this group constituting a scant 3 percent of the Millennial population.[22] This illustrates how a cumulation of advantages has flowed down a "funnel of privilege" that only the luckiest enter.[23]

The consequence is more people renting into middle age—and because the likelihood of buying for the first time decreases once we get through our forties, more people will rent into retirement, which has widespread implications.[24] The Australian academic Alan Morris has charted the impact of private renting versus home ownership on older people. The higher housing costs cut into their pensions, leaving them with less money for socializing and therefore exacerbating isolation and loneliness.[25] The idea that all older people are lonely is one of the laziest generational stereotypes, but it *is* true for some groups, especially where resources are scarce or living arrangements are unstable. Morris's analysis identifies trends among a relatively small proportion of older people, but if generational changes in home ownership hold, they will become much more common in the next few decades.

There are many reasons people prefer to own their home; academics often break these down into a home's *use value* (the value you get from using it), its *exchange value* (its stored wealth), and its *symbolic value* (including feelings of achievement, status, and belonging).[26] Within these, there are a number of specific behavioral benefits, including the fact that mortgages are a form of "forced saving."[27] Some of these benefits apply wherever you live, while others are modified by national economics and culture. In countries such as Germany, many of the motivations for ownership are relatively weak; in the UK, the United States, and Australia, the motivations make home ownership a near-universal aspiration.

This wasn't always the case. It's true that for the past twenty years, around 80 percent or more of every generation in Britain have said that they'd choose to own their home rather than rent, but prior to this there was much less of a consensus. In the early 1990s, only half of the Pre-war generation said they'd ideally like to buy. We have been socialized into thinking of buying as the clear best choice, and this began when prices started to take off.

The real societal threat is the gap between aspiration and reality among younger age groups and the bleak future for the growing numbers of people who are locked out of the system. The geographer Joel Kotkin sees these recent trends as part of a return to something akin to a feudal system, where "this generational gap between aspiration and disappointment could define our demographic, political, and social future."[28]

This is a cause for concern, because the financial pressures faced by renting retirees will make them more dependent on state support: according to one calculation, it would increase the cost of retiree housing benefits by over £3 billion per year in the UK.[29] This future additional cost should provide the impetus to improve the housing situation now.

The aftermath of the COVID-19 pandemic will most likely bring further disruption. In the early stages of the crisis, the focus in the UK was on the extent to which home prices were holding up or even increasing, bolstered by massive government stimulus packages that supported businesses and incomes, and direct support for the housing market, such as the stamp duty (a tax paid when buying a home) holiday. Analysts' predictions are for significant drops in property prices as the longer-term economic effect of the pandemic plays out, but this may, once again, underestimate governments' desire to prop up housing prices.[30] We shouldn't count on there being a price correction to make housing more affordable for younger generations.

## STUCK IN THE NEST

Although owning your own place remains the clear aspiration in many countries, an increasing number of young people are not even making it out of their childhood bedrooms. The vision may be of a fashionable downtown apartment or a cozy suburban house, but the reality for increasing numbers of young adults is sleeping in their old single bed, surrounded by tattered posters of pop bands from their teens. As one twenty-eight-year-old who had recently moved back in with her parents said, "It's hard to feel like an adult when you're living with the people who used to brush your teeth."[31]

Of course, living at home into adulthood is not uncommon in many countries. In fact, the main pattern that stands out in the global data is the incredible variety of circumstances across the world. For example, around half of Italians aged twenty-five to thirty-four still live with their parents, compared with around 5 percent in Norway and Sweden; the UK and the United States fall between these two extremes.[32] For such a key influence on formative experiences, that's a huge range.

But our main interest here is how this is changing generationally and how people are adjusting, particularly in countries where it's an increasingly common outcome. The reaction has not been sympathetic. The subtitle to an infamous 2013 *Time* magazine cover story that branded Millennials the "Me Me Me Generation" was "Millennials Are Lazy, Entitled Narcissists Who Still Live with Their Parents."[33] The term "boomerang generation" implies that, no matter how hard their parents try, they can't get their kids to stay away. And a Pew survey from 2019 suggests many are still not getting used to the shift, with 64 percent of the American public thinking you should be financially independent from your parents when you reach the age of twenty-two—when only 24 percent actually are.[34]

It is, however, a new reality that increasing numbers of families in a number of countries are having to come to terms with. As Figure 2.4 shows, around 18 percent of American Gen Xers were living at home in 1999, when they were an average age of twenty-seven, but this had increased to 31 percent for Millennials by 2014. Millennials are finally moving out now that their average age is over thirty, with only 16 percent still living at home. But this is

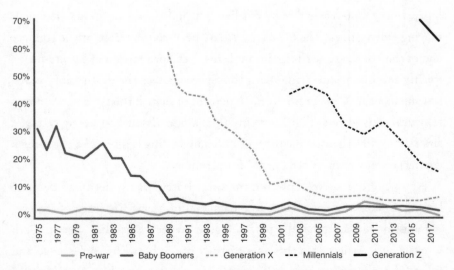

Figure 2.4: Percentage of American adults living in parents' home. Source: General Social Survey, 1975–2018.

not the end of the trend: it looks as though Gen Zers will be even more likely to be stuck at home than previous generations.

In the UK the pattern is almost identical. Only 20 percent of my generation were still living at home in their late twenties, but this had increased to 31 percent for Millennials by 2014. As in the United States, British Millennials have started to move out as more of them have edged into their thirties, and by 2016 the percentage was down to 19 percent—but again, the trend is continuing with Gen Z. In total, *over one million* more young adults in the UK were living at home in 2019 than in 1999, which is an extraordinary change in how we live.[35]

We can even see a similar story in Germany. According to the World Values Survey, 40 percent of German Millennials said they were living with their parents in 2013, versus 26 percent for Gen X in 1999. The historical base level of young adults living at home in Germany may be higher, but the direction of generational travel is the same.

It's true that sons are more likely to live at home in adulthood than daughters, for all sorts of reasons: women tend to form relationships with older men, and men tend to have less access to housing benefits because they are less likely to be caring for children on their own.[36] But, contrary to how it is often portrayed, this trend isn't simply the result of increasing numbers of hairy, thirty-four-year-old manboys living happily in their parents' basement playing video games. The big changes have been concentrated at the younger end of the age range, with significant leaps in the proportion of twenty-five to twenty-seven-year-olds living with their parents over the past twenty years, now up to a third. In contrast, only 6 percent of British thirty-three to thirty-four-year-olds were still at home in 2018, a figure that had barely changed since 1996. For the vast majority of individuals, this is more of a short-term coping strategy than a permanent lifestyle choice.

At an aggregate level, however, the shift in how we live seems to be more lasting. Some even consider it to be a signal of a new life stage of "emerging adulthood," as coined by Jeffrey Jensen Arnett, a psychologist at Clark University.[37] Arnett sees this as a distinct phase between adolescence and full adulthood, a time of identity exploration "in love, work and worldviews" between the ages of eighteen and twenty-nine. The theory has attracted some criticism from developmental psychologists, partly because it casts a limitation of a person's financial circumstances as an active choice.[38] As one US study shows, individuals in households that had incomes in the bottom half of the distribution were less likely to move out before the age of twenty-seven than those in the top half, and those who have home-owning parents were more likely to move out than those who don't.[39] "Delayed adulthood" is a better description than "emerging."

## DRIFTING APART

The fact that young people are living at home for longer in countries like the United States and UK, and the parallel increase in the number of multigenerational households over the past decade or so, should not been seen as all bad. It is a sensible strategy in tougher economic times, and in some circumstances it helps to bolster connections between generations.

However, this increased intergenerational contact is dwarfed by larger forces pushing the young and the old apart. Over the past century, the United States has gone from being one of the most age-integrated societies in the world to one of the most age-segregated, so much so that in many parts of the country, age segregation is as stark as ethnic segregation.[40] In one study, Americans over the age of sixty said that only a quarter of the people they had discussed "important matters" with during a six-month period were thirty-five or younger; if they didn't count relatives, the number dropped to just 6 percent.[41]

The separation of ages came from the gradual introduction of all sorts of reforms: formal education became more finely grained, from a single school-room to distinct stages; the workforce became specialized through industrial methods; young people moved to cities while older people separated into their own communities, as they went into senior centers, care homes, and retirement communities. As the author Marc Freedman, an architect of a number of intergenerational programs, says, we began to "warehouse" older people, who were "viewed increasingly as useless drains on the economy, families and our collective resources."[42]

This separation seemed to meet a latent demand. When the real estate developer Del Webb opened Sun City, America's first large-scale self-contained retirement community, in the Arizona desert in 1960, it promised "graying as playing," free from the annoyance of younger generations. It was a way to forestall thoughts of mortality—as Freedman suggests, a nostalgic "trip back to summer camp." It might even have felt like a "low-tech attempt at the fountain of youth"—after all, "if everyone is old, no one is old."[43] On its opening weekend, a hundred thousand people flocked to the new town, producing the largest traffic jam in state history.

These trends have become so widespread that it's easy to forget that this is a relatively new phenomenon, in contrast with centuries during which generations lived in close proximity. As the Cornell professor Karl Pillemer says, "We're in the midst of a dangerous experiment. This is the most age-segregated society that's ever been."

The United States is far from alone in testing a radically different way for generations to live. A study in the UK shows that in 2001, just 15 local council areas out of 343 had an average age that was 10 percent higher than the national average, and 17 areas had an average age that was 10 percent lower than the national average. But by 2018 these figures more than doubled. We're drifting apart.[44] As the authors of the report point out, we tend to characterize countries as either "young" or "old," but to do so hides the extent of variation within countries. For example, there were sixty local authorities in the UK—mainly rural and coastal areas like North Norfolk—in 2015 that had a higher average age than the oldest country in the world, Japan (at forty-six years of age). At the other end of the scale, there were twenty-three local authority areas—including university cities like Oxford—with an average age lower than in Chile (at just thirty-four years of age), one of the youngest OECD countries.

Longer-running analysis stretching back to 1981 by the Centre for Towns, a British think tank, illustrates how new a phenomenon this is. Figure 2.5 shows the old-age dependency ratio, which measures the ratio of people over sixty-five to those of working age. There was little change until 1991, but since then different sorts of areas have gone in different directions, with villages getting older and cities getting younger.[45]

What is causing this rapid separation of young and old? The average age of any locale can only really be affected by a few factors: the rate of births, deaths, and immigration and emigration, either from other countries or within a country. And the analysis suggests that a combination of these effects is responsible, depending on which direction the area is going. Rural

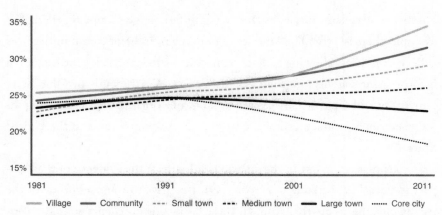

Figure 2.5: Old-age dependency ratios in different types of locations, 1981–2011. Source: Centre for Towns reanalysis of UK Census data (1981–2011).

areas are particularly affected by a lack of immigration and the lower birth rates that result from an exodus of people of child-rearing age, while an influx of younger migrants from other parts of the UK and abroad are the key causes of cities becoming younger. This, in turn, is driven by the increasing concentration of economic opportunities in cities, along with their growing student populations.[46]

The physical separation of generations is demonstrably affecting our ability to develop positive relationships with each other. The US social psychologist Gordon Allport pioneered "intergroup contact theory," the idea that well-managed contact between different groups—if they have equal status in the interaction and common goals—can reduce stereotyping, prejudice, and discrimination.[47] Time and again, and in different contexts, experiments have shown that this type of contact works: familiarity breeds favorability, not contempt. This approach has been mostly applied to building connections across racial and religious divides, with much less focus on bridging the gaps between generational groups. But the same principles apply, and the growing physical separation of age groups makes action increasingly necessary.

The research is clear: there are significant benefits to contact between different age groups, at all ages. Large numbers of studies have shown that seniors in retirement homes benefit from spending time reading to children and playing with them, while young people gain the chance to absorb wisdom and life experience.[48] These mutual needs of old and young are the basis of a number of excellent initiatives that bring different age groups together. For example, there is a trend in America of building retirement communities near college campuses, allowing seniors to attend events alongside students, even incorporating schools into their original design. A 2018 study by Ohio State University and Generations United, a nonprofit organization promoting intergenerational contact, established 105 shared-site programs in the United States.[49]

Two things stand out in these various initiatives: the evidence of their impact is clear, but the scale of activity is tiny relative to the magnitude of the trends pushing us apart. Although these social entrepreneurs should be applauded, it's depressing that there hasn't been more systematic government support, particularly because we've known about the problems for so long. In the UK, a 1949 report by the National Old People's Welfare Council said, "It is essential that old people should not be segregated from the rest of the community, but that dwellings should be included as part of the general housing. This will prevent the feeling of loneliness and isolation from which the aged tend to suffer." The problem has crept up on us because we have failed to pay attention.

## UNMET EXPECTATIONS

Our collective memory plays tricks on us. This isn't just the blatant reimagining that some, like Monty Python's four Yorkshiremen, indulge in to promote a heroic image of their own past. Instead, it is seen in our misunderstanding what is truly different now compared with the past and our false sense that how things have turned out were always destined to be.

Our susceptibility to this "hindsight bias" was brought to prominence in a seminal paper by Amos Tversky and Daniel Kahneman in the early 1970s.[50] It has since been shown to exist in all sorts of areas, from the financial sector to the judiciary to medicine. It's even been found on *Wikipedia*, where articles written before disasters barely mention the vulnerability of, for example, the Fukushima nuclear reactor to a tsunami, but articles written afterward point out the inevitability of the outcome.[51] The same tendencies have emerged with governments' responses to the COVID-19 pandemic—all missteps look absurdly incompetent in retrospect, regardless of how justifiable they may have seemed at the time.

This same bias infects our view of how and where we live. The increasing separation of old and young into different communities feels natural, when it is in fact an entirely new way of life. The good fortune of older generations, with their high rates of home ownership and the wealth this has brought them, now seems like it was inevitable. The reality is that they neither had it entirely easy nor knew how uniquely lucky they were destined to be, relative to what would follow. When they were young, housing pressures led to some extreme measures that would draw a lot of attention today. For example, the BBC tells the story of young couples camping out in muddy fields for four days in 1964, in a bid to be first in the queue for a new housing development that was being built in Sunbury-on-Thames, near Heathrow Airport.[52]

There was no indication then that they were going to strike it rich, despite how it looks today. Indeed, there were times when home ownership looked more like a burden than a wise investment—for example, nearly four hundred thousand homes in the UK were foreclosed on between 1990 and 1996, after interest rates spiked to 15 percent.[53] However, once something has happened, we are much more likely to believe that we "knew it all along." Our resentment at the apparent inevitability of Baby Boomers' good fortune is partly a trick of our minds.

But that is how it turned out, and it has created one of most serious and urgent problems we face. Our generational lines demonstrate the scale of the massive deflections from the paths experienced by previous cohorts. We are in a situation where expectations of independent living and home ownership have been raised far beyond any attainable reality, and this promises a lifetime of unmet aspirations. Given the importance of housing to our lives, this regression is a key factor that undermines our belief in progress. Our own path is increasingly related to the resources we can draw on from our families. In fact, it is hard to see how governments can revitalize the social contract between generations without finding a solution to the problem.

Though the approach required will vary, it boils down to a choice between meeting current aspirations for home ownership and changing them. If we view the good fortune of older homeowning generations as an unsustainable decades-long aberration, then we are in for a difficult period of readjustment. Furthermore, given the higher cost of renting and the wealth gaps that would continue to grow between owners and others, we will be baking further intergenerational inequality into the system. Instead, our post-COVID recovery schemes should have housing at their heart if we are to "build back better." This will not, however, be achieved simply by increasing the supply of homes to buy; it will require a comprehensive range of measures. We need increased public housing support and a better-regulated private rental sector for those struggling to move out of their childhood homes, and we should help those trying to get a foothold on the ownership ladder by providing more direct support to those first-time buyers who can't rely on the Bank of Mom and Dad.

# CHAPTER 3

# REACHING HIGHER, FALLING FLAT

"There is . . . a disconnect between young people, their hopes, goals and expectations, and what companies think young people want. I see my role as a translator." This is the view of a self-ascribed "generational consultant" who advises large corporations how to better engage with younger members of their workforce. "Generational consulting" has become its own mini-industry: in 2015, US companies spent up to $70 million on it, with some experts making as much as $20,000 an hour, and more than four hundred LinkedIn users describing themselves solely as "Millennial expert" or "Millennial consultant."[1] Of course, you may also call it, as one of the contributors to a *Wall Street Journal* article on the phenomenon suggests, "a racket" built on "pseudo-expertise, playing to bureaucrats' anxiety that they don't have their fingers on the pulse."

It's easy to understand this sentiment when you see the insight being peddled by some of these consultants—and eagerly bought by major companies. The US retail chain Target gave managers a single sheet of paper with a guide to each generation's work style, view of authority figures, and attitude toward balancing work and family. For example, managers were told that Pre-war generation workers liked to get "personal acknowledgement . . . for work well done," compared to the "public praise" preferred by

Millennials. Baby Boomers were deemed to be greedy in terms of salary expectations compared to Gen X, who were said to be happy to trade more money for more time off. As a reporter who got hold of a copy of the guidelines said, "Coaching tips for every single generation: patronise everyone in their own way."[2]

In some respects, there is nothing unusual or particularly egregious about this particular branch of consulting. Consultancy often involves gilding advice with a sheen of rigor borrowed from frameworks based on not particularly rigorous research. But this generational stereotyping has a destructive force. The money there is to be made provides a clear incentive for the exaggeration of generational difference, which is not just wasteful but harmful. The distracting "insights" from this generational consulting also crowd out discussion of some of the biggest shifts between generations in modern times. We get clichés about today's young workers being particularly lazy and disloyal that immediately collapse under scrutiny but still divert us from real and dramatic changes in the worlds of education and work.

There are more important dilemmas than whether to give praise by email or in a group. And by carefully separating life-cycle, cohort, and period effects on our experience of work and education, we can gain insight into important questions of social progress—whether higher education still pays, how increasingly precarious employment affects both young and old, and how artificial intelligence (AI) and automation are set to transform the nature of work.

## THE MOST EDUCATED GENERATION

When you ask Britons what areas of life they expect will be better for young people than for their parents, education is one of only four where more people still expect improvements rather than a decline. The only areas where the outlook is more positive are the freedom of self-expression, the ability to travel abroad, and access to information and entertainment.[3]

This relative optimism is based on incredible rises in education levels around the world over the past few generations, particularly in emerging economies. For the older generations in these countries, access to secondary—let alone tertiary—education was limited. China provides a particularly vivid example. Secondary school enrollment leapt from 64 percent in 2006 to 94 percent in 2016, and the increasing numbers of students completing secondary school has had knock-on effects. In 1999, just 6.4 percent of China's young people were studying at a tertiary level. This number had more than tripled, to 21 percent, by 2006, and nearly doubled again, to 39 percent, by 2014.[4] The raw figures are staggering: eight million Chinese students graduated from college in 2017—ten times more than in 1997.[5] Until 1998 there were twice as many US students enrolling in higher education each year than Chinese students, but just ten years later, the situation had reversed. The expansion was far from an accident. Starting in 1999, the Communist government rolled out a series of reforms to increase both the rate of enrollment (at home and abroad) and the quality of secondary and higher education in China—it clearly worked.

Other countries have also experienced an enormous growth in higher education, even without this level of centralized planning.[6] Figure 3.1 shows the proportion of birth-year cohorts with a tertiary-level qualification when they were aged twenty-five to thirty-four. The top bars are roughly representative of the older half of Gen X, the middle bars of the younger half of Gen X, and the bottom bars of a large proportion of Millennials.

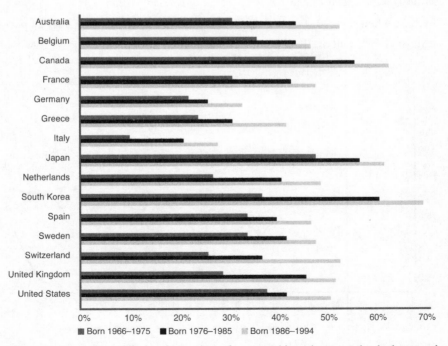

Figure 3.1: Percentage of twenty-five to thirty-four-year-olds with tertiary-level educational qualifications in 2000, 2010, and 2019. Source: OECD 2000, 2010, and 2019.

The pattern is the same in every country: each cohort has a higher level of education than the previous one, and there are some remarkable shifts. For example, in South Korea, 37 percent of those born between 1966 and 1975 had a tertiary qualification in their late twenties or early thirties; a generation later, nearly 70 percent do. A similar near-doubling of graduate numbers can be seen in the UK. When that first half of Generation X were in their late twenties or early thirties, around one-quarter had university degrees. Britain lagged way behind most countries, particularly Canada and Japan, where over 40 percent of young people had degrees at the same age. But by the time the first wave of UK Millennials made it through to their late twenties and early thirties, the proportion with higher education qualifications had shot up to 50 percent. Australia and Switzerland have followed a similar trajectory.

These trends can be seen in Figure 3.2, tracking what proportion of different generations reached degree level in Britain. Millennials have already overtaken Gen X, and the gap will continue to grow in the next few years, as some in the Millennial cohort are still making their way through the education system. This is easier to see when you compare each generation at the same average age: for example, 40 percent of British Millennials had a degree in 2018 when they were on average around thirty years old, while only 26 percent of Gen X had one at the same average age in 2002.

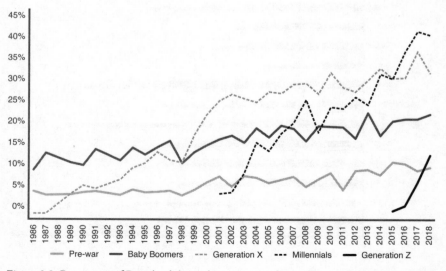

Figure 3.2: Percentage of British adults with a university degree. Source: British Social Attitudes (1986–2018).

There is a very similar pattern of expansion in the United States, with only a few variations. There was a much later boom in university education in the UK, with bigger gaps between the Pre-war, Baby Boomer, and Gen X groups. Older generations of Americans had much greater access to college than their British peers, with US Baby Boomers on a par with UK Gen Xers in educational qualifications. Some of this difference in educational history between the countries will be due to America's GI Bill, passed in 1944 to help soldiers returning from the Second World War gain a university degree. More than two million members of the US Pre-war generation—nearly half of those who served in the Second World War and about 43 percent of those who served in Korea—had taken advantage of the opportunity by 1956, confirming a tertiary degree as part of the American Dream. After Vietnam, nearly 80 percent of veterans enjoyed the education benefits.[7] In contrast, the later surge in higher education in the UK is clearly visible in the Gen X line from the late 1990s, following the commitment of Tony Blair's Labour government to get half of young people into college.

Another feature stands out when you look at this generationally: the slow but steady upward drift of the proportion of older generations with degrees. For example, in 1986, when the youngest was forty-one years old, just 5 percent of the Britain's Pre-war generation had a degree; by 2018 this was 10 percent. It would be misleading, however, to interpret these data as a minor revolution in continuing education. Rather, differences in education-related life expectancy are a more important explanation. For example, men with a tertiary education can expect to live an average of seven years longer than those who didn't finish high school, owing to a series of factors that drive unequal health outcomes for different social and economic groups.[8] Older cohorts are, on average, gradually becoming more educated—but, sadly, this is mostly because the less well educated die younger.

Despite these very long-term advantages, questions are growing over whether the return on our increased investment in higher education pays off, both for individuals and for nations. A plethora of articles has asked whether it is still "worth it" following the huge expansion in the number of people going through higher education and an equally significant increase in cost. In the United States, for example, for a student in the 1940s and 1950s, registration at a state university cost around $300, and a year's tuition cost around

$600, or around $6,000 in today's money.[9] Today, the average cost of a year's tuition alone is around $20,000. The Federal Reserve Bank of New York calculated that the average student debt for a twenty-five-year-old has more than doubled between 2003 and 2015, the total figure owed by US graduates is a staggering $1.5 trillion. Graduates of the class of 2017 owe an average of $28,650.[10]

Even with their frightening costs and growing prevalence, on the face of it, a college degree still pays off. Graduates earn significantly more, on average, than their peers: in the UK, men with a degree can expect to earn an extra £130,000 over their lifetime, factoring in taxes and tuition repayment, while the figure for women is £100,000.[11] The pattern is the same in the United States. The "average rate of return" for a university degree there has come down slightly in recent years, but it is still 14 percent—nearly double the rate of return for the same level of education in 1980.[12] Although university students often forgo three to four years of full-time work to pursue their degree, the extra earnings balance the costs in relatively little time, compared with the length of working life. In the United States, on average, graduates pay off the costs of higher education by age thirty-three, a pattern also seen in other countries.[13]

These calculations are not the full picture, however. First, this graduate dividend may reflect the preexisting abilities or resources of graduates: they may have done just as well without a degree, because of their own skills or support from their typically wealthier families. There is some evidence that this does explain quite a lot of the difference. For example, the Institute of Fiscal Studies (IFS) in the UK calculates that the graduate dividend for men, once these factors are taken into account, is only 8 percent.[14]

Second, there are very large variations depending on where and what you studied. Another IFS report has identified twelve institutions in the UK where graduates have earned *less* by the time they get to twenty-nine than those who didn't go to college at all and subject areas such as the creative arts for which the relative return is negative, regardless of the university. In stark contrast, men who study medicine or economics can expect to earn an additional £500,000 over their lifetime.[15] Overall, while 80 percent of graduates see a net return, 20 percent don't. This variety of outcome is mirrored in the

United States, which helps explain the varied view of graduates when they are asked whether it was worth it: a quarter each say "definitely yes," "probably yes," "probably no," and "definitely no."

Finally, there is the question of whether a degree adds value or skills, or is instead an expensive vetting process for employers, who use it as a signal of desirable underlying characteristics. The latter is what Bryan Caplan argues in his book *The Case Against Education*. When access to higher education expands, some seek other distinguishing markers—more advanced degrees or more prestigious institutions—and others end up working in jobs that don't require a degree. Caplan draws an analogy with a concert. If a few audience members stand up, they will be better able to see the performance, but when those around them start standing too, the result is that everybody is less comfortable and nobody has a better view. The challenge is that it becomes impossible to convince people to sit down, particularly (to stretch the analogy) new generations who are arriving at the back of audience.

It's no surprise then that, despite the huge expansion of higher education, there is still significant appetite for it, particularly among the young. Levels of support have fallen away among Baby Boomers in Britain, for example, but around half of Gen X, Millennials, and Gen Z say they would like increased access to higher education. Few in any generation—at most around 16 percent of both Baby Boomers and the Pre-war generation—say they would like to see it *reduced*.

We continue to prioritize university education in part because of the value we put on the broader experience, not just the economic payoff. At an individual level, higher education provides exposure to new ideas and people beyond lectures and tutorials, and the space to explore new interests, find new talents, and develop broader skills. The benefits from this are hard to quantify, but some have attempted to measure the cognitive benefits of attending university. Based on thirty years' research, psychologists Ernest Pascarella and Patrick Terenzini have found that those who attend college show greater development in critical thinking skills than predicted simply by their preuniversity potential and family characteristics. And it's not just what happens in the classroom that matters: out-of-classroom experiences contribute about half of the increase in critical thinking skills.[16]

This doesn't mean that returns aren't falling or that better systems would not provide even greater benefits. In countries like the UK and United States, we have become so focused on higher education that we have neglected support for nonacademic education and training. As David Goodhart argues in *Head, Hand, Heart*, "Isn't it better to widen the sources of achievement and to try to raise the status of 'not university' rather than send as many people as possible to university, and in the process raise expectations of professional success that in many cases are likely to be disappointed, while starving the economy of the middling technical skills it needs?"[17] The rapid rise in young people with degrees is a success that should be celebrated, but it is difficult to make such a fundamental change without knock-on effects. Key among these effects seems to be a neglect of those not following this route, which partly explains why education levels have become such a key social divide.

## REAL CHANGE AND LAZY MYTHS AT WORK

The labor market has transformed in just a few generations. One of the clearest examples can be seen in the extraordinary changes in women's employment levels in just three or four generations. There have been enormous increases in women's participation in the labor force in nearly all countries.[18] For example, in 1941, only 22 percent of Canadian women aged fifteen or over were economically active, but by 2016 this had shot up to 61 percent.

Immediately prior to the COVID-19 pandemic, the UK was at record levels of employment among the working-age population, at 75 percent, largely driven by increased employment among women.[19] Each generation of women has made gains, particularly in their midtwenties to midthirties, largely due to higher rates of employment during the child-rearing years. For example, nearly 70 percent of women Baby Boomers were employed when they were around twenty years old—but this then dropped to 56 percent by their late twenties. Employment rates for Gen X and Millennial women hit 70 percent when they were slightly older, because of their increased participation in higher education, but didn't dip at all as they moved into their child-rearing years.

The importance of shifting gender roles, reduced birth rates, better maternal health, and increased childcare in supporting higher female employment is clear from the fact that nearly all the generational increases in female employment are concentrated among married women. For example, the participation of married women in the American labor market went from around 30 percent in the 1950s to around 60 percent by the 1990s, accounting for the vast majority of the overall change in women's employment rates.

The other major shift in recent generational employment patterns is the extraordinary rise of older workers. The United States has seen a huge increase in the total number of people employed in the past couple of decades, up twenty-two million since 1998. But, as Lynda Gratton and Andrew Scott, the authors of *The 100-Year Life*, point out, this has relatively little to do with the dynamism of Silicon Valley or the (largely invented) entrepreneurial obsession of today's young people.[20] In fact, 90 percent of the increase is due to higher employment levels of workers aged fifty-five and over. And this isn't just because there are more old people—the bigger part of the change is that a greater proportion of older individuals are staying in or entering workplaces.

The employment rate for this same age group has doubled in the UK and tripled in Germany. Across Germany, Japan, the UK, and the United States, some twenty-nine million of the thirty-three million jobs created have gone to these older workers. The change is particularly striking among older women: the number of working women aged fifty-five to sixty-four in Germany has increased from around one in four to two in three.

However, while employment has become more evenly spread by age and gender, work has become less secure—and it is the younger generations who are more often the victims. Youth unemployment is always higher than overall unemployment, but the young were hit particularly badly in the recession that followed the 2008 crisis. At the lowest point of the downturn, over 20 percent of young people across thirty-five countries were unemployed, while total unemployment remained at around 8 percent. And some countries saw incredibly dramatic swings—for example, youth unemployment in Italy surged to over 40 percent, while overall unemployment was around 12 percent. The same pattern is playing out with the COVID-19 crisis. An incredible 25 percent of young people lost their jobs in the first three months of the crisis in the United States, twice the level of other age groups.[21]

Younger workers also tend to be affected first by structural changes in the nature of work, because they can't afford to be choosy when they're starting out in their careers. Millennials are, for example, more likely than older generations to be working in "nonstandard" or "insecure" employment. One in forty of the UK workforce are on so-called zero-hour contracts—a form of employment on demand that does not guarantee work hours—but among people under twenty-five, the figure is around one in twelve. These changes help explain why overall earnings are often flat for younger generations, despite all those years of extra education. In countries like Spain, Italy, France, and the United States, earnings are rising for most cohorts, but not nearly as much as they did in the past. And in countries like Greece and the UK, real earnings have been falling for most cohorts, and each successive generation is doing worse than the previous one at the same age.[22]

With this increased precarity of work and tighter finances, it's no surprise that young people who have permanent jobs are holding on to them as tightly as ever—in stark contrast to their image as disloyal job hoppers. *Forbes* declared in a 2017 piece, "Millennials and the Death of Loyalty," that "Millennials are coming to have no faith in the concept of loyalty. Instead, they're playing games of leap frog, going from here to there and staying on the move, thinking that when you stand still, you get crushed."[23] However, although it is true that young Americans spend less time with each employer—on average three years when they are in the twenty-five to thirty-four age group than older employees—that has been true since at least 1983, when the young people were Baby Boomers.

In fact, it's older workers who have become more mobile, with particularly big declines in long-term job tenures for those aged fifty-five to sixty-four. These figures are for all job moves, so some may have been forced rather than voluntary, but similar analysis in the UK that looked only at voluntary moves suggests this is not the key factor. Millennials are 20 to 25 percent less likely to switch jobs voluntarily than Gen X were at the same age, and Gen X moved less than Baby Boomers. Far from flightiness, successive generations are staying put longer—largely because secure jobs are harder to come by and so people hold on to what they have.

This generational myth is even worse than the usual one of young people being blamed for changes in their situation, not only because it is not true but because changing jobs infrequently actually reduces your income. Being loyal is typically not good for pay progression—you need to move out to move up, particularly in the early stages of a career. In 2016, the average pay raise for someone who stayed in their job was just 1.7 percent, but a switcher received an average hike of 7.8 percent.

When younger generations aren't being wrongly accused of disloyalty, they are being called lazy. Laziness was cited on the *Time* magazine "Me Me Me" cover, and "lazy" is one of the top adjectives associated with younger cohorts in our global survey of the public. These themes are frequently tied to the workplace, in headlines like "Millennials Work Far Fewer Hours Than Our Parents—So Why Are We Much More Stressed?" However, these interpretations are based on a partial reading of the data that mixes up period and cohort effects.[24]

The reality is that the number of hours worked per week has fallen significantly for all age groups in the long term, reflecting shifting types of employment and increases in productivity. For example, the average working week in France in 1870 was 66 hours; by 2000 it was 37.5.[25] In the UK, the normal working week during the Industrial Revolution was six days—the common usage of the word "weekend" to refer to two days, rather than a single day of rest, did not appear until 1878, according to the *Oxford English Dictionary*.[26] The government didn't restrict the working day to ten hours until 1847, and that was only for women and children. These historical trends have continued into modern times; for example, the average hours worked in Germany has fallen from 41.5 in 1984 to 39 in 2017. As Figure 3.3 shows, *all* generations

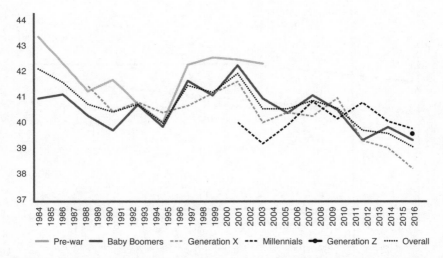

Figure 3.3: Average number of hours worked per week, including overtime, by German adults. Source: ALLBUS (1984–2016).

are working fewer hours—this isn't about lazier younger people dragging down their more assiduous elders. And similar patterns are seen in other countries, including the UK.[27]

Indeed, younger people say they'd like to work *more* rather than less—if they could earn more. Norway offers a typical example: each generation's enthusiasm for working longer hours is likely to decline as they age. This seems to contradict trends that Twenge outlines among senior-year high school students in the United States, an increasing proportion of whom say they "don't want to work hard": from around 25 percent in 1976 to around 40 percent in 2015. But the US data for the question on "working longer to earn more" show the same pattern as elsewhere, with the youngest adults keenest on the idea. It's easy for high school kids to *say* they'd like to work less, but when they need to earn a living, they're at least as motivated as previous generations.

This doesn't mean that younger generations are driven purely by the financial reward that work offers. In fact, they are much less likely to agree that "a job is just a way of earning money," as the example of Japan in Figure 3.4 shows. This also seems to contradict a trend that Twenge identified in the United States of big increases in the proportion of high school seniors who agreed that work is "nothing more than making a living" between 1976 (Baby

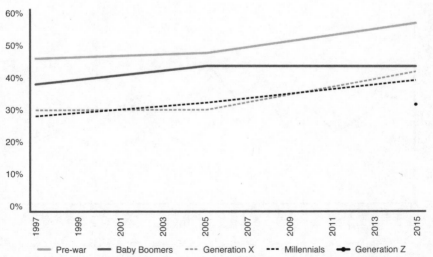

Figure 3.4: Percentage of Japanese adults saying that a job is just a way of earning money. Source: International Social Survey Programme (1997–2015).

Boomers) and 2015 (Gen Z). But again, when they get to adulthood, the pattern in the United States is the same as elsewhere: Gen Z are the least likely to agree that work is just about the money. This demonstrates the power of life-cycle effects that change the views of each generation as they go through various life stages—and the dangers of generalizing about what a generation of adults will be like from their views when they were kids.

## THE END OF WORK?

This bigger question of what work is for is increasingly occupying academics and policy makers as we start to face up to the prospect of a world with a lot less for coming generations of humans to do, due to the acceleration of automation and AI. The list of affected occupations no longer solely includes those that we'd previously have viewed as "routine" or easy to automate but also highly specialized roles we'd expect to require judgment and even intuition, such as medical diagnoses. For example, where a highly skilled dermatologist can draw on hard-won skills developed over many years in determining whether a mole is cancerous, a program can search through hundreds of thousands of cases and come to a more accurate diagnosis.[28]

Of course, we've been here before: we are often leery of technological changes that, in the end, result in significant progress and growth in employment. In Germany, when Anton Moller invented the labor-saving ribbon loom in 1586, the Danzig city council didn't just turn down his request for a patent; it apparently issued an order that he should be strangled! More recently, great leaders and thinkers, from John F. Kennedy to Albert Einstein, have warned that automation will be the cause of a dislocation that may overwhelm its creators. But at each turn, so far, the growth created has far outstripped the direct loss of jobs.

But there are reasons to think the future could be different. In *A World Without Work*, the economist Daniel Susskind outlines how automation has always been a balance between the "substitution" effect, where the machines take the work away from humans, and "complementing" forces that lead to increased productivity, lowering the price of goods and services, creating growth and wealth.[29] As Susskind puts it, these innovations make a "bigger pie," so there is more for humans even if the robots take some of it. These advances can also free up humans to provide goods and services that we couldn't have conceived of at the time. For example, the extraordinary expansion in service-sector jobs, from finance to health to entertainment, could not have been envisaged during our previous industrial ages.

However, Susskind believes that we will inevitably reach a tipping point in the balance between these substitution and complementing effects, because there seems to be no limit on the progress of technology. This won't come as a big bang but as a withering away. The end of work is likely to happen in spurts, where particular sectors are affected greatly, but overall it will be gradual, if relentless. A study by McKinsey & Company examined the trends in around fifty countries and across eight hundred occupations and estimated that four hundred million, or 15 percent of all jobs, could be displaced by 2030. And as with so much else, COVID-19 is likely to accelerate this existing trend, as businesses look to make their operations "pandemic-proof." Long-term social distancing measures, as well as the fear of future novel viruses, will make investment in robots a more attractive proposition.

The advice for us now is uncertain, because so much is unknown. Saying that one profession is safe while another is doomed fails to acknowledge how wrong such projections have been in the past. As Susskind points out, it's often not whole jobs that are automated but tasks within them. We, therefore, need to be suspicious of the simple lists and league tables of "zombie jobs" that the media and commentators love to focus on. However, we still need to prepare ourselves for a huge realignment, learning lessons from a careful examination of the past. Although the overall effect of progress in the Industrial Revolution was incredible, the short-term effects on individuals were often catastrophic—wages stagnated for decades, infant mortality rose, and life expectancy fell. Even those who have an optimistic view of the future recognize that there will be what economists call "frictions." People's existing skills, their connection to their current occupation, and their physical location mean they can't instantly pick up new opportunities.

On the surface, it might seem as though automation will have a genuinely generational impact, in the sense that it will hit particular cohorts much more than others. This could be dramatic, if it came about as a singularity moment, where the machines either launch a hostile takeover or free us from the burden of work. We could then be talking about a "Golden Generation," with a life full of meaningful leisure time, or a "Terminator Generation" if things don't turn out so well. But given the more likely gradual nature of the shift, the consequences will be spread over generations. And as with all major shifts in how we live, its effect will depend on where you are in your life and career. Older groups will struggle more to adapt and retrain, while younger generations are likely to see the more routinized early career roles that they depend on to get started dry up.

## THE SHOCKING SCAM OF GENERATIONAL WORKPLACE RESEARCH

With such transformational change in the pipeline, it's hard to believe that the focus of discussion about generations and work is so often on nonsense about how different each wave of new workers is. This is pushed by those generational consultants who have helped popularize unfounded stereotypes through seminars called things like "Dude, What's My Job? Managing Millennials in Today's Workforce."[30]

Their advice usually starts with big generalizations:

"Generation X are cynical and independent. Millennials are optimistic and focused on themselves. Gen Z are open-minded, caring, with a sense of integrity and tenacity."[31] [These descriptors work just as well for star signs—incredibly, Taurus, Aries and Sagittarius, respectively, have exactly the same attributes. Maybe. I just guessed.]

They then move on to similarly sweeping workplace implications that flow from these character insights:

"Millennials like a collaborative workplace and might not be excited about Gen Z's desire to work independently. Millennials' group lunches, pod workspaces and collaborative projects may not be what many in Gen Z prefer."[32] [Can't Gen Z hang out with the also independent-minded Gen Xers and leave Millennials to their team-building exercises?]
"Praise is the name of the game. When it comes to Millennials, we're talking about a generation where everybody got a trophy, everybody got praised, and everybody got rewarded for showing up."[33] [I also like praise.]

"The national surveys proved that Gen Z was not at all like the Millennials. In fact, they were quite different. One thing was for sure: Gen Z is ready and eager to kick some serious butt at work."[34] [The surveys did not prove this.]

"Dream big with them. Dreams are a big part of a Millennial's life. They were encouraged to dream ever since they were children, and they keep doing it on a daily basis. . . . If they see that your dreams are not as big as theirs, it can be demotivating for them."[35] [Generational consultants focus *a lot* on hopes and dreams.]

"Research does show that Gen Z's attention span was shorter than previous generations' was at their age. Gen Z has on average an eight-second attention span, which is down from 12 seconds in 2000."

This last claim is an undying zombie of generational myths. It has been used for many years now, and it was first applied to Millennials. It's since been bequeathed to Gen Z, but there appears to be absolutely no reliable evidence to back it up. The most frequently cited source is a report in 2015 by Microsoft Canada's Consumer Insights team, which in turn points to the Statistic Brain website, which provides no actual data on generational attention spans.[36] In practice, "attention spans" are complex concepts. The tests by which they are usually measured aren't straightforward and can't give you one simple average in seconds for each generation.[37] In the end, there are no trend data that allow us to accurately compare the average human attention span in the way claimed.

Each of these stereotypes is risky and damaging, as they color our view of whole generations. As the American professors of organizational psychology David Costanza and Lisa Finkelstein have pointed out, "generational membership" is not a protected category. While most people would feel uncomfortable saying that older people can't concentrate, that Black people are cynical, or that women are addicted to praise, it's acceptable to brand entire generations with the same attributes.[38]

So what generational differences truly exist in the workplace? Virtually none. As a meta-analysis of twenty studies that focused on differences in job satisfaction, organizational commitment, and intended job moves concluded, "The pattern of results indicates that the relationships between generational membership and work-related outcomes are moderate to small, essentially zero in many cases."[39] As Jennifer Deal, author of *Retiring the Generation Gap*, concluded in a *Harvard Business Review* podcast, "Fundamentally, Millennials want what older generations have always wanted: an interesting job that pays well, where they work with people they like and trust, have access to development and the opportunity to advance, are shown appreciation on a regular basis, and don't have to leave."

## NOT EVERYTHING IS GENERATIONAL

The separation of cohort, life-cycle, and period effects is the best guard we have against falling for generational myths. Some of the clichés peddled as generational insight, such as those that focus on how different cohorts behave and respond in the workplace, are so gratuitous that they're easy to bust. Of course, people at different stages of their career are looking for different things, but there is no conclusive evidence that these life-cycle effects have shifted greatly over recent decades.

The danger of workplace myths is not just wasted time and money; they also allow employers to blame whole cohorts for their own failings. If companies have a problem with the motivation and retention of younger or older people, they should look to themselves rather than to magic answers based on astrological thinking. It seems bizarre that the workplace has been the context for the frothiest generational claims—it's almost as if there's money to be made in fabricating and then troubleshooting generational challenges.

Life-cycle effects, particularly at key transitions in our lives such as at the start of our careers, pull us into line as we pass through them. This is important because a lot of the myths about each generation's attitudes to work start early, drawing on findings from when they were still teenagers. Unsurprisingly, these differences flatten out when people grow up—people change with experience in these formative years, and this often blows away unreliable signals from our teens. Mark Twain may not actually have said the following, but whoever did had a point: "When I was a boy of fourteen, my father was so ignorant I could hardly stand to have the old man around. But when I got to be twenty-one, I was astonished at how much he had learned in seven years."

The shame of these myths is that they distract us from the extraordinary recent changes in education and work, many of which have been truly generational. Women born just a few decades apart have had incredibly different experiences of the labor market, older people today are staying in the workforce far longer than their parents did, and younger workers face new forms of employment precarity. The extraordinary gradients in our generational lines of graduates should be a cause for celebration, but such a rapid change is bound to create tensions and raise questions. Most importantly, it has distracted us from supporting alternative routes in education and training. In future years we need to see similar growth path for young people completing high-quality apprenticeships and other types of technical education, to avoid a further widening of the generational divide in life chances.

# CHAPTER 4

# HAPPY NOW

It seems blindingly obvious that happiness should be a core aim of life. Even govern-ments are increasingly seeing it as part of their role. Following the lead of Bhutan, France and the UK attempted to make "gross national happiness" a national priority, alongside GDP. In 2019, the New Zealand government developed its first "well-being budget."[1] The United Arab Emirates now has a minister solely dedicated to implementing its National Program for Hap-piness and Well-Being, and the UK has appointed a "minister for loneliness."

These latest interventions may seem like a logical response to a deep and constant human ambition to be happy—but the active pursuit of happiness is actually a relatively recent development. The ancients viewed suffering as a natural condition. The Greek historian Herodotus grimly captured this idea in the fifth century BC: "There is not a man in the world, either here or else-where, who is so happy that he does not wish—again and again—to be dead rather than alive."[2] That's my next inspirational Facebook post sorted.

Historians generally agree that the notion of happiness as an attainable emotional state, rather than an earned outcome of a virtuous life, traces back to the Enlightenment. These changes accelerated in the twentieth century, with improvements in the basics of life, allowing space for greater emotional focus and a growing sense of individual entitlement to happiness. In the

1920s, a spate of books started appearing in America, with titles like *Happiness Is a Choice* and *A Thousand Paths to Happiness*.[3] In later decades, happiness was tied to growing consumerism and formalized as a method of selling more stuff. Major corporations like Disney set out their mission statement to "make people happy," and Coca-Cola urged people to "have a Coke and a smile." Happiness also became a new aim of parenting. Work and obedience had previously been the focus, but parenting manuals began to include well-meaning, if plainly wrong, advice that happiness is "as essential as food."[4]

These shifts reflect the acceleration of human progress in the past couple of centuries, as we left behind millennia of subsistence and moved from survival toward self-expression. This comes with downsides, of course—the pressure to be happy can produce frustration when expectations aren't matched. The shuddering halt in generational progress has had far-reaching implications, including a loss of hope for the future among whole sections of society and even resulting in the tragedy of suicide.

We have developed our understanding of life satisfaction since the 1970s and 1980s, when psychologists suggested humans are stuck on a "hedonic treadmill," where nothing that befalls us—neither lottery wins nor losing a limb—will shift our individual happiness levels significantly in the long term.[5] This assessment now seems somewhat dubious. Although there may well be a baseline that each individual will tend to hover around, happiness levels can fluctuate as a result of what happens to us. However, happiness remains a complex and mysterious subject, and a lot around it is still contested and unexplained. We are constantly looking for new and simple answers, but they often lead us astray.

This confusion is not helped by the abundance of casual myths and stereotypes around generations. We caricature whole decades as having different relationships with happiness, from the swinging 1960s, to the dour 1970s, the greedy 1980s, and the hedonistic 1990s. We overlay these eras with cohort characterizations, from the stoic Pre-war generation, carefree Baby Boomers, and morose Gen Xers, through to the emotionally damaged "snowflakes" of today's younger generations. We hold exaggerated ideas of how our relationship with happiness changes through our life course, spurred on by sensationalist headlines about the anxiety of youth, the misery of middle age, and the loneliness of the elderly.

There is often an element of truth in these different images of periods, cohorts, and life stages, but we are poor at separating them and understanding what is really important. As we will see, proclaimed "epidemics" of suicide among the young or loneliness among the old give a greater sense of threat and change than the actual trends warrant. When we more carefully separate the different effects, it's often a less frightening picture than we're led to believe—but these myths also obscure important, often tragic, realities.

One of these hidden truths is that a lot of the most important stories around happiness are not about the young or old but about those in the middle.

## MIDLIFE MISERY?

"This is the worst day of my life," Bart Simpson groans. He'd earlier been goaded by Homer into skateboarding to Krusty Burger and back while "fourth-base naked." Bart was initially reluctant ("girls might see my doodle"), but he had no choice when Homer threatened to declare him "chicken for life." It was going surprisingly well, until the police stopped him "in the name of American squeamishness" and cuffed him to a lamppost while they went for a burger. Homer, of course, arrived to rescue his son, bringing a T-shirt and socks but, crucially, no pants or shorts. But although Homer had failed in every practical way, he did bring his usual reassuring wisdom, as he corrected Bart: "the worst day of your life *so far*."

And Homer is correct—the likelihood is that things will go downhill for Bart. This is not just because of the bad individual life choices or unfortunate paths awaiting grown-up Bart, where he's nearly always pictured still mooching off his family or working through a fraught divorce. Beyond a cartoon character's imagined futures, there is significant evidence from a number of studies that younger people tend to be happiest.

The best-known model is the "U-shaped happiness curve," where we begin adult life happy, bottom out in our late forties or early fifties and then gradually get happier again.[6] Two of the key analysts of life satisfaction, Andrew Oswald, a UK academic, and David Blanchflower, a former Bank of England policy maker, have examined this relationship for decades, across a wide range of countries and surveys. In his latest study, Blanchflower covered 132 countries and concluded, "No ifs, no buts, well-being is U-shaped in age."[7]

Blanchflower found that in the dozens of richer countries included in his study, the absolute low point of happiness is at 47.2 years. This is where I should confess that this is my exact age as I'm writing this chapter. It may help explain my current dark mood about the book-writing process—but looking on the bright side, by the time you're reading this, I'll be on the upward curve. I can recognize a lot of the features that are often held up as explanations for unhappiness in middle age. It's a life stage that is often defined by pressure, when we tend to be caught between responsibilities to kids, parents, and careers, which puts a strain on time for ourselves and our personal relationships. It's also the point when we begin to reassess our lives; more is behind us than in front, and the reality doesn't always live up to what we dreamed of in our youth. The Irish comedian Dylan Moran boiled down Shakespeare's seven ages of man to just four, and perfectly captured the ennui in the middle: "Child, failure, old, dead."[8]

The relative consistency of Blanchflower's U-shaped pattern across many countries raises the intriguing possibility that this is a pure age effect attributed to our biology. This explanation was reinforced in a study by Oswald and four other scholars, in which zookeepers and other animal caretakers rated chimpanzees' and orangutans' state of mind over time in Australia, Canada, Japan, Singapore, and the United States. The apes' well-being bottomed out at ages that were comparable to between forty-five and fifty in humans. As the authors conclude, "Our results imply that human well-being's curved shape is not uniquely human and that, although it may be partly explained by aspects of human life and society, its origins may lie partly in the biology we share with closely related great apes."[9]

The U-shaped happiness curve attracts significant controversy. Other studies find relatively flat lines, a U shape with happiness trailing off again for the oldest group or even *inverted* U shapes.[10] These different results sometimes occur because studies are looking at different measures of well-being or are conducted in different countries: the U-shaped pattern is more clearly seen in more developed Western nations, while other parts of the world see more variable patterns. But even in Western countries, it is hotly disputed. An exhaustive review of published research across economics, psychology, and gerontology concluded that it is not possible to say with any certainty whether the happiness relationship is really U shaped, because it depends on how you approach the analysis.[11]

There are three points that help us come to grips with the real changes in happiness as we age. First, it is not always clear from reports that these analyses are often not a simple presentation of survey results. Most analyses, including Blanchflower's study identifying the age of 47.2 years old as the height of misery, control for other factors that relate to life satisfaction, to try to identify the pure impact of age on happiness.

For example, we know that there is a relationship between happiness and characteristics like employment, wealth, health, and relationship status. We also know that your place within each of these categories depends to a large degree on your age. Some analysts, therefore, take the view that, if we want to understand how *just our age* relates to our happiness, we should strip the effect of these other factors out of the data. This typically increases older people's "adjusted" happiness, because they tend to have worse health and are more likely to be widowed and live alone. For example, Figure 4.1 shows one chart from Blanchflower's study that uses Eurobarometer data from thirty-five European countries, and you can see that the U shape is more pronounced after these controls are included; without them, the data show a much less dramatic bounce back in later years.

Some regard these controls as "fiddling with the data," as the results don't reflect the actual life satisfaction levels of different age groups. Richard Easterlin, another prominent analyst of happiness, has said, "If one wants to know

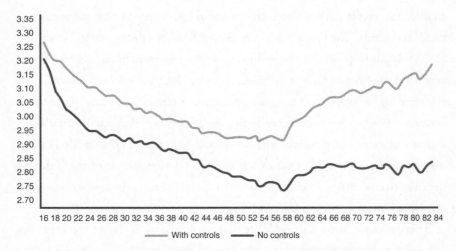

Figure 4.1: Life satisfaction (scored out of four) by age in Europe, 2009–2019. Source: Blanchflower reanalysis of Eurobarometer data 2009–2019.

whether a person is likely to be happier in his or her golden years than when forming families, one would not want to set aside the fact that older people are likely to have lower income, and be less healthy and are more likely to be living alone."[12] This is true, but understanding the pure age effect is also useful. As Blanchflower points out, when we look at the risks to our health from smoking, we control for other factors that relate to both smoking and illness, such as income, in order to gain a true idea of the effect of smoking alone. The real problem is how the findings are reported and the fact that they are simplified into those "middle-age misery" headlines.[13]

The second important point we need to understand is how big the midlife dip in our happiness actually is. The differences are statistically significant—partly because the surveys are so large—but we also need to know what statisticians call the "effect size."[14] If you look back at Figure 4.1, you can see that, through the vast majority of our lives, we tend to bobble around between 2.8 and 3.1 out of a possible score of 4. These small changes are not to be dismissed: from peak to trough, they sometimes approach the average impact of losing a job, for example. But we shouldn't interpret the changes as guaranteed midlife despair—this is a dip, which partly reflects the nature of happiness in humans: it doesn't vary greatly between most people, our own individual happiness is pretty well established, regardless of circumstances, and we tend to adapt when the context changes.

The final point these reviews make clear is that part of the reason for the conflicting results is that there are an awful lot of things that influence our happiness levels. The focus is overwhelmingly on age effects, but other studies find a relationship between happiness and when we were born (cohort effects) and what was happening in our countries at the time (period effects). The evidence for cohort effects is messy and inconsistent across countries, mostly because when you were born tends to have a fairly small impact.[15] One study stands out as an exception: Blanchflower and Oswald found that life satisfaction among US men decreased with each successive decade of birth during the twentieth century. We'll return to this pattern later when we examine the growth of "despair" in the United States.[16]

There is more consistent evidence that particular periods of time are either happy or unhappy for entire populations of countries. Not surprisingly, the onset of the COVID-19 crisis had a particularly dramatic effect on happiness levels; for example, the proportion of people in the UK giving themselves the lowest score increased to 21 percent as the lockdown started, compared with just 8 percent at the end of 2019.[17] However, these scores also started to recover within a few weeks. Our happiness is resilient, even in extreme circumstances.

However, this is unlikely to be the end of the pandemic's impact on happiness. It is clear that there is a link between how the economy is doing and our life satisfaction, and it is clear that economic busts make us much sadder than booms make us happy. In a study of over 150 countries, the economists Jan-Emmanuel De Neve and Michael Norton showed that recession years are significantly associated with losses in well-being, but the relationship between positive growth years and increased well-being is much weaker.[18] For example, drawing on the same Eurobarometer study as Blanchflower, they found that our subjective well-being is around six times more sensitive to the negative effects of recessions than the positive influence of booms. Greece provides an extreme example: life satisfaction there barely shifted from the 1980s through much of the 2000s, despite the economy growing by over 50 percent. But well-being then plummeted to historic lows following the 2008 recession.

This asymmetry can be partly explained by the trends we've seen in earlier chapters: ordinary people have not benefited significantly from economic growth in recent decades, as wage growth has stalled—while downturns have continued to hit them hard. But it is also partly related to our strong "loss aversion": we feel losses keenly, while we tend to bank gradual gains without really noticing them.[19] We also have a "complaint bias"—when things are going well, we keep pretty quiet about it, in the hope that it continues or even increases. But when things go wrong, it makes sense to make our feelings known, in order to encourage change.[20]

You get a much clearer image of the relative importance of these competing age, period, and cohort effects when you plot our happiness along generational lines. For consistency with Blanchflower's analyses, I used the same Eurobarometer data, looking across more than thirty countries—and what stands out is not a large midlife dip in life satisfaction but rather its undulation for all age groups over time, with relatively small gaps between generations. There is only one clear and repeated exception: each generation of young people tends to start out notably happier than older generations.

Spain is typical of these patterns, as shown in Figure 4.2. First, you can see the roller coaster of period effects among all Spanish generations, with significant falls around recessions in the early 1990s and in 2008 and then a gradual recovery from 2012. There is no clear sign of a cohort effect, where generations are different and stay different over time. There also doesn't seem to be much of a midlife trough, where, for example, Gen X become notably more miserable than other generations in recent years as they reach their late forties.

The one age-based pattern that does stand out is that as each new generation comes into the data, they start off as the happiest of all cohorts—before being dragged down into the pack. Gen X arrived relatively bright eyed in the late 1980s, just as Millennials did in the early 2000s and Gen Z did in the past few years—but these repeated waves of positivity soon dissipate. We see the same sort of pattern in the Netherlands, Italy, and the UK, among other countries.

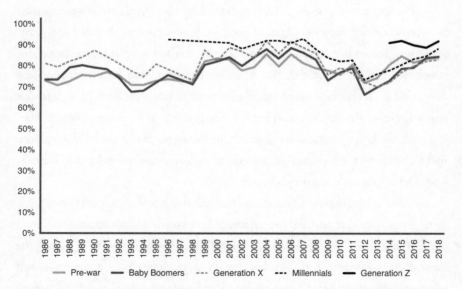

Figure 4.2: Percentage of Spanish adults who are "very satisfied" or "fairly satisfied" with the life they lead. Source: Eurobarometer (1986–2018).

So overall, those of us who are in middle age can stake a decent claim to being the most miserable but not by as much as some media reports imply. A chunk of our reported relative unhappiness is because most of the models correctly assume that worse is to come as we age, in terms of our health and relationships. It highlights significant truths about middle-aged angst and the resilience of older age, but the generational lines show how much is going on, both between groups and across time. Reassuringly, there is not much evidence of big differences between cohorts; instead, it's the repeated relative happiness of youth that stands out, regardless of when they were born. Despite all the difficult circumstances facing young people, there is no sign of a wholesale decline in happiness among our current generation of young people compared with previous ones, in the large majority of countries.

## ARE THE KIDS ALRIGHT?

This relatively rosy picture may seem at odds with concern for the mental health of younger generations. Headlines abound on how first Millennials and now Gen Z are "the most mentally ill generation" or "so anxious and unhappy."[21]

But this apparent mismatch between our data on happiness and the narrative presented in the media is not a straightforward generational myth. Although happiness and mental health are clearly related, they are distinct dimensions.[22] For example, those with a severe mental illness can still have a high level of well-being if their condition is managed well. And even where mental health conditions do reduce an individual's happiness, they still affect only a relatively small proportion of the population, and these trends may not move the average happiness level for young people as a whole.

This seems to be what's happening in the United States. A 2019 study by Jean Twenge and colleagues showed that the proportion of US adolescents reporting symptoms consistent with major depression in the past twelve months increased from 8.7 percent to 13.2 percent between 2005 and 2017.[23] Young adults saw an almost identical trend, in both major depressive symptoms and serious psychological distress. There were no corresponding increases among other age groups over this period—it looks like a pattern that's emerged in the past few years among the current generation of young, rather than a more general period effect.

These are large proportional increases in severe mental health conditions, but as they only affect relatively small proportions of the young, they don't mean that young people are, on average, less happy than older groups. Indeed, Twenge shows in her book on Gen Z that overall happiness levels have remained relatively high among young people.[24]

The picture for young people in England is starting to show worrying parallels with the picture in the United States. Figure 4.3 traces our generational lines from 1991 to 2016 on a measure called the General Health Questionnaire–12, part of the Health Survey for England. This widely used measure covers twelve items on general levels of depression, anxiety, sleep disturbance, and self-confidence; the chart below tracks those with a score that indicates a high likelihood of a common mental health disorder.[25]

For the most part, different generations hover around the same level throughout the period, and there are few significant changes in the trend (with a notable blip in 2009, following the global financial crisis). There is, however, an indication that something may be different with Gen Z. Over a fifth of this latest generation of young people (22 percent) are starting out adult life with signs of a common mental health disorder, compared with 15 percent of Millennials back in 1998, when they were the same average age.

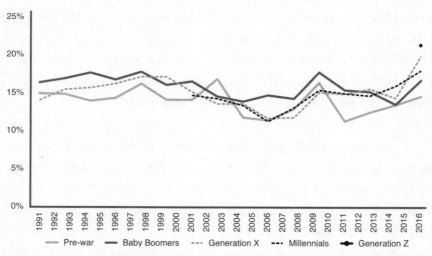

Figure 4.3: Percentage of young people in England with a score of 4 or higher on the General Health Questionnaire–12 measure of common mental health disorder. Source: Health Survey for England (1991–2016).

This is just a single data point that uses a simple, nonclinical survey measure of possible mental health disorders, so we should be cautious about placing too much emphasis on its results. However, it is reinforced by other British studies that suggest underneath this overall trend a more worrying pattern for recent generations of young women and girls. For example, the Mental Health of Children and Young People survey uses a detailed diagnostic tool for mental disorders, and all cases are reviewed by clinically trained professionals. Again, on first glance it is not that worrying. Emotional disorders, such as anxiety and depression, did increase among children aged between five and fifteen, from around 4 percent in both 1999 and 2004 to around 6 percent in 2017. But there are some startling differences between age groups and genders, with 22 percent of seventeen- to nineteen-year-old girls and women classified as having an emotional disorder.[26]

Other studies in England suggest that this is an emergent trend. The Adult Psychiatric Morbidity Survey includes people aged sixteen to twenty-four; as Figure 4.4 shows, there has been a stark increase in young women classed as having severe anxiety or depression, from under 10 percent in 1993 and 2000 to around 15 percent by 2014, while the figures for boys and young men have

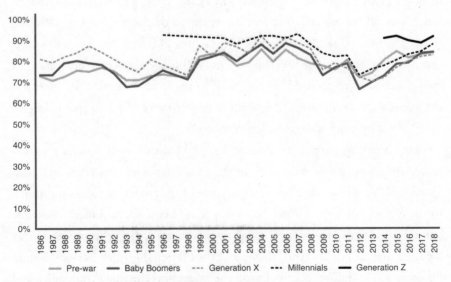

Figure 4.4: Percentage of English people aged sixteen to twenty-four with severe anxiety and depression. Source: McManus, S., and E. Fuller (2009). Adult Psychiatric Morbidity in England: Results of a Household Survey. Health and Social Care Information Centre.

barely changed. The study also highlights the extraordinary rise in reported self-harm over the same period, from around 6 percent of young women to nearly 20 percent, with young men also increasing but to a much lower level of around 8 percent.[27]

These gender-specific findings are eerily similar to results in the United States, where the prevalence of major depressive episodes shot up for teenage girls, from around 12 percent in 2011 to around 19 percent by 2015, with boys remaining quite stable at around 5 to 6 percent.[28] The overall trend in Britain may be less marked, but it seems to be following a worryingly similar path. Nor is this just a UK and US phenomenon: the World Health Organization has flagged its concern about the "increasing rate of mental health and behavioural problems" in adolescents and young people across Europe.[29]

Early reviews of the mental health impact of the COVID-19 pandemic suggest that the direct effects of social isolation and the longer-term consequences for the economy will accentuate these worrying trends. In fact, a number of studies have already shown increases in mental health disorders across the population.[30] The president of the Royal College of Psychiatrists in the UK believes it will be the "biggest hit to mental health since the second world war," with as many as ten million people requiring new or additional mental health support as a direct result of the crisis.[31] However, as with so much around the effect of the pandemic, this is disproportionately affecting those who were already vulnerable—including children and young people: one tracking study in the UK showed that eighteen- to twenty-four-year-olds were twice as likely to feel "hopelessness" as result of the pandemic than was the population as a whole.[32] How these huge shocks affect people is largely determined by much slower, longer-term shifts.

One culprit in particular is often blamed for this shift among the current young generation: the advent of the smartphone and social media. Jean Twenge believes this is the "worm at the core of the apple," and she's not alone. In the UK in 2019, the Health Secretary Matt Hancock proposed a new law banning under-thirteens from using social media, citing the consequences for their mental health. And the head of the National Health Service, Simon Stevens, was unequivocal in pointing the finger at technology companies and social media platforms for leaving "the National Health Service to pick up the pieces—for an epidemic of mental health challenge for our young people."[33]

On the surface, the evidence seems clear-cut. For example, my own analysis of British data shows that children who spend three or more hours on social networking sites on a weekday are more than twice as likely to have mental disorder symptoms than those who spend no time on them (27 percent compared to 12 percent).[34] Other studies show even larger effects for high-level users. For example, one study of more than ten thousand fourteen-year-olds showed that 12 percent of light social media users and 38 percent of heavy social media users had depressive symptoms.[35] This explanation is particularly tempting because it also provides a logical rationale for the growing gap between girls and boys: 40 percent of girls use social media for three or more hours a day, compared with only 20 percent of boys.

It seems like a closed case—but it's not.

First, these associations don't account for other factors that could cause both higher social media use *and* mental health issues. When researchers include a wider range of factors in their models, the influence of social media and technology becomes much less dramatic. In one major study covering more than 350,000 interviews in the UK and the United States, smoking marijuana and bullying, for example, have much larger negative associations with adolescent well-being than technology use.[36] And simple activities, such as getting enough sleep and regularly eating breakfast, have much more positive associations with well-being than the average effect of reduced technology use.

In fact, the association between well-being and regularly *eating potatoes* was nearly as negative as the association with technology use—but it's much harder to find articles bemoaning how potato consumption is "destroying a generation."[37]

A separate UK government study, focusing specifically on the effect of social media, also showed its use was only marginally related to psychological health when the researchers controlled for other factors.[38] The effect of getting enough sleep and seeing friends was about three times larger, and the effect of being bullied, whether online or offline, was about eight times larger. When the researchers accounted for these other factors, social media use had a minimal unique association with psychological health.[39]

In the end, the best conclusion is that social media use has a relatively small association with well-being for children and young people overall; although there may be stronger links between social media and mental health among specific groups, such as teenage girls, there is evidence that it is the wider effects associated with high use that are more important. For example, time spent on social media is associated with more sedentary behavior, which is related to a range of poor health outcomes. Social media may also expose young people to more opportunities for bullying, and it might also interfere with sleep hygiene, both of which are associated with mental health problems, including depression. You might think that limiting social media use is a good idea if it improves sleep and activity levels and reduces bullying. However, the crucial point is that social media use is not even a particularly good predictor of these mediating factors, when you compare it with the effects of family, social life, social class, educational status, genetics, and so on.

It is vitally important that we get this right, given the significant risks in being wrong. Little in the current evidence suggests that encouraging parents to take away mobile phones, or legislators to restrict social media platforms, will significantly reduce the problem. Our tendency to accept a simple answer that seems right is a strong human trait, but these are complex issues, which hardly ever yield a single solution. Even with all the details we know about young people across these studies, we can only explain around 30 to 40 percent of the variation in happiness levels. There is a lot that we just don't know.

We need to be particularly suspicious of simple answers to big questions when they relate to an emergent technology. "Moral panics" have ensued from all sorts of innovations: everything from the mass translation and printing of the Bible, to novels, bicycles, and electricity, to violent video games have been seen as threats to the established social order. At its root, this is a deeply generational phenomenon. New generations are more proficient at adapting to innovation, which can create a perception among older generations that they are losing control of the culture they helped shape.[40]

I was surprised by the certainty of senior politicians and officials in their calls for legislative action on social media, given the paucity of evidence, but it's a repeated pattern. In 2005, Hillary Clinton attempted to introduce a bill to strengthen the regulations on violent video games, citing evidence that they "increase aggressive behavior as much as lead exposure decreases children's IQ scores." But the Supreme Court ruled that the evidence did not support the action. And Clinton was far from the first to pick up on the video game threat. In 1983, the US surgeon general suggested that games like Asteroids, Space Invaders, and Centipede were a leading cause of family violence.[41] The reason that older examples of these panics sound more ridiculous to us than the latest ones is *not* that the world is getting worse—it's just that we're getting old.

## ONLY THE LONELY

It's understandable why the head of the National Health Service in the UK would talk about a "mental health epidemic" among young people—even prior to the COVID-19 pandemic, which seems set to accelerate the trend. The few percentage points' increase in prevalence that we'd already seen represents hundreds of thousands of additional young people accessing support, which places an enormous strain on already stretched services.

However, the hundreds of media articles over the past few years that claim we have been experiencing a "loneliness epidemic" are more misleading. It doesn't seem to matter that sometimes this loneliness epidemic was focused on young people and sometimes the old—both versions are increasingly accepted truisms across many countries.[42] This is strange, because the evidence is almost entirely absent. I would love to present a compelling generational chart of a loneliness measure, but I have been unable to find data for the general public in any country over an extended period of time.

The trend data that do exist tend to be for specific sections of the population and suggest little change over the long term. For example, a study by a group of US psychologists and social scientists examined of loneliness among Baby Boomers relative to a Pre-war cohort; they found no evidence that loneliness is substantially higher among the Baby Boomers or that it had increased over the previous decade.[43] Studies of other rich countries have yielded similar results. In Sweden, repeated cross-sectional surveys with adults aged eighty-five, ninety, and ninety-five found no increase in loneliness over a ten-year period.[44] Using data from the Berlin Aging Study, researchers found that loneliness levels were substantially *lower* among seventy-five-year-olds in more recent birth cohorts, while another study found lower rates of loneliness in more recent Finnish cohorts of seventy-year-olds compared with earlier ones.[45]

At the other end of the age spectrum, a team of psychologists analyzed long-term trends among teenagers in the United States and found no signs of

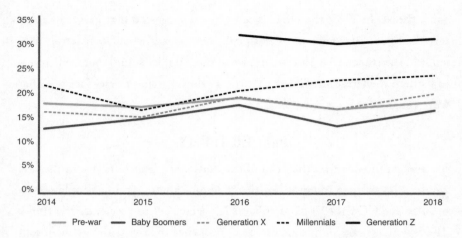

Figure 4.5: Percentage of English adults who say they "sometimes" or "often" feel lonely. Source: Community Life Study (2014–2018).

increasing loneliness between 1976 and the 2010s. In fact, they found a statistically significant *decline* in loneliness among high school students, but the size of the effect was small.[46]

Loneliness does vary between age groups, but these patterns seem to be constant over time. Perhaps surprisingly, given the focus in recent years on loneliness among the old, it is clear that younger adults are more likely to feel lonely, as studies in the UK, United States, New Zealand, and Japan confirm.[47] You can see this in generational lines from a study in England, in Figure 4.5. This is too short a run of data to tell us anything about generational change, but you can see why a casual reading generates headlines about rising loneliness among young people: Gen Z are around twice as likely to say they feel lonely than older age groups are. However, the scant evidence available suggests that this is the norm for young people.

On a personal level, it's easy to recall feelings from our own youth that suggest why the young feel loneliness the most—it's a time in life when socializing is more important to us and social isolation hurts more. Loneliness, properly defined, is the subjective discrepancy between our actual and our desired level of social connection: it depends on our expectations.

Even with this more precise definition, it may seem surprising that there is not at least some evidence of a long-term increase in loneliness, given the enormous changes in how we live. As the sociologist Eric Klinenberg put it, "Our species has embarked on a remarkable social experiment." Humans are now living apart more than at any time in our history.[48] For example, 2018 estimates from the Census Bureau show that 28 percent of all US households are made up of a single person, compared with just 9 percent in 1950. And this is a common pattern across countries. My own analysis of Eurobarometer data from more than thirty countries shows an increase from 11 percent in 1971 to 24 percent in 2019.

Solitary living is not an entirely recent phenomenon then, and it has caused waves of similar concern over many decades. As Julianne Holt-Lunstad, a US psychologist who has focused on the impact of loneliness, explains, "We have worried about loneliness since the rise of industrial society. Since we started moving away from the village and we agglomerated into towns where we didn't know as many of our neighbors, we worried about loneliness. . . . We worried about the loneliness of apartment dwellers, of people driving in cars, of people who went to movies, of people who got the telephone instead of going into social life."[49]

Drawing on a similarly long-term perspective in *A Biography of Loneliness: The History of an Emotion*, the British historian Fay Bound Alberti suggests that loneliness is a product of our industrialized society, noting that the term hardly ever appeared before 1800.[50] Modern loneliness, in Alberti's view, is the product of capitalism and secularism, and it is caused by the divisions between "the self and the world" that have developed since the eighteenth century. Living alone and feeling alone have been driven by the politics and economics of individualism. As with so many of the other patterns we've seen, the most important trends are the result of long-term cultural evolution rather than overnight epidemics.

This is not to say that the effects of loneliness are unimportant. The American psychologist John Cacioppo produced some of the most important work in understanding its mechanisms and effects, and he likened it to a biological drive similar to hunger or thirst. Loneliness plays a useful role in motivating us to seek out others, as a form of protection and a more effective use of effort. The feeling of loneliness is a signal to us to participate in social life, but it can also increase our sense of threat, which can in turn lead to biological responses, like higher blood pressure.

Beyond these direct biological impacts, some researchers see loneliness as being behind other destructive behaviors. US surgeon general Vivek Murthy advocates raising the profile of the consequences of loneliness: "When I began my time as Surgeon General, I started to recognise that many of the stories that I was hearing from people in small towns and big cities all across America were stories about addiction, about violence, about depression and anxiety. But behind them were threads of loneliness."[51]

There have been some attention-grabbing studies that seem to confirm these dire consequences of loneliness—including the suggestion that loneliness is as likely to kill you as smoking fifteen cigarettes a day. The claim has circulated widely, even cited by Murthy. The source of the claim is a meta-analysis of 148 studies across North America, Europe, Japan, China, and Australia.[52] The study finds that people who were more socially connected had a 50 percent increased chance of survival over time, a figure that is indeed comparable to quitting smoking. Crucially, however, the researchers were measuring the impact of *all* social connections rather than loneliness specifically. This included a wide range of measures, for example, whether subjects received practical support from others and their perceptions of how supported they were, as well as whether they were married, the size and depth of their network of friends, and whether they lived alone. We also need to remember that these studies can prove only an association rather than a causal relationship. The comparison with smoking is eye catching, but it's difficult to be as sure about the causal link.[53]

However, given its prevalence and likely importance, attending to loneliness is ultimately a good thing, even if the epidemic rhetoric is sometimes overblown. Raising the profile of a relatively hidden issue may be a benefit in itself, and the effect of COVID-19 may actually help bring the discussion to the fore. Tracey Crouch, the first "minister for loneliness" in the UK, said, "I think we are in loneliness where we were with mental health a decade ago. People didn't talk about poor mental health, whereas now we are removing the stigma." This increased focus must translate into action that builds practical and emotional connections between people, including creating spaces for people to meet and interact, and finding new ways to reach those who would most benefit. For example, a significant proportion of doctor visits have their root cause in loneliness; as Crouch suggested, "social prescribing," where people can be connected to local organizations that provide support networks, might be more effective than pills.

## KILLING OURSELVES SLOWLY

I have much less patience with claims that we are facing yet another "epidemic"—of suicide among young people. For example, a *Sunday Times* headline in 2019 called Gen Z a "suicidal generation," citing a doubling in the death toll among teenagers in the UK over the previous eight years. However, as journalist Tom Chivers succinctly put it, this reading of the data and the broader claims of an epidemic are "absolute bollocks from top to bottom."[54]

The first point to bear in mind is that suicide is incredibly rare. Fewer than seven in one hundred thousand young people kill themselves each year in the UK, a lower rate than for just about any other age group. In contrast, for example, around eighteen in one hundred thousand of those aged forty-five to forty-nine killed themselves in 2018. The common misconception that suicide is more of an issue among young people is partly because it *is* one of the top killers among the young—it's the second–most common cause of death in teenagers across many countries, including the UK, Canada, the United States, and Australia, behind cancer—but this mostly reflects the fact that young people don't die very often.

Of course, the focus on youth suicide is in some ways understandable because of this rarity and because each case is a particular tragedy, given each victim had so much life ahead of them. It would be a real concern if the rate really were consistently doubling, but examination of the data shows this to be a gross misdirection. The *Sunday Times* article picked the lowest available point to compare the latest figures with, in order to show the largest possible short-term increase. When you look at the actual trends, as in Figure 4.6, the real pattern has been a long-term decline in suicide among younger people, from a high in the late 1980s and 1990s.[55]

The danger of this sort of sloppy reporting is that it distracts us from the real pattern in the data. This is much clearer in a striking analysis by the UK Office for National Statistics (ONS), which plots suicide by age over the long term.[56] In the early 1980s, suicide was spread across all age groups in England and Wales and, if anything, affected those in their sixties and seventies more. But from around 1986, a wave of higher suicide rates started to make its way through the age ranges, starting with a peak for people in their early twenties, exactly when those born at the start of Gen X would have reached this age. By 1998, the peak shows up when people are in their late thirties,

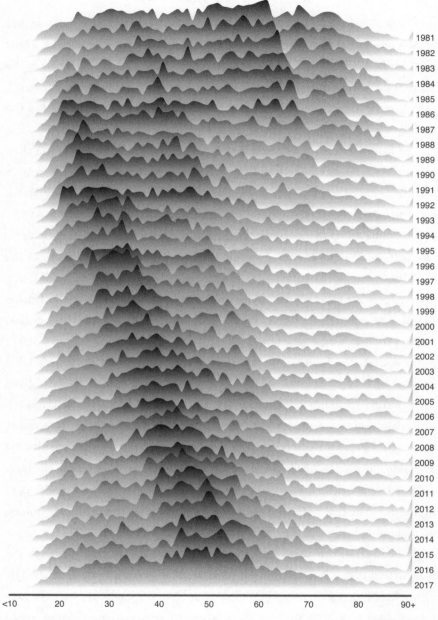

1981
1982
1983
1984
1985
1986
1987
1988
1989
1990
1991
1992
1993
1994
1995
1996
1997
1998
1999
2000
2001
2002
2003
2004
2005
2006
2007
2008
2009
2010
2011
2012
2013
2014
2015
2016
2017

<10   20   30   40   50   60   70   80   90+

Figure 4.6: Age-specific suicide rates by broad age groups, UK males. Source: Office for National Statistics, National Records of Scotland and Northern Ireland Statistics and Research Agency (1981–2018).

and in 2018 it straddled those in their forties and fifties. Each of these points marks a perfect trail of Gen X making their way through life. I've been trying to identify cohort effects for over a decade, and this was an awful one to find. Gen X, sadly, can be much more accurately described as "the suicidal generation."

Of course, this is still a grossly overblown epithet; even among this cohort, suicide is still extremely rare, and it varies hugely between men and women and rich and poor. For example, in the latest figures for the forty-five to forty-nine age group, men make up three-quarters of all cases. Suicide rates are also more than twice as high in the most deprived areas of the UK than in the least deprived.[57] It seems that being born a man, in a poor area of Britain, and as part of Gen X is a particularly toxic combination.[58]

As for why there might be such a strong cohort connection between Gen X and suicide, one theory relates to the "middle child" position of Gen X: they straddle two distinctive cultural and economic periods, and some have ended up getting the bad from both. They've borne more of the brunt of economic stagnation and austerity than older UK cohorts but are more reticent in seeking help when they're struggling than younger cohorts.[59]

Another sad element of the story of Gen X is shown in further analysis by the ONS, tracking deaths from overdose. These tightly trace the same horrible path, following Gen X over time—the peak of drug deaths moves from people in their early twenties in 1992 to those in their mid-forties by 2017.

This might be explained by the greater availability of opioid drugs, particularly heroin, from the 1980s in the UK, just when Gen X was just coming into their teenage years. Heroin was responsible for more than half the deaths from overdose in 2017.[60] A further life-cycle element makes this increasingly tragic over time. Deaths from overdose in each year cohort within Gen X have tripled, from around 50 in the early 1990s to around 150 now. The government report speculates this could be partly a life-cycle effect; the older bodies of drug users from this generation are less able to cope with the effects of long-term use.

Crucially, economists Anne Case and Angus Deaton have shown that these apparently separate phenomena of suicide and overdose are connected in the United States. They suggest that the relationship between them is blurred, given the difficulty of identifying motives in deaths caused by drugs and the reticence to classify any death as suicide. Their suggestion is that, along with deaths related to alcoholism, they should be considered "deaths of despair," which are increasing significantly in the United States.[61] These self-destructive trends are having an extraordinary impact on sections of society and are even affecting overall life expectancy, which after decades of consistent improvement has started to *fall* in the United States. Their analysis shows that the phenomenon is not population-wide; the reversal is concentrated almost entirely among less-educated white people.

Case and Deaton show that "deaths of despair" among white men and women aged forty-five to fifty-four without a bachelor's degree tripled between 1990 and 2017, while those among middle-aged white American graduates held steady. They focus their analysis on middle age, but the cohort effect in the United States is quite different from the one I've just described in the UK: each cohort is doing progressively worse than the one preceding it. For example, at age forty-five, white Americans without a bachelor's degree from the cohort born in 1960 faced a 50 percent higher risk of dying from suicide, drugs, and alcohol than the 1950 birth cohort, and the 1970 cohort faced a risk that was more than twice as high again. This is a true generational tragedy; when less-educated white Americans were born has really shaped who they are.

There is no single accepted explanation as to why this is happening. Case and Deaton's main argument is that deaths of despair reflect a long-term loss of a white working-class way of life. This is not solely about poverty, inequality, or the financial crash, although each has played a role. For example, they echo Robert Putnam in suggesting that after the great recession, "capitalism began to look more like a racket for redistributing upward than an engine for general prosperity."

Case and Deaton's analysis is deeply generational, and not just in the sense of the relentless decline in life chances for successive cohorts. It also highlights how embedded the expectation of generational progress had become and how its failure to appear contributed to the despair. As they outline, "Progress in health and living standards in the twentieth century was prolonged enough that, by the century's end, people could reasonably expect it to continue and to bless their children's lives just as it had blessed theirs. . . . Not only that, but the rate of improvement since the end of the Second World War had been so steady and so prolonged that it seemed obvious that future generations would do better still." Alongside the immediate tragedy of so many lives cut short, the sense of betrayal from this shocking reversal has threatened society's faith in the system.

Whether this is a peculiarly American phenomenon is a key question. Perhaps the problem is really one of contemporary capitalism, and the United States is setting a trail that other countries will soon follow. But either way, there are certainly contributing factors that are particular to the United States: Case and Deaton suggest that its history of racial tension and prejudice, lower levels of social protection, and particular health-care system are all significant.

As Case and Deaton conclude, this trend may be particular to America or one that might be seen elsewhere in the future. They point to the fact that, while the United States currently dwarfs other countries in its total number of deaths of despair, countries including Canada, Ireland, Australia, and Britain (particularly Scotland) are showing increases. More encouragingly, our analysis of British data suggests that this tragedy is specific to Gen X, and we are not yet seeing it spill over into the kind of generation-on-generation increases in deaths of despair seen in the United States. It is not yet inevitable that Britain will follow America's lead.

## SIMPLE ANSWERS ARE WRONG

We are programmed to look for patterns and explanations—the countless examples of people seeing the face of Jesus in a tortilla or the Virgin Mary in a grilled cheese sandwich testify to our need to make sense of randomness. This relates to the "clustering illusion" explained by the Cornell University psychology professor Thomas Gilovich. In one study, he presented the sequence "oxxxoxxxoxxoooxooxxoo" to hundreds of people and asked them whether they thought it was random. Most believed there was a planned pattern, because when we see clusters, we tend to think there is a design or meaning behind them (it is random).[62]

It takes very little to convince us that there is a reason for patterns, particularly if that reason seems straightforward. We want to know *the* single cause, but this preference for simplicity is not just mental laziness—it also gives us a clear target for action. For example, Europeans in the Middle Ages believed that lice were good for your health, because they were rarely found on sick people. When illness struck, they would therefore try to deliberately catch lice. They reasoned that people got sick when the lice left, when the real explanation was the lice left when people got sick. Lice are extremely sensitive to body temperature—a small increase in a fever will make them look for a new host. The thermometer had not yet been invented, so this temperature increase was rarely noticed, giving the impression that the lice had left *before* the person got sick. Cause and effect were reversed, but it felt good to have one single source of the problem to blame and one single achievable action to take.[63]

We've seen some clear generational shifts in this chapter. There is strong evidence, for example, that mental disorders have increased among sections of young people in some countries in recent years. But there is only superficial evidence that mobile phones or social media are the cause—and there is good reason to think that there are more important, and complex, things going on. It's vital that we resist the lure of these simple answers, as they are likely to distract us from taking necessary action. As American journalist H. L. Mencken put it, "For every complex problem there is a simple answer, and it's wrong."[64]

Causes can also take time to reveal their true nature. The hump of suicide among young people in Britain in the 1980s will have appeared as a blip at the time, but the longer-term picture suggests a generational effect on a particular subset of Generation X. It is important that our responses reflect the reality to get that particular cohort the support it needs rather than grasp for an immediate simple answer.

The importance of these generational patterns should prompt us to question the view that history jumps rather than crawls. As the work of Case and Deaton suggests, even where the jumps are vitally important, like the 2008 global recession and now COVID-19, the consequences depend on the particular set of circumstances that have developed for different groups over a much longer period. Understanding long-term generational trends is as vital in times of rapid change as it is in the quiet periods in between.

# CHAPTER 5

# A HEALTHY FUTURE?

Improvements in health and longevity play out as a series of grinding battles between the aging process on the one hand and medical and social advances on the other. Our life cycles exert a powerful force: our risk of dying is pretty high when we are babies and young children, drops to a low in our teens, and then increases each year for the rest of our lives. Here's a cheery fact: from our thirties, the probability of dying doubles every decade (sorry if that adds to your midlife misery).[1]

But our life expectancy is also highly dependent on what era we were born into. In 1800, for example, the average life span around the world was around thirty years; even in the most developed nations, it was only around forty. Despite the massive economic growth of the Industrial Revolution, this picture didn't change much until the start of the twentieth century, when economic progress combined with advances in medical science, increased health-care provision, and better sanitation to create a long surge. And this remarkable rise has continued through our more recent past. In 1950, life expectancy was still only sixty-three years in Spain, sixty-six in France, and sixty-eight in Canada, but by 2015 it was at least eighty-two years in each of these countries.[2]

This has also been a truly global trend, and less developed countries have experienced even more dramatic improvements. For example, at the start of the twentieth century, life expectancy in India was only around twenty-five years, but by 2019 it was seventy years. Today, most of the world can expect to live as long as those in the richest countries did in 1950, with the poorest regions improving recently and quickly.

Life-cycle and cohort effects are, then, central to our shifting health. The collective health of whole countries is seldom directly affected by huge shocks—the type of sudden period effect we associate with an economic crash or a terrorist attack. But the COVID-19 pandemic is an extraordinary exception. The pandemic has had massive consequences for global health, despite the unprecedented measures to contain its spread. It seems set to become a true generation-defining moment, with aftereffects that will shape the future of whole cohorts. This will take some time to play out, but a generational perspective on the pandemic can also help to understand how it is affecting us *now*.

Firstly, the probability of dying from COVID-19 is fundamentally related to when you were born. In Italy, for example, those aged seventy-five or over when the pandemic struck made up around 12 percent of the population, but they accounted for around 70 percent of all deaths. The age gradient of fatalities was exceptionally steep: over 70 percent of Italians were under sixty, but they accounted for only 3 percent of COVID-related deaths.

The course of the pandemic has also been shaped by the period of history it occurred in. Although COVID-19 is the archetype of Nicholas Nassim Taleb's historical "jump," its impact has been shaped by slower evolutions of the economy, society, and medical technologies that have affected our response. This becomes particularly clear when you compare the direct health effects of COVID-19 with the Spanish flu pandemic in 1918. The death toll of the Spanish flu is estimated to be as high as fifty million, or around 3 percent of the entire world's 1.7 billion population at the time.[3]

The immense impact of the Spanish flu pandemic reflects how different a time that was, with poverty, malnutrition, overcrowding, and poor sanitation much more widespread. Many deaths from the disease were linked to secondary bacterial infections rather than the initial viral infection—antibiotics could have significantly reduced death rates if they had been widely available.[4]

We've also seen a transformation in global communication, which has meant that our response has been swifter and more consistent internationally. The actions of many governments in response to COVID-19 have been very far from perfect, but the suppression of information carried out during the Spanish flu pandemic just isn't possible today.[5]

However, the changes in our health have been far from entirely positive. Although our living conditions have improved hugely and medical advances have been extraordinary, some lifestyle drivers of disease have gone in the other direction. We're also seeing new interactions between health and inequalities that were not present even a few decades ago. If we look at our health generationally and separate cohort, period, and life-cycle effects, we can see new patterns that show your chances of a long and healthy life are no longer automatically increasing for some of the less-well-off groups in wealthy countries like the UK.

But let's start with smoking, which is one of the real success stories, where a long-term, generational outlook has been vital to our progress.

## SMOKING KILLS

Smoking has killed almost unimaginable numbers of people. One estimate suggests that more than 100 million have died prematurely during the twentieth century because of smoking.[6] It is still responsible for around 8 million deaths a year, around 15 percent of all deaths. In more developed countries, the proportion of deaths from smoking is even higher: in the United States for example, it accounts for more than 480,000 deaths every year, around 1 in 5.[7]

These awful figures would have been so much worse without a sustained fall in smoking levels. For example, in 2018, only 14 percent of adults smoked in England, down from 46 percent in 1976.[8] Smoking is down to 14 percent in the United States too, from a similar peak.[9] Of course, this trend is not universal—countries as diverse as Croatia, Egypt, and Indonesia have seen an increase in the proportion of smokers over the past decade. Global population growth has also meant that the total number of smokers has held up, driven by increases in developing countries. But in the past few years, even the total number of cigarettes sold (a terrifying 5.7 trillion in 2016) has finally started to fall.[10]

Within this overall decline, the generational patterns on smoking are another example of combined life-cycle, cohort, and period effects. Taking England as an example, it's clear in Figure 5.1 that every generation is smoking less over time, with each line drifting downward. But each generation tells its own story. The Pre-war generation have the lowest level of smoking, despite having grown up before the links between smoking and cancer were unequivocally proved. This will, sadly, partly reflect higher death rates among those who continued to smoke, but it is also the result of the high propensity of this older generation to quit. One study suggested that over 40 percent of the Pre-war generation are former smokers.[11]

The relative positions of the Gen X and Millennial lines are the most fascinating. At the start of the series, Gen X were slightly more likely to be smokers than Millennials, but then the lines cross over, and for much of this period, particularly from 2009 until the past couple of years, Millennials were more likely to smoke. Millennials were still quitting during this period: 33 percent smoked in 1999, and now it's 22 percent. But they've been kicking the habit more slowly, with a shallower line than other generations, until the past few years. This fits with the "delayed adulthood" theme that we've seen elsewhere. Some of the spurs to giving up—getting married and having

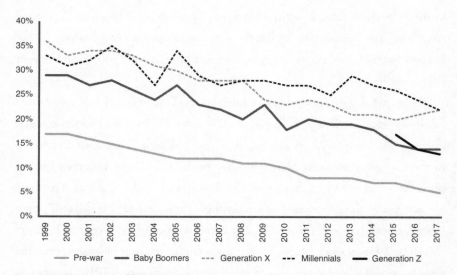

Figure 5.1: Percentage of English adults who are current smokers. Source: Health Survey for England (1999–2017).

children, for instance—are happening less and later. Millennials are acting younger for longer.

The generational pattern of smoking in the United States is remarkably similar to that seen in England, with the same slow decline across all generations and the same hierarchy between them. American Millennials started out with a smoking rate similar to that of Gen X in 2000, but this then increased slightly and stayed above Gen X for a number of years, before falling closer into line. The trend of delayed adulthood seems to have played out in the United States too.

But the most important (and encouraging) generational pattern in both the United States and England is the utterly different starting point of Gen Z. In both countries, this cohort is much less likely to smoke cigarettes, only around 12 to 13 percent—an incredible generational break in the habit.

Of course, this trend can be partly explained by the extraordinary rise of e-cigarettes. These relatively new products contain nicotine and flavorings and create a water vapor that users inhale. Vaping has exploded in the United States in particular, with one 2019 study showing that 27 percent of American seventeen- and eighteen-year-olds had vaped in the prior thirty days.[12] Concerns about this rapid rise in use, combined with a spate of lung conditions and deaths among vapers toward the end of 2019, led to fierce debate about its safety. As a result, the Trump administration raised the legal age to buy tobacco products, including e-cigarettes, to twenty-one and banned some flavored products that were seen to particularly appeal to young people.

This is a tricky public health line to tread, and it is partly a generational trade-off. The health gains from existing smokers switching to vaping are clear—one independent review concluded that they were 95 percent safer than regular cigarettes—but the counterbalancing risk is that vaping will lead otherwise nonsmokers into tobacco use.[13] These concerns have exercised many in the United States, including former secretary of health and human services Alex Azar, who said, "We will not stand idly by as these products become an on-ramp to combustible cigarettes or nicotine addiction for a generation of youth."[14]

Age is key here, as smoking illustrates how we form attitudes and behaviors in our teens and early adult years: around 90 percent of daily smokers first used cigarettes before they were nineteen.[15] Vaping raises a generational choice between converting older smokers to a less harmful be-havior, on the one hand, and exposing younger generations to riskier behav-ior, on the other.

The stakes are high precisely because it seems that we may be turning a corner on cigarette smoking with Generation Z. This success has been built on a long-term series of robust measures, including increases in the legal age of smoking; raising prices; bans in public spaces; and changes in tobacco pack-aging, sponsorship, and advertising. Canada introduced picture-based health warnings on cigarette packets in 2000, and Australia mandated entirely plain packaging in 2012, both measures that have been taken up in a number of other countries. As David Hammond, a professor of public health focused on tobacco control explains, these measures were *not* primarily designed to get current smokers to quit—rather, as generational investments, "the expec-tation is that the benefit will accrue and grow over time as children grow up without the positive brand imagery on packages."[16] This makes sense to me, as an ex-smoker of around twenty years who still has strong associations with "my" brand's design. This idea will be completely alien to my children, who will never have seen a designed cigarette pack. The generational investment is paying off.

## THE LAST SUPPERS?

Our relationship with alcohol is also strongly related to when we were born. In fact, regular drinking is one of the clearest examples of a cohort effect we'll see in this book. Figure 5.2 tracks the proportions of cohorts in England who have said they drink alcohol on five or more days a week over the past twenty years. The lines are incredibly flat, with a strict generational hierarchy and extremely consistent gaps between each.

Around three in ten of the Pre-war generation drink alcohol five or more days a week; as far as we can tell, they always have and always will. I know I shouldn't be impressed, but I can't help thinking that's a great effort for a cohort the youngest of whom is now seventy-five years old. Baby Boomers are not that far behind, at around one-fifth. The rate drops to 10 to 15 percent for Gen X, and then down again for Millennials to around 5 percent. And it has become a near-extinct behavior among Gen Z, with less than 1 percent drinking this regularly.

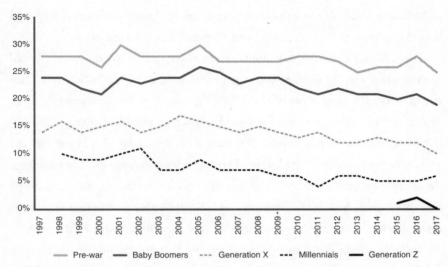

Figure 5.2: Percentage of English adults drinking alcohol five or more days per week. Source: Health Survey for England (1997–2017).

Being from a cohort in the middle of this range, I am slightly perplexed by either end of this generational spectrum. I can't imagine being part of a co-hort where so many of my peers have the dedication required to drink nearly every day, nor can I picture a world where *no one* does.

I was similarly surprised when looking at the generational patterns of those who have even *tried* alcohol as teenagers. Among Millennials when they were aged thirteen to fifteen, in 2000, around seven in ten said they had tried alcohol. But by 2016 this had *halved*, to 36 percent of the thirteen- to fifteen-year-old slice of Gen Z. That's an incredible shift in just one generation, and this is not just seen in the UK. The CDC Youth Risk Behavior study has tracked alcohol use among young people in the United States since 1991, and it shows a similar trend. In that first year of the study, which covered the tail end of Gen X, 82 percent of high school students said they'd tried alco-hol, but by 2017 this had trailed off to 60 percent among Gen Z teenagers (a higher figure than in the UK because it includes older kids).

Of course, "ever tried" and highly regular drinking represent the extremes of alcohol consumption. Tracking the total volume of alcohol consumed by each cohort over a long period is less straightforward, partly because the definition of an alcohol "unit" is relatively new, but evidence suggests that younger cohorts are drinking less overall. For example, in 2014 only a quarter of Millennials drank more than fourteen units of alcohol per week, compared with 31 percent of Baby Boomers and 30 percent of Generation X.[17]

The UK and United States are far from alone in this trend—total alcohol consumption among current younger generations is falling in Sweden, Germany, Australia, and most of the OECD group of richer countries.[18] There are no definitive explanations for why this has happened in so many different national contexts—it is almost certainly a combination of factors. For example, many countries have adopted stronger legal enforcement of underage drinking laws, and many have significantly raised taxes on alcohol. Combined with the tighter financial circumstances facing younger people in many countries, this increased expense has made alcohol less affordable for the young.

There is a long-standing academic theory that the popularity of alcohol ebbs and flows in "long waves."[19] It may feel like a fixed part of our culture, but levels of consumption actually vary significantly over time. For example, the per capita consumption of alcohol in the UK doubled between the 1960s to the 2000s but has since fallen back. This fits with the view that above a certain level, society reaches a "saturation point" at which the harm resulting from alcohol leads to greater concern among both individuals and politicians. Consumption then declines, in tandem with increasingly restrictive government policies that pick up on and reinforce this cultural shift. Eventually, consumption is suppressed to a point where previous concern seems exaggerated, which leads to a relaxation of attitudes and an increase in drinking, and the cycle repeats.

This also fits with what we've seen in the shifting perceptions of risk among the young. As a whole, Gen Z have a reputation for being "more mild than wild," reflected in their lower smoking, drinking, criminal behavior, and, as we'll see in the next chapter, sexual activity. But for the most part, there have been no big increases in the risk they attach to smoking, sex, or illegal drugs. The one exception in the UK is alcohol. In 2018, 70 percent of Gen Z teenagers saw binge drinking as very risky, compared with 56 percent of Millennial teenagers in 2004. A quarter of Gen Z teenagers now say even just *having* an alcoholic drink is risky. The fact that this wasn't a question that seemed worth asking in 2004 is a clear sign of how far cultural norms have changed.

Of course, this is good for our collective health. Alcohol was implicated in 5.3 percent of global deaths in 2016.[20] A more measured attitude toward alcohol is a positive change, particularly when it appears to be a long and steady cultural shift rather than a fad.

## JUST SAY NO

Although the downward generational trends in both smoking and drinking are crystal clear, the changes in patterns of drug use are as murky as the bong water at a college party. Headline writers, hungry for a simple message, must find this complexity frustrating, but they still have a go. As one *Vice* article put it, "Being a teen today is the same as joining a sanctimonious monk-cult, obsessed with organic food and extreme yoga. Yet, turn the page and teenage ecstasy deaths are spiralling, laughing gas and Spice are all over the schoolyard."

The actual picture depends on where you're looking and what you're measuring. There are different, and often contradictory, patterns, both within and across countries. Beyond the recent opioid crisis concentrated among particular populations in the United States and the terrible toll drug addiction seems to be taking on some members of Gen X in the UK, there are few clear-cut patterns and no real sign of consistent generational shift in either direction. Taken as a whole, there have been small declines in harder drug use among recent generations of young people, with marijuana use remaining fairly steady or falling in some countries.

For example, an "ever used" measure for a collection of illegal drugs—marijuana, cocaine, methamphetamines, or heroin—in the United States over the past ten years shows a pretty stable pattern across generations. There are some differences between the cohorts and over time, but they are all in a range of 50-odd to 60-odd percent, and there is no clear direction of travel.

Looking just at marijuana use among American teens over a longer period, we can see why there is such confusion in reporting on generational drug trends. For example, the percentage of US seventeen- and eighteen-year-olds who had tried the drug in the previous twelve months has gone from a high of around 50 percent in the late 1970s, through a sustained decline in the 1980s, to a deep low of 20 percent at the end of that decade and the start of the 1990s, before bouncing back up and bobbing around 35 percent from the start of the 2000s until today. It is the late 1980s and early 1990s that stand out as different, and commentators now seem to be exaggerating relatively small short-term changes.[21]

The lower level of marijuana use in America in the 1980s is mirrored by a steep decline in support for its legalization, as shown in Figure 5.3. These trends in use and attitudes coincided with the height of the country's "war on drugs," a key focus of the Reagan administration, and the "Just Say No" campaign, which lasted for a decade from the early 1980s. Support for legalization started to rise again almost immediately afterward, an illustration of how attitudes can reflect an interplay between general cultural trends and the tone set by political leaders.

After that more uptight period, the United States saw astounding increases in support for the legalization of marijuana among all generations; over 60 percent of all generations except the Pre-war generation were in favor by 2018. Since 2012, eleven US states have fully legalized it, with many others decriminalizing it and allowing medical use. There's little evidence that this has changed how many people partake, and some studies in states that have legalized have claimed reductions in opioid use and related deaths.[22] Looking at the generational opinion trends, relaxation in further states seems a safe bet.

Similarly, six in ten Britons thought cannabis use was "morally wrong" in 1989, but this collapsed to 29 percent by 2019. This decline has been driven by a generational change, with a steeper drop in concern between those aged

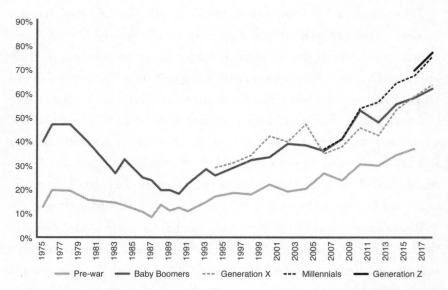

Figure 5.3: Percentage of American adults who approve of legalizing marijuana. Source: US General Social Survey (1975–2017).

fifty-five and over from the two eras. This reflects the fact that, over this thirty-year period, we are comparing two very different generations of older people, with very different formative experiences—one born in 1934 or before and one born in 1964 or before.[23]

These changing views on the morality of marijuana are also reflected in the shift in the perception of the risk associated with the drug. In stark contrast with the increased likelihood that young people see alcohol as risky, there have been steep falls in their assessment of the threat posed by marijuana. For example, nearly 80 percent of American seventeen- to eighteen-year-olds in the late 1980s thought there was a great risk in regularly using marijuana; this had collapsed to under 30 percent by 2019.[24] There have been similar drops across many other countries, including the UK and New Zealand.[25] Today's young people are not a particularly drug-fearing generation.

## THE GIRTH OF NATIONS

Although the generational breaks in smoking and drinking are extremely good news for our health, the trends in obesity levels are not. The most striking pattern is driven by life-cycle effects. Figure 5.4 shows the slow downward drift of each generation in England as they age. I can track my own generation's progress to fatness in the Gen X line; in 1992 70 percent of us were a healthy weight, but now that we are in middle age, only around a quarter of us have managed to maintain it.

Our downward drift means we've joined the previous two cohorts, ending up at a remarkably similar end point to those of Baby Boomers and the Pre-war generation. I find this a mildly motivating thought: if I can make it to my fifties at a healthy weight, there is a good chance that I'll stay there. Of course, the reality is more complex and less comforting; the chart shows only an average, with people flowing in and out, including by dying. The harsh truth is that many of us will continue to get flabbier, even while the proportions of those who are at a healthy weight within each older generation seem to remain stable—because the overweight tend to die younger.

Despite the dominance of life-cycle effects, we can also see significant generational differences in our chances of being a healthy weight. Comparing Gen X with Millennials in England when they were both an average age of twenty-six, 53 percent of Gen X were a healthy weight, compared with 48

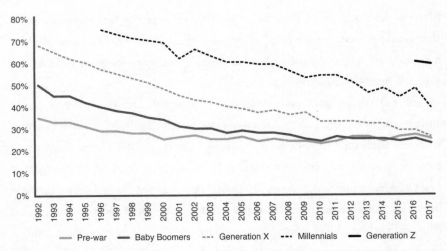

Figure 5.4: Percentage of English adults with a healthy weight (defined as BMI score between 18.5 and 24.9). Source: Health Survey for England (1992–2017).

percent of Millennials. Millennials are the first cohort in England to reach their midtwenties with a minority at a healthy weight, and the trend seems to be continuing: in the latest data from 2017, 62 percent of Gen Z were a healthy weight, compared with around 70 percent of Millennials at the equivalent age. We need to treat this with some caution as this represents just an early slice of Gen Z, but it seems that we haven't reached the bottom of the generational slide into weight problems.

There is a similar generational pattern among adults in the United States when we look at the proportion classed as obese, meaning they have a body mass index (BMI) of at least 30. For example, 40 percent of US Millennials were obese by 2018, compared with around 30 percent of Gen X when they were a similar average age in 2004. It's too early to draw conclusions about Gen Z, but current data suggest their obesity levels are rising even faster than Millennials'.

However, you wouldn't think these were the trends from looking at the endless spurious articles proclaiming either Millennials or Gen Z to be the "wellness generation." Some are unintentionally funny. One article called American Millennials the new "health-conscious" generation simply because they watch a lot of videos on "how to consume turmeric . . . apple cider vinegar, cauliflower rice, bone broth and avocado oil."[26] Another article, inexplicably, pointed to the fact that "54 per cent of Millennials . . . expect ancient grain to be included in their foods." But this kind of thinking also infects more serious analyses, including from one of the most famous financial investment companies in the world. Goldman Sachs suggests that "for Millennials, wellness is a daily, active pursuit. . . . '[H]ealthy' doesn't mean just 'not sick.' It's a daily commitment to eating right and exercising."[27]

These spurious generalizations are damaging, because they distract us from the consequences of generation-on-generation weight increase, which has become a global issue. Worldwide, obesity has tripled since 1975; in 2016, 650 million adults were obese, and a further 1.25 billion were overweight.[28] This has serious consequences on our collective life expectancy—a World Health Organization report suggested it "has the potential to negate many of the health benefits that have contributed to the increased longevity observed in the world."[29]

There is also a growing variation within the population, particularly in more developed countries like the United States and UK: childhood weight is becoming increasingly intertwined with inequality. For example, one study draws on a series of cohort surveys that track UK residents born in a particular year throughout their lives. It compares slices of the population born in 1946, 1958, 1970, and 2001, providing a vitally important resource for understanding how life is really changing between generations. It highlights two important trends in our weight. First, it confirms that children in the latest 2001 cohort are heavier than children in previous cohorts. However, it also shows a new pattern of increasing divergence between those born into the highest and lowest social classes, with the latter having significantly higher BMI scores in 2001 than the former, unlike previous cohorts, which exhibited little difference between classes.[30] Being born into lower social classes now is more damaging to your relative chances of making it through childhood at a healthy weight than in the past.

This pattern isn't confined to the UK; in Europe and North America, some of the strongest correlations with childhood obesity are to income and social class—and this gap appears to be widening. A survey of children covering thirty-four countries across Europe and North America has shown that the impact of the social class you are born into on your weight nearly doubled between 2002 and 2010. Socioeconomic differences, it seems, are becoming a more significant influence on childhood obesity.[31]

On one level, the causes of the generational increase in obesity and its growing link to inequality are straightforward: we have been increasingly consuming more calories than we are burning, and the less well-off have been more affected. The stubbornness of childhood obesity levels in the face of endless initiatives, and the fact that it is increasingly skewed between different social groups, reflects how tightly tied the outcomes are to a number of societal conditions that are very difficult to shift. These "obesogenic" factors can be found in all aspects of young people's lives and are often transferred between generations. Many more of the adults that children interact with are now obese or overweight themselves, and there are also important environmental factors such as the accessibility of safe places to exercise and what food is available at school and at home. The conditions shaping the current generation of young people promote obesity more than those their grandparents experienced did, and many of these conditions are worse for the poor.[32]

When you're born increasingly interacts with the socioeconomic circumstances you're born into. We've already outlined that in the United States, for example, life expectancy has actually started to fall again in the past few years, in the longest downturn since Spanish flu.[33] As Case and Deaton have demonstrated, this is entirely due to decreases among subsets of the population, particularly white Americans without a bachelor's degree. Although the UK has not seen an actual reversal in life expectancy, progress has stalled for the first time in a hundred years.[34] The trajectories of different communities are startling and explain much of the slowdown. For example, we have seen drops in life expectancy among women in the most deprived areas in England and for both sexes in deprived areas of some regions, such as the Northeast of the country.[35] Meanwhile, those in the least deprived areas continue to see gains in life expectancy. In the United States and England, as well as elsewhere in Europe, being born into a poorer background shapes your life in a more negative way than it would have in the recent past.

## WOULD YOU STILL CHOOSE TO BE BORN NOW?

The extraordinary medical and social advances of the past century have tilted in our favor with disease and old age. We'll see further gains in the future, as medical innovations continue at pace and our investment in breaking the smoking habit, the biggest recent cause of preventable death, continues to pay off.

Toward the end of his presidency, Barack Obama regularly returned to the theme of progress and the resilience it brings. In his introductory piece to an edition of *Wired* magazine that he guest-edited in 2016, he emphasized his faith in scientific and social innovations: "We are far better equipped to take on the challenges we face than ever before."[36] He later expanded on his belief in the benefits accrued to those born today: "If you had to choose a moment in history to be born, and you did not know ahead of time who you would be—you didn't know whether you were going to be born into a wealthy family or a poor family, what country you'd be born in, whether you were going to be a man or a woman—if you had to choose blindly what moment you'd want to be born, you'd choose now."[37]

Even at the time of writing, in a world that is largely "locked down" during a global pandemic, Obama is still correct. Despite the immediate health risks, and the unknown long-term impact of the pandemic, such has been the scale of improvement across the world that choosing now is still a smart bet.

However, the calculations have gradually shifted. First, generational progress in health across society as a whole has faltered, with trends such as the rise in obesity acting as a drag on our gains. Second, we have seen starker reversals in health and life expectancy among particular subsets of the population. If you were destined to be a white nongraduate in the United States or a woman living in a deprived area of northern England, it is less clear that being born now would be the best choice. This is a shocking thought, particularly when we have grown to take progress for granted. Health inequalities, of course, have always existed, but they are more startling and harder to accept when they are accompanied by actual reversals for significant proportions of the population in wealthy countries like the UK and United States.

It also means that although medical and social advances have allowed us to deal with the COVID-19 pandemic more effectively than we would have at any time in history, even the best-equipped countries have huge inequalities in terms of vulnerability to both the direct threat of the virus and the longer-term effects of the measures taken to control its spread. The tragic consequences of this were clear from the start of the pandemic: deaths from

COVID-19 were twice as high in the most deprived areas of England than in the least deprived, a larger gap in death rates than in normal times.[38]

We expect to enjoy a healthier, longer life than our parents, and we expect our children to enjoy the same. But the actual trend has become clear: when it comes to health, generational progress is increasingly reserved for those who can afford it.

# CHAPTER 6

# THE SEX RECESSION, BABY BUST, AND DEATH OF MARRIAGE

In *Everybody Lies*, Seth Stephens-Davidowitz draws on the vast swathes of thoughts we happily share with Google in our internet searches but no one else. As you might expect, sex features prominently in the book—it contains insights such as "Men's top Googled question related to how their body or mind would change as they aged was whether their penis would get smaller" and "Men make as many searches looking for ways to perform oral sex on themselves as they do how to give a woman an orgasm."[1]

Although these insights are in equal parts grim and predictable, they only give a partial picture. To truly understand our sex lives, we need careful measurement in rigorous and sensitive surveys, and to understand how generations are changing, we need these to go back a long way. We also need to be mindful that people don't always tell the whole truth in surveys, particularly on sensitive subjects like sex, but the good studies provide insights we can't get anywhere else.

Unfortunately, high-quality studies of reported sexual attitudes and behavior are rare today, and they were even rarer thirty years ago. Instead, we tend to get an endless stream of spurious polls and attention-grabbing headlines, which often attempt to sum up whole generations in pithy but misleading ways. These are sometimes based on serious studies that point to important changes, but it's a reflection of our sensationalist approach to sex that they often overreach. Taking each generation in turn, here are some of the key messages you might pick up from a casual reading of the articles:

Gen Z: "The Kids Are Boning Less."[2] No explanation is required for this article, and the trend it describes is based on a real pattern in the United States, as we'll see.

Millennials: Here it gets confusing, as there are two contradictory groups of pieces that both somehow manage to blame Millennials for killing something. The first emphasizes the rise of "hook-up" culture, aided by new technology, which is killing serious relationships.[3] The second accuses Millennials of killing sex because they are too wrapped in their devices to be bothered: these pieces suggest that "Netflix and chill" has become a literal description rather than a euphemism.[4]

Baby Boomers: "Silver Shaggers Risk STDs."[5] These pieces pick up on a genuine trend of higher rates of sexually transmitted disease among Baby Boomers. However, it represents a very niche behavior, far from the impression of a wave of wrinkly, unprotected orgies given by the headlines.

The eagle-eyed reader will have spotted the gap in the above generational lineup; Gen X are virtually nonexistent in generational discussions of sex, true to their forgotten-middle-child status. There are plenty of pieces on the difficulty of maintaining an interest in sex during midlife, but very little that is about the cohort's unique character. The one piece I found may not be most rigorous, but it is based on analysis from a US academic, who suggests, "Generation X . . . were influenced by the sexual revolution and ruled by the blowjob, while Millennials embraced anal sex . . . and Gen Z is into pegging. . . . [T]he next generation will likely be the masturbation generation."[6] I guess being "ruled by blowjobs" or "embracing anal" are more colorful generational clichés than being narcissistic or materialistic.

Of course, it's easy to mock, particularly when we still have a slightly embarrassed attitude toward sex. But it's a literally existential aspect of human

life, and one that shows significant differences over time and between generations, which can sometimes get lost in the noise.

These generational shifts in our sex lives have been linked to one of the
biggest challenges facing many countries over the coming decades: our low
or declining birth rates will create increasingly unbalanced populations, with
many more retirees and fewer of working age. The tendency in some commentary is to blame this trend on recent generations of young people, for
their supposed lack of interest in sex and child-rearing. But this is a gross
misreading of a longer-term decline in fertility rates and a simplification of a
much more complex pattern.

A future with fewer kids is not the only challenge that our shifting family lives present. As the writer David Brooks points out, the "nuclear family" of two parents and 2.5 children (or *2point4 Children* to take the title of a
long-running British sitcom) seems like the natural order "even though this
wasn't the way most humans lived during the tens of thousands of years before 1950, and it isn't the way most humans have lived during the 55 years
since 1965." This stripped-back model of family life has worked well for some
but not for those who have fewer resources to draw on, and this has all sorts
of ripple effects.

The resilience of marriage itself should not be underestimated, however.
As Stephanie Coontz, author of *The Way We Never Were: American Families
and the Nostalgia Trap*, points out, people have unsuccessfully predicted the
death of marriage for decades. In 1928, John Watson, a prominent child psychologist, predicted that marriage would be finished by 1977. And in 1977,
the sociologist Amitai Etzioni suggested that if then-current trends continued, by the 1990s "not one American family will be left."[7] More recently, and
predictably, headlines have accused Millennials of "killing marriage."[8] The
reality is that the history of marriage has always been a mix of continuity and
change.

## A SEXUAL RECESSION?

Let's start at the beginning, by looking at trends in first sexual experiences
from a US study of high schoolers. They show a clear decline in the proportion of young people aged between fifteen and eighteen who have lost their
virginity, from 54 percent for Generation X in 1991 to 40 percent by 2017.

Two downward steps in the trend coincide quite neatly with the periods when different generations were reaching their late teens—Millennials in the late 1990s and Gen Z in the mid-2010s. On this measure, it seems perfectly reasonable to believe that "the kids are boning less."

We don't have the same sort of studies in the UK, but there are indications that we are seeing a similar pattern, with a higher proportion of young adults in recent generations delaying sex for longer. For example, a study tracking a cohort of people born in 1989 and 1990 and interviewing them at various points as they grow up showed that by age twenty-five, 12 percent of these late Millennials were still virgins. This is significantly higher than the levels seen in previous generations, which hovered around 5 percent by their midtwenties.[9]

Is this a universal trend across countries or just an American and British phenomenon? Long-term, robust surveys of teenagers' sexual behavior are rare, but a study in six African countries, for example, showed a slow but steady rise in the age of first sexual experience over the past few decades, with particularly significant effects in Uganda, Kenya, and Ghana.[10] The country most widely seen as the archetype of the trend, however, is Japan, where the level and longevity of virginity is of quite a different order. In 2015, 26 percent of men and 25 percent of women aged eighteen to thirty-nine had no experience of heterosexual sex (disappointingly, Japanese sex surveys don't measure same-sex experiences). As seen with US teenagers, this has been a slow evolution rather than a sudden shift—the figures were already 20 percent for men and 22 percent for women in 1992. Reflecting this, long-term virginity is increasingly affecting the oldest age groups within the survey: for example, the proportion of thirty-five to thirty-nine-year-olds who have not had heterosexual intercourse roughly doubled between 1992 and 2015, to nearly 10 percent.

A gradual increase in the age of virginity loss is a relatively narrow measure of declining sexual activity. It tells us very little about the sex lives of most people: after all, virginity is still rare by the time we get to our thirties, even in Japan.

Counting the number of sexual partners people have had in the past year gives a more representative perspective on trends in sexual activity. We'll start again at the inactive end of the scale, with those in the United States

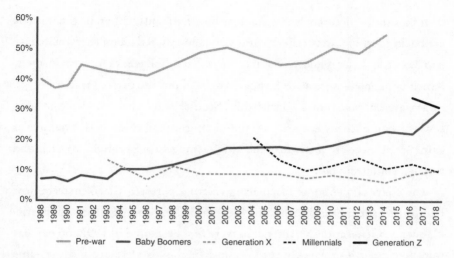

Figure 6.1: Percentage of American adults who report no sexual partners in the past year. Source: US General Social Survey (1988–2018).

who've had none (Figure 6.1). We can see that each line, from Gen X through Millennials and then Gen Z, starts with a higher proportion of young adults saying they've had no sexual partners in the past year. It was around 12 percent for Gen X, 21 percent for Millennials, and 34 percent for Gen Z. These are enormous increases over the course of just three generations.

But, unlike the trends among teenagers in the previous section, we can now take a fuller generational perspective. In particular, we can track Millennials further through their life cycle, with the oldest around thirty-eight by the time of the latest survey in 2018. We get a different picture of their sex lives from this longer view; after years of lagging behind, Millennials are now perfectly in line with Gen X, with just 10 percent having had no sexual partners in the previous year. Once again, the story of their development is of a delayed arrival at the same destination.

However, the chart also makes it clear that Gen Z have a big gap to close with the level of sexual activity of previous cohorts. I'm trying hard not to dismiss this possibility—after all, the path Millennials have followed is a clear demonstration of how powerful human life cycles are in pulling us back into line. It's possible that the same thing will happen for Gen Z, but it seems more likely that they'll struggle to close the gap completely. We may be heading for a new norm of sexual abstinence among young adults in the United States.

It's a similar picture when we look at how frequently different generations are having sex. Figure 6.2 on the next page shows US data on those who have had sex at least weekly over the past year. Each line tracks a pretty content bunch of people—once a week appears to be about the perfect amount of sex to achieve happiness in a relationship. Studies show that couples who have sex less than once a week are less content, but we fail to show real happiness gains from more frequent sex, and this seems to apply equally to men and women, young and old.[11]

The chart shows some fascinating shifting patterns that illustrate how tied up our sex lives are with life-cycle, period, and cohort effects. In particular, when Generation X Americans were first measured in 1992, 66 percent were having at least weekly sex. When Millennials were around the same average age in 2006, only 50 percent were having sex this frequently, which at the time would have looked like a collapse in sexual activity. However, the shape of the Millennials' line is entirely different—rather than falling in these early adult years, it rises to around 60 percent, before stabilizing. By 2018, 53 percent of Millennials are having sex at least weekly, which is not too different from the 58 percent among Gen X at a similar average age in 2002. After a slower start, regular sex for Millennials is a bit lower than Gen X but not a lot. Again, the story for Millennials is mostly of a delayed life cycle—they came later to regular sex but ended up in a not dissimilar place.

As with their sexual abstinence, Gen Z have taken a further step down, with only around 35 percent having sex at least weekly. They are nearly half as likely to have weekly sex as Gen X were when they were young adults. As with their number of sexual partners, the different sexual life cycle Millennials have followed means that we can't be sure that this is an utter break from the past—but it seems increasingly unlikely Gen Z will catch up with previous generations' levels of sexual activity.

Recent changes in our sex lives are often described as a "sex recession," as coined by *Atlantic* journalist Kate Julian at the end of 2018.[12] Her article focuses on how this "recession" is being driven by younger generations, with vivid stories of young people forlornly "swiping left" on dating apps with no real interest in meeting a match, terrified of initiating real-life contact, and distracted by their smartphones and internet porn. It gives the impression that a whole generation is giving up on sex, but this is misleading.

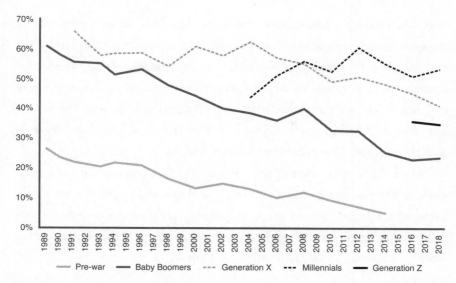

Figure 6.2: Percentage of American adults having weekly sex in the past year. Source: US General Social Survey (1988–2018).

Part of the problem with the term "sex recession" is that it treats the decline in sexual activity as a single trend that stems solely from changing behaviors among the young, despite having several strands running together. In particular, this portrayal glosses over the fact that older age groups have often seen larger falls in sexual activity. In fact, the frequency with which the US population as a whole are having sex has declined in recent years, from around sixty times a year in the 1990s to around fifty by the mid-2010s.[13] In Britain, the median number of times adults had sex in the previous four weeks fell from five in 1990 to three by 2010.[14] A similar generalized decline in the frequency of sex has also been recorded in Sweden, Australia, Finland, Spain, Italy, and, of course, Japan.[15] The studies show significant differences in which groups are driving the change, but it's actually mainly *not* the young who are to blame. Data from the United States, UK, Australia, and Finland consistently demonstrate that the largest declines in frequency are actually among married people and those in early middle age.[16]

These are long-term, multifaceted declines, and no single generation or individual factors such as the rise of mobile phones, dating apps, or Pornhub fits the timing of the trends.

On top of these period effects, younger generations have also experienced shifts in their life cycle. Delayed adulthood is writ large in their stalling sex lives. The trends for Millennials have shown how this can be a pause rather than an outright rejection of sex. For example, it's still the case that by the time people in the United States and UK reach their midthirties (where Millennials are now), one in twenty or fewer remain virgins, which is not hugely different from past patterns.[17] However, Generation Z may be the first to snap this stretched life cycle and settle at a lower level of sexual activity—we will get a clearer picture of this in the next few years.

This, I think, gets closer to the point of why "sex recession" doesn't quite work as a term—it suggests a temporary and unusual phase that we would bounce back from if young people could only get their act together. But a fuller understanding of the generational trends suggests that its causes are more varied, and it's likely to be more permanent.

## BABY BUST?

The later start to our sex lives is mirrored in significant increases in the average age at which women give birth to their first child. For example, in the UK it has gone from around twenty-six years in the 1950s to over thirty, with a steady upward trajectory starting in the mid-1960s. France, Australia, and America followed a similar pattern, although the United States settled at a lower twenty-nine years old.[18] In Germany, the average age that women first give birth decreased from nearly twenty-eight to twenty-six between the 1950s and early 1980s, but then rose to around thirty-one.

These small increases may not seem dramatic, but they hide utterly transformed distributions across age ranges. For example, in England and Wales in 1985, six times as many babies were born to teenagers as to women over forty. But by 2015, the number of children born to women over forty was larger than the number born to those under twenty for the first time in history.[19] This same tipping point was reached in Canada and Australia in the early 2010s.[20] Of course, a large part of the explanation is the massive fall in teen pregnancies, but the number of "geriatric births" (until recently the official medical term for births to older women) has also risen significantly. It's no accident that Bridget Jones, the chronicler of shifting female lives, was forty-three in the film *Bridget Jones's Baby*.

As with our declining sexual behavior, these trends have often been mispresented as a failing of current generations of young people, as headlines like "Will Childless Millennials Turn America into Japan?" illustrate.[21] But the reality is that the average age at childbirth has increased in almost all countries since at least the 1980s, when Baby Boomers and then Gen X were in their prime child-rearing years. These are not sudden generational shifts driven by a particular cohort.

As for the number of children people are having, the judgments on today's younger generations are similarly unfair. It is true that birth rates have plummeted globally; the worldwide total fertility rate (the number of children born for every woman of childbearing years) halved from around 5 in the 1960s to around 2.5 by 2015.[22] But more recent drops have been driven by lower-income countries, with relative stability elsewhere. For example, total fertility rates in the UK have moved only between around 1.7 and 1.9 per woman since the 1980s.[23] It's true that we have had six years of slightly decreasing rates in the UK and the United States has seen small but consistent falls since 2008, but the main pattern in the long-term trends is a much steeper drop in the 1960s and 1970s.[24] The rate in richer countries seems to settle around 1.7; the latest projection from the Office of National Statistics in the UK is that the average completed family size for each woman will still be 1.78 children in 2043.[25]

Of course, although this is not the generationally driven plunge in the number of children that you might assume from the headlines ("Baby Bust! Millennials' Birth Rate Drop May Signal Historic Shift"), it is significantly below the replacement rate of around 2.1 children.[26] And combined with our increased longevity, we are going to see severe and sudden increases in the old-age dependency ratio, or how many working-age people there are compared with those over sixty-five.[27] In fact, in the United States, this ratio is expected to *double* between 2010 and 2050, from nineteen older people per one hundred working-age people to thirty-six. Of course, we need to be careful not to overstate the threat: improved health and longer working lives mean that many of these older people won't be "dependent." But it is still an enormous societal shift.

COVID-19 will also have a significant impact on our birth rates—but not in the way some people have expected. In the initial stages of the "lockdown" in March 2020, the UK health minister Nadine Dorries even tweeted, "As the minister responsible for maternity services, I'm just wondering how busy we are going to be nine months from now."[28] These expectations were based on a widespread misperception that events that leave people stuck at home, such as blackouts or blizzards, result in more babies. But these myths are not supported by the data.[29] Stress and anxiety in crises generally outweigh the boredom of being at home.

The real effects of COVID-19 are more likely to accentuate the "baby bust." The economists Melissa S. Kearney and Phillip Levine have drawn on trends from previous recessions and the 1918 Spanish flu pandemic to estimate between three hundred thousand and five hundred thousand fewer births in the United States, a drop of up to 14 percent.[30] Their analysis also shows a 12.5 percent decline in birth rates nine months after each wave of the Spanish flu pandemic. This was not primarily an economic effect—the economy barely contracted—but was instead driven by the anxiety and public health effects of the crisis. The Spanish flu killed or sickened more people in their childbearing years than COVID-19, so this effect is likely to be less marked with the current pandemic. Social distancing measures will reduce birth rates in the short term, but the key longer-term effect of the current pandemic will be economic, as birth rates are procyclical, rising and falling with economic growth and decline. Analysis of the 2008 recession suggests that a one percentage point increase in unemployment rates was associated with a 0.9 percent decrease in birth rates.

A protracted period of social separation and the even longer-lasting economic "scarring" will mean not just a delay but a permanent loss. As with so much about COVID-19, it seems it will hasten preexisting trends; the resulting slowing of birth rates could have long-term repercussions for Western countries already struggling to support aging populations.

## SAVING OURSELVES

What do Britney Spears, Miley Cyrus, and Justin Bieber have in common? As a Gen X dad of two daughters who have at times listened incessantly to each pop star's music, I could think of a few sweary phrases to connect them. But beyond their responsibility for my aural torture, they've all at one point pledged to "wait"—before subsequently admitting that they didn't. Miley Cyrus, who originally opined a "true love waits" mind-set, later concluded that "virginity is a social construct."

The American "purity industry," which includes jewelry, elaborate events, books, T-shirts, and DVDs, as well as government programs that reinforce it, appears very alien from the UK. But when we look at the differences in attitudes toward premarital sex between the two countries, it's much less surprising.

Each generation in the United States, with the exception of the latest figure for Gen Z, is significantly more concerned about sex before marriage than the equivalent generation in Britain, as we can see in Figures 6.3 and 6.4. For example, nearly three in ten US Baby Boomers consider premarital sex always or almost always wrong, compared with just 8 percent of British Boomers. If you were to look only at the overall population's disapproval of premarital sex in Britain, which has gone from 27 percent in 1983 to 9 percent by 2017, you may think this was due to a gradual shift in views and not the deeply generational trend that it actually is. There has, in fact, been remarkable consistency among the views of most British generations since the question was first asked in the early 1980s: with the exception of the Pre-war generation, only one in ten or less of all generations have ever thought it was wrong. The Pre-war generation has also been slowly catching up with this general view, and now only one in five are concerned, less than half the level of the equivalent American generation.

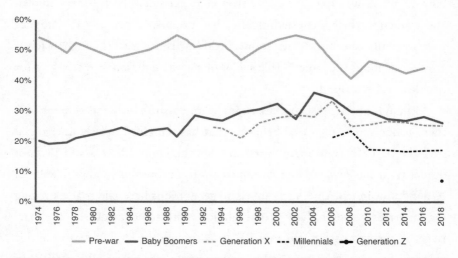

Figure 6.3: Percentage of American adults who say that having sex before marriage is "always" or "almost always" wrong. Source: US General Social Survey (1974–2018).

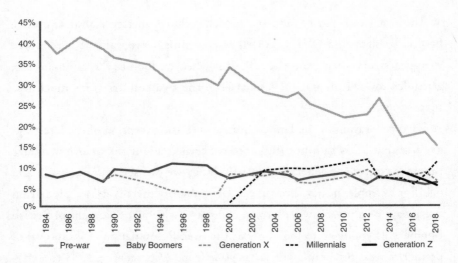

Figure 6.4: Percentage of British adults reporting that having sex before marriage is "always" or "mostly" wrong. Source: British Social Attitudes (1984–2018).

Some raise concerns about how this perspective impacts on women's sense of their value. As Jessica Valenti suggests in *The Purity Myth*, using "purity" as shorthand for not having sex means that women who have sex before marriage are impure or tainted: "While boys are taught that the things that make them men—good men—are universally accepted ethical ideals, women are led to believe that our moral compass lies somewhere between our legs."[31]

The reality is that it's not just Britney, Miley, and Justin who fall short—hardly anyone lives up to the ideal. Around 95 percent of both American men and women in their forties admit they had premarital sex, and this applies pretty equally across the generations, including those with the highest levels of concern about the issue.[32] That's a lot of cognitive dissonance or regret for people to carry around.

Although so many sexual attitudes seem to shift between generations, there is one aspect of sexual behavior that has remained utterly unchanged over the past thirty to forty years, in both the United States and Britain: infidelity. It has always been wrong to cheat, and probably always will be. Around nine in ten Americans across all generations have said that it's wrong for a married person to have sexual relations with someone outside the marriage, all the way back to the mid-1970s. Although the level of disapproval is lower in Britain, there is incredible consistency between 1989 and 2019 in majority condemnation.[33] In fact, levels of objection in Britain have increased slightly, mostly driven by men coming into line with views among women—a pattern that applies equally across generations. With so much change in sexual attitudes and behavior, it's strangely striking how universal this one view is across time and generations.

## MARRIAGE CAN WAIT

But although people value fidelity, it's less clear they think it requires marriage. People are getting married later and less around the world, as Table 6.1 shows: for example, the average age of marriage for French women in 1980 was twenty-three, but by the 2010s it was thirty-two. The average age of marriage in African countries is lower, but the direction of change is the same. Across countries, the age of first marriage for women has generally increased more than for men, closing the age gap and reflecting women's increasing financial independence.[34]

| Country | Gender | Mean age of marriage (1980–1982) | Mean age of marriage (2011–2016) | Difference (Years) |
|---------|--------|----------------------------------|----------------------------------|--------------------|
| France | Men | 25 | 34 | 9 |
| | Women | 23 | 32 | 9 |
| UK | Men | 26 | 33 | 7 |
| | Women | 24 | 32 | 8 |
| Sweden | Men | 26 | 33 | 7 |
| | Women | 24 | 31 | 7 |
| Australia | Men | 26 | 31 | 5 |
| | Women | 24 | 30 | 6 |
| Japan | Men | 29 | 31 | 2 |
| | Women | 25 | 29 | 4 |
| USA | Men | 24 | 29 | 5 |
| | Women | 22 | 28 | 6 |
| Rwanda | Men | 25 | 27 | 2 |
| | Women | 17 | 24 | 7 |

Table 6.1: Average age of marriage for men and women, 1980–2016. Source: UN World Marriage Data, Singulate Mean Age at Marriage, 2017.

Although these figures point to a clear trend, they tell us nothing about changes in the proportions of people who don't marry at all or the source of the changes across generations. This is clearer when you track generations over time. Figure 6.5 first demonstrates how universal marriage has been for our current older generations in Britain, and this is mirrored in other countries: almost all of the US Pre-war generation and over 90 percent in Britain and France were married at some point in their lives. This fell slightly for American Baby Boomers but more for British and French Boomers, to around 85 and 80 percent, respectively. Around 82 percent of US Gen X have been married at some point, compared to 70 percent in Britain and 60 percent in France. But the chart also shows the Millennial line stays much flatter for longer than the Gen X line: marrying in their late teens or twenties was much rarer for Millennials than for Gen X. Millennials did pick up the pace, but by 2017, with many of them well into their thirties, only around 40 percent were married, compared with 50 percent of Gen X at a similar age.

We can't yet be certain about the future end point for Millennials: as we saw with their sex lives, they are late bloomers. However, by current trajectories it seems reasonable to expect that some 75 percent of US Millennials will at some point marry, compared to a little over 60 percent of British Millennials and less than 50 percent of French Millennials. These are big generational changes but hardly the death of an institution.

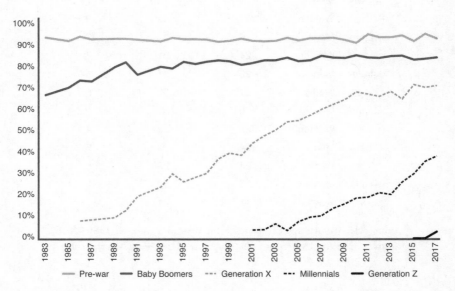

Figure 6.5: Percentage of adults in Britain who were married at some point in their life. Source: British Social Attitudes (1983–2017).

It is too early to say whether Gen Z will continue this trend, but it seems likely, as their marriage rates are at least as low as those of Millennials in their early adult years. There are also clear signs that teenagers are deprioritizing marriage for other goals. As Jean Twenge outlines in surveys of high school students, marriage has slipped down the order of life priorities, with financial and career ambitions on the rise.[35] As Twenge suggests, this is partly due to greater economic uncertainty, but it also reflects a cultural change in perceptions of how marriage fits into our lives. As the sociologist Andrew Cherlin outlines, marriage is no longer a first step in adulthood but a celebration of what a couple has already achieved: "The wedding is the last brick put in place to finally complete the building of the family."[36]

Of course, young people are not giving up on intimate relationships; a great deal of the change is explained by increases in unmarried couples living together. For example, 25 percent of British Millennials were living with a partner in 2017, twice the level of Gen X at a similar age. This no doubt reflects the narrowing distinction younger generations make between marriage and cohabitation.[37]

This is despite efforts by governments around the world to incentivize marriage. According to the US Government Accountability Office, there are 1,138 perks in federal law available to married couples.[38] Many are pretty niche: Title 18 of the US Code, Section 879, for example, makes it illegal to threaten certain individuals guarded by the Secret Service, including the president, the vice president, and their families.[39] Jared Kushner, Ivanka Trump's husband, was covered—but Kimberly Guilfoyle, Donald Trump Jr.'s partner, was not. This is unlikely to coax Gen Zers down the aisle, but the real benefits include substantial tax breaks, property rights, and inheritance rules. Of course, one spouse needs to die to get the full value from many of them, which may also explain why they're less enticing to the young.

The shifting state of marriage is not all about delay and decline, however—recent years have seen remarkable progress in the recognition of same-sex marriage. Since the Netherlands became the first country to legally recognize same-sex marriage in 2001, around thirty other nations have followed. There is still a vast distance to travel, but it represents an incredible turnaround in a relatively short time.

The extent of the change in attitudes is clear in the generational trends in US support for gay marriage, as shown in Figure 6.6. This is one of the most remarkable shifts we'll see in the whole book: in 1988 barely 10 percent of people agreed that homosexual couples should have the right to marry, a figure that increased to over 60 percent by 2018. Both period and cohort effects are clear in the chart, with every generation moving significantly over time and each new cohort more supportive than the last. This is a clear illustration of both the capability of societies to shift quickly and the power of socialization in our early years.

These two trends—the declining relevance of marriage and its hard-won expansion among a previously excluded group—may seem at odds, but they reflect the increasing diversity of our relationships.

However, as with other aspects of life, this generational increase in freedom has played out differently depending on your resources.[40] Americans with at least a bachelor's degree, for example, are now more likely to get and stay married compared to those with lower educational attainment. This is new: in the 1960s, marriage and divorce rates in these groups were nearly identical. Similar divisions between income groups have arisen in other countries too, including the UK.

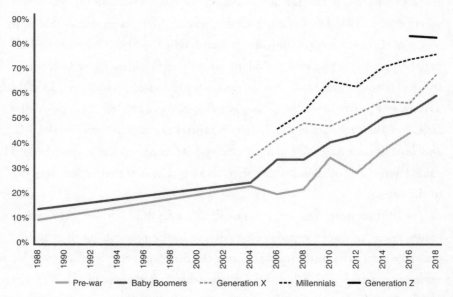

Figure 6.6: Percentage of American adults supporting homosexual marriage. Source: US General Social Survey (1988–2018).

In our more individualized times, when we are less connected to extended families, affluent nuclear families can buy support that helps keep families together, from childcare to couples counseling. Less-well-off families are on their own, and the results are startling: college-educated women aged between twenty-two and forty-four have a 78 percent chance of their first marriage lasting at least twenty years, while women with a high-school education have only about half that chance.[41]

This divergence also transfers across generations, as the shape of families does seem to affect life outcomes for children. Simplistic assertions that a two-parent model is always best are clearly false: studies show that high-conflict two-parent households can be a lot worse for children.[42] But study after study has shown that children in households with their married parents, on average, do better than the alternatives.[43] Of course, cause, effect, and intervening factors are impossible to untangle, and many studies show that the indirect financial implications of single parenthood or relationship breakups may be more important than the relationship itself.[44] But in the end, stability matters, and it tends to be greater in married households, despite claims that long-term cohabitation is equivalent.[45] Children in France, for example, are 66 percent more likely to see their parents break up if they are cohabiting rather than married.[46]

## SPLITTING UP

It is good news, then, that recent declines in divorce rates suggest that break-ups are becoming rarer. For example, in England and Wales there was a twenty-eight percentage point fall in the number of divorces between 2005 and 2015. In Germany, 2016 saw the lowest rate of divorce since 1993.[47] In the United States, the rate fell from a peak of five divorces per one thousand people in the 1980s to around three by 2017, its lowest since 1968.[48]

This change appears to be at least partly generationally driven, with younger cohorts particularly likely to be divorcing less. In fact, the trend resulted in one of the few positive headlines I've found about Millennials in years of research, from the World Economic Forum: "The United States Divorce Rate Is Dropping, Thanks to Millennials."[49]

You can see the signs of this when tracking the proportions of British people who say they're divorced or separated. Only around 3 percent of

Millennials were divorced in 2017, compared with 6 percent of Gen X when they were a similar age. Of course, as we've seen, fewer Millennials were married at the same age, but that does not entirely explain the lower divorce rates. Instead, later marriages tend to be more stable, partly because the additional time allows people to build up financial resources and establish careers, reducing some of the key sources of marital stress.[50]

Accordingly, older people seem to be bucking the trend of fewer divorces.[51] In England and Wales between 2005 and 2015, the number of men over sixty-five who divorced increased by 23 percent, and the number of women increased by 38 percent.[52] Part of the reason is that there were many more older people in 2015. Looking at the number of men and women divorcing as a proportion of the married older population shows that their divorce rate has remained broadly consistent over the past decade.[53] Of course, in the context of falling divorce rates in other age groups, this bucks the trend and reflects a bulge of divorces among Baby Boomers that is making its way through the age range. In 2008, divorce peaked among those in their late forties and early fifties, but by 2018 it had shifted to those in their sixties. There's a similar trend in the United States, too: the divorce rate was 12.5 percent among fifty-five- to sixty-four-year-olds in 2017, compared with 5 percent in 2008.[54]

Many explanations have been proposed for these "Silver Splicers"—from increased economic independence of women and greater focus on individual happiness, to rising longevity prompting panic at the prospect of spending several more decades with the same person. As one sardonic *Guardian* article put it, in the old days, an unhappy partner "could just die, and avoid all that paperwork."[55]

There has also been speculation that the COVID-19 crisis will both reverse the trend toward lower divorce rates and encourage the shift to delayed marriage. Some short-term impact on marriage rates is inevitable: most countries banned weddings for several months, and restrictions remain on ceremony sizes. Similarly, the stress of the crisis is likely to be too much for some relationships: Citizens Advice, a UK-based charitable network, reported that visits to its divorce webpage were up 25 percent in the first week of September 2020 compared with the same week in 2019.[56]

But there are reasons to be hopeful that the longer-term effects of the crisis and its economic fallout will be less dramatic than their impact on birth rates.

Analysis of previous recessions show limited effects on marriage and divorce rates. There were plenty of headlines that claimed people were delaying marriage as a direct result of the recession in 2008, but the evidence cited generally mistook the long trend toward later marriage for a short-term economic effect.[57] As University of Michigan economist Justin Wolfers points out, the decline in the marriage rate following the 2008 financial crisis was the same as in the preceding boom and the previous bust. He concludes, "The patterns of marriage and divorce rates have remained remarkably immune to the ups and downs of the business cycle."[58]

## AM I THE ONLY ONE WHO . . . ?

Although the pandemic may have put a temporary block on marriage, it has had the opposite effect on the use of internet porn: Pornhub, for example, reported a 22 percent increase in traffic in the early months of the crisis. This is likely to play out very differently for different generations, as attitudes toward porn are very generational. Figure 6.7 shows the proportion of each American generation who think it should be illegal, and while over half of the Pre-war generation have consistently called for outright prohibition, the number falls to one in five among Millennials and Gen Z. Interestingly, Baby Boomers in

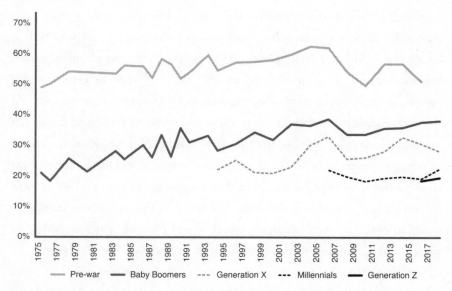

Figure 6.7: Percentage of American adults who say that pornography should be illegal. Source: US General Social Survey (1975–2018).

particular have become increasingly prohibitive over the years. This seems to reflect a life-cycle effect rather than a general period effect, as other cohorts are not moving in the same direction.

There are signs of a similar generation gap in British attitudes toward porn. Back in 1989, four in ten Brits thought the sale of soft porn magazines at newsstands was "morally wrong." This collapsed to only 22 percent by 2019, though it may reflect the fact that buying hard-copy porn in a store now seems incredibly quaint as much as a relaxation in attitudes. However, the change has been driven by a shift among older age groups, with more permissive Baby Boomers replacing the more concerned Pre-war generation, in a similar pattern to that seen in the United States.

Brits are also much more relaxed about full-frontal male nudity on TV than in the late 1980s; the proportion of people who disapproved halved from around four in ten to 23 percent by 2019, with women driving a lot of that change. Male nudity has become much more common on TV in recent years, but there still remains a distinct gender imbalance. As the ardent auditor of TV nudity, "Mr Skin" (who runs a website that records the number and nature of naked scenes on popular programs) points out, of the eighty-two nude scenes in the first seven seasons of *Game of Thrones*, only twenty-one were of men, and there were ten pairs of breasts for every penis shown.[59]

Although it's clear our exposure to nudity has increased, it is surprisingly difficult to say exactly how widespread pornography use is, or how it has changed. This is partly because of our ongoing reticence about all sexual behaviors, but also the myriad and shifting forms of sexually explicit material, which makes consistent measurement tricky. However, most studies find that between seven and eight in ten men, and between three and five in ten women, have viewed porn in the past few months. Not surprisingly, studies of younger people give higher figures: for example, one Dutch study of fifteen- to twenty-five-year-olds found that 88 percent of men and 45 percent of women had viewed sexually explicit material in the past twelve months.[60] One Canadian academic studying the effects of porn on men's attitudes toward women ran into a problem with the control sample for his research design: "We started our research seeking men in their twenties who had never consumed pornography. We couldn't find any."[61]

The main driver of this ubiquity of porn use is, of course the incredible reach of internet porn sites. In 2018, *109 billion* videos were watched on Pornhub alone (which ranks as the twenty-second most popular of all websites among UK internet users, just behind Microsoft.com).[62] Pornhub has analyzed its users by demographic—splitting out Millennials and comparing them with Generation X and above. Although it is in no way representative of general use—this is only one website and it is difficult to accurately account for users who do not register their age—the data do offer some insight into pornography use by age, across a range of countries.[63]

Overall, Millennials are easily Pornhub's largest user base, accounting for 60 percent of global traffic. However, the Millennial share of the Pornhub audience varies widely from country to country—eight in ten Indian users are Millennials, while in Denmark and Japan, older generations account for 52 percent of the traffic. However, rather than suggesting that older Indians have no interest in porn, it more likely reflects the much younger age profile of the Indian population and relative rates of internet access.

Life stage is also reflected in the viewing habits of different generations. Splitting search terms by generation, the Pornhub data reveal that Millennials are more likely to search for clips that are relevant to their age, such as "teacher," "party," and "college," as well as expressing a knowledge of relatively emergent trends such as "cosplay" and "hentai." But plenty more niche interests are revealed by searches, including "humping stuffed animals" and "snot fetish."[64] Our private internet porn tastes are among the clearest demonstrations of Ugol's Law, named after the software developer Harry Ugol, who said, "To any question beginning with 'Am I the only one who . . . ?,' the answer is no."[65]

With a new technology bringing such an easy outlet for these types of fantasies, it is unsurprising that it raises many concerns about its effect on our patterns of thought and real lives. There has been a particular focus on younger generations, who are both heavier consumers and in their more formative years.

The first point to make is that we have always seen this pattern with the use of, and reaction to, new communications technologies. John Tierney, a US journalist, called it the "erotic technological impulse," and it's a constant throughout history. For example, there is a sketch of a reclining female nude on the wall of a cave at La Magdelaine in France from 12000 BC. Sumerians wrote sonnets to vulvas as soon as they discovered how to write cuneiform on clay tablets. Among the early books printed on a Gutenberg printing press was a sixteenth-century collection of sex positions. Ivan Bloch, the German physician who coined the term "sexology," asserted in 1902, "There is no sexual aberration, no perverse act, however frightful, that is not photographically represented today."[66]

The growth of internet porn, then, reflects nothing new in human nature, but given the variety and ease of access, it is right that we look carefully at its possible impact. The *Journal of Sexual Medicine* thoroughly reviewed the many different dimensions of the effect of porn on sexual satisfaction, the quality of intimate relationships, aggression and sexual aggression toward women, lowered libido, and erectile dysfunction. The key words used throughout the review are that the evidence is "mixed" or "inconsistent," with a number of "flawed" studies showing negative consequences and just as many showing no effect, while some even show positive outcomes. The authors also point out that divorce rates have fallen and numbers of sexual crimes have declined while the viewing of porn has exploded. They find little relationship between how these increasingly positive outcomes vary across countries and levels of porn use. The review is called "Pornography Viewing: Keep Calm and Carry On," which is a fair summary of their view of the evidence.

Of course, this is not to say that porn does not have any negative effects. Part of the problem with the media coverage about and the political discourse around porn is that it is presented as something that can have only good or bad effects, but not both or neither. In practice, just as there are many different kinds of porn, people engage with it for many different reasons. The meanings that porn has for people, and the ways they use it, seem likely to be crucial in determining whether it is a positive, negative, or neutral influence in their lives.

The most thorough studies of the effects on children and youth present a similar picture. A literature review of more than forty thousand academic studies by the children's commissioner in the UK found very little robust evidence of the effect of pornography on children and young people. The wider assessment was how much was still unknown, which echoed a review by the

Dutch government that determined that evidence confirming harmful effects on minors is just "not available."[67]

## IT'S TOO LATE TO PANIC

My approach to generational analysis is to identify and understand continuity and change by carefully separating period, cohort, and life-cycle effects. Because shifts in our sex lives and family structures are so emotionally charged, this is especially important: the moral panics that result can mess with our memory of the past and color our judgments of the present. There is a reason therapists spend so much time carefully exploring our sexual and family experiences: the private choices and very personal consequences involved, combined with the moral and religious overtones surrounding each, make them difficult subjects.

This also means that we tend to blame current generations of young people for a decline in sexual activity, birth rates, and marriage, and we fret that new innovations are damaging them. The reality is a much more interesting blend of consistency and change both within and between generations, driven by long-term period effects, delayed life cycles, and generational shifts. Panic over porn and the death of marriage, as well as the blame that is directed at young people for the sex recession and low birth rates, are all misplaced.

The blame may be misplaced, but low birth rates still present one of our biggest generational challenges, as the balance of our populations tips inexorably from young to old. If we think we have reason to focus on the balance of contribution and support between young and old now, wait till the middle of the century. The problem is that there are no apparent solutions. As Darrell Bricker and John Ibbitson outline in *Empty Planet*, none of the interventions introduced to encourage higher birth rates, from subsidized childcare to tax breaks, seems to have much traction in the face of powerful forces such as increased education, urbanization, and choice.[68] This is not a sudden baby bust that we can turn around but the end of a long-term trend driven by some of the largest changes of the past few decades.

In the shorter term, we face similarly intractable problems with the families we already have. We need to avoid a fake nostalgia for a supposed golden age of the nuclear family, as Stephanie Coontz points out. We forget that that "during its heyday, rates of poverty, child abuse, marital unhappiness and domestic violence were actually higher" than in our current, more diverse times.[69] But this is only half the story. The fact that we have a rosy view of the past doesn't mean we're in a better place now, and this is particularly true for those who have fewer resources to draw on.

Just as happens with insufficient birth rates, tiny, targeted interventions to increase marriage rates are rightly dismissed as inadequate to the increasingly unequal consequences of our diverse family structures. Robert Putnam has suggested an extremely large menu of measures, from direct financial support for poorer families, reduced incarceration, and an increased focus on rehabilitation, improved early childhood education, school and community college investment, and neighborhood regeneration. Analysts at the Brookings Institute similarly conclude that the answer, rather than directly supporting marriage, is encouraging the factors that lead to stability in families and planning for parenthood, which mainly come down to increasing education and raising incomes for those at the bottom.

The task is not to attempt to bolster a constantly changing institution but to improve how family life can support opportunity across future generations as a whole, not just for those who already have resources. As Putnam suggests, at the heart of the programs that achieved this in the decades following the Second World War was a "commitment to invest in other people's children. And underlying that commitment was a deeper sense that those kids, too, were our kids."[70] This is a generational challenge about how we see our collective future.

CHAPTER 7

# MANUFACTURING A GENERATIONAL CULTURE WAR

"**N**ot cool, University of Manchester. Not cool."[1] This was how Jeb Bush, former governor of Florida, responded to a 2018 story about a student union that had "banned" applause at its events. Students had argued that clapping might trigger anxiety among some audience members, and that there were less startling ways for people to show appreciation. Students were encouraged to instead use "jazz hands"—the British Sign Language gesture for applause.

It may seem odd that such an eminent American politician felt compelled to comment on a minor decision by a handful of students thousands of miles away. In fact, former governor Bush was making a self-deprecating reference to his own excruciating experience of asking his audience to clap after a flat speech during his unsuccessful campaign for the 2016 Republican presidential nomination.[2] But the joke was missed in the international media storm that blew up around the story. Overnight, Manchester University's jazz hands became a cri de coeur among those who despaired at the character of the day's youth ("What a Load of Clap" was a popular headline), without any hint of Bush's irony (Piers Morgan tweeted "Britain's losing its mind").[3] One

professor opined that "it symbolises our culture's slide into infantilised deca-
dence, where enfeeblement is celebrated and learned helplessness indulged."[4]

It's not just students in Manchester who have been the subject of such attention: whenever similar incidents crop up, whether at US political conferences
or Australian schools, the furor is similar.[5] The reason is that it provides a
simple but vivid example of a complicated issue that is seen entirely differently
by different groups. On one side, these sort of measures are just a sensible attempt at the inclusion, in this case, of autistic people for whom applause, as the
University of Manchester disability officer said, can feel like a bomb going off.[6]
On the other side, it's a sign of a generation that is coddled in a way that will
cause them to be utterly unprepared for the real world.[7]

The clapping controversy is one, admittedly slightly ludicrous, example of
the "culture wars," which are most often presented as being waged between
the "snowflake" young and the "out-of-touch" old. The culture wars are increasingly the prism through which we see generational differences, so it's
important to figure out whether we are experiencing a real sea change in the
attitudes and beliefs of today's youth.

The first point to recognize is that there is *always* tension between generations, and this is a good thing. We can think of it as a type of "demographic
metabolism," as outlined by the Canadian demographer Norman B. Ryder
in the 1960s. Ryder regarded society as an organism where this metabolism
makes change inevitable. As both Karl Mannheim and the French philosopher Auguste Comte concluded, social, political, or technological innovation
would likely stall if we lived forever, as individuals get stuck in their ways.
As Ryder says, "The continual emergence of new participants in the social
process and the continual withdrawal of their predecessors compensate the
society for limited individual flexibility. The society whose members were im-
mortal would resemble a stagnant pond."[8]

Despite the benefits of generational change, it is a constant challenge for
society to cope with this unending churn of membership, and, as Ryder put it,
"the incessant 'invasion of barbarians.'" Although this may seem like a harsh
description of our delightful children, Ryder means that each new entrant is,
by definition, not "configured" to the attitudes and behaviors of their parents'
society. Traumatic shocks, like wars, economic crises, or pandemics, may utterly change the direction of new generations in their formative years, but

there is *always* cultural tension between generations. As Ryder says, we are "pulled apart gradually by the slow grind of evolutionary change."[9]

This is also the impression we get when we look at the actual data: there have been some incredible changes in our cultural attitudes over the past few decades, but this did *not* start with the arrival of Millennials or Gen Z. Instead, we can see that there is often not a great deal of difference between generations, except for the oldest. High-profile examples of extreme views and behaviors on both sides of the generational divide are amplified, but they do not reflect a break across generations as a whole. Rather than a cohort effect, this looks more like a period effect, where the greater polarization in society today sensitizes us to differences.

More than this, painting whole generations of young people as battling for "social justice" misses the fact that less "progressive" values persist among significant minorities of them. Generational analysis is to some extent part of the problem, as it can give the impression of an unstoppable march toward greater liberalism. In reality, cultural change is neither smooth nor unidirectional. Social values change as a result of a constant and messy struggle both between and within generations, and a fuller understanding of cohort, life-cycle, and period effects is vital.

## THE BELOVED COMMUNITY

The Black Lives Matter (BLM) protests around the world, at the height of a global pandemic, will be remembered as one of the most extraordinary events of recent times. The murder of George Floyd in Minneapolis sparked an outpouring of anger that linked a number of debates about race around the world. It also had a particularly strong generational element in the profile of campaigners (at least two-thirds of protestors in four major US cities were thirty-four or under) and the methods of protest and organization. BLM started in 2013, first as a hashtag following the acquittal of George Zimmerman in the killing of Trayvon Martin, and quickly evolved into a movement with a loose organizational structure and Gen Z leaders.[10] The president of BLM Greater New York, nineteen-year-old Nupol Kiazolu, made the generational nature of the protest clear to the government: "You've fucked with the last generation. . . . Young people have been carrying every single movement we've seen across the world, so it's time for adults to step aside and uplift us."

This is not new, however: young activists have always played a leading role in civil rights struggles. John Lewis, one of the most important figures in the fight for racial equality in America, was only twenty-three when he spoke alongside Martin Luther King Jr. at the March on Washington in 1964. His own speech possessed the same urgency that comes from emergent generations, ending: "We will not and cannot be patient."[11] In his final essay before his death in July 2020, Lewis urged the protestors to continue with nonviolent direct action: "When you see something that is not right, you must say something. You must do something. Democracy is not a state. It is an act, and each generation must do its part to help build what we called the Beloved Community, a nation and world society at peace with itself."[12]

The discrimination faced by minority ethnic groups that sparked such passion is rooted in attitudes, beliefs, and values. At its heart, it is based on how people see different races. Long-term survey measures can help us understand how views have changed, but it is difficult to gain a true measure of racial prejudice from surveys, particularly over a long period. "Social desirability bias" means that people respond to some extent in the way they think they're expected to or that puts them in a good light. This happens with all sensitive social issues, but it's likely to be particularly marked on measures of racism, given the highly charged nature of the issue.

For a while, it seemed like we may be able to access our unconscious bias through a tool called an Implicit Association Test, where the speed at which we associate good and bad things with different racial groups was supposed to provide a "window into our souls."[13] The only problem is that it doesn't really work: people who score high on the test don't seem to be any more racist in practice than people who don't. The same people can also achieve very different scores at different times, as Jesse Singal pointed out: "If a depression test, for example, has the tendency to tell people they're severely depressed and at risk of suicidal ideation on Monday, but essentially free of depression on Tuesday, that's not a useful test."[14]

Despite their limitations though, surveys of attitudes remain key measures of racist views. Some simply ask whether people think of themselves as prejudiced against other races, or whether they think people in the country as a whole are. In Britain, a long-time series survey has asked these questions, with incredibly stable responses: around three in ten have said they are a little or very prejudiced since 1983, with no discernible generational pattern.[15] But it's difficult to judge the meaning of this, as our standards of prejudice have shifted.

Perhaps more useful are "social distance" questions, which ask people how comfortable they are connecting with people of other races in specific ways. In Britain, respondents were first asked whether they would "mind if a relative married a person of black or West Indian origin" back in 1983, when 51 percent said they would, which was a balance of quite different views between the Pre-war and Baby Boomer generations. The overall figure had more than halved to 22 percent by 2013, and generational differences are important to this trend, as we can see in Figure 7.1. In particular, a lot of the Pre-war generation retained their view while Baby Boomer concern halved, and Gen X and Millennials came into the population with few saying they'd mind. The good news is that the very high levels of concern we've seen in the recent past will fade away with the oldest generation. However, generational analysis also makes it clear that these attitudes won't entirely disappear: significant minorities of younger cohorts are holding on to this mind-set.

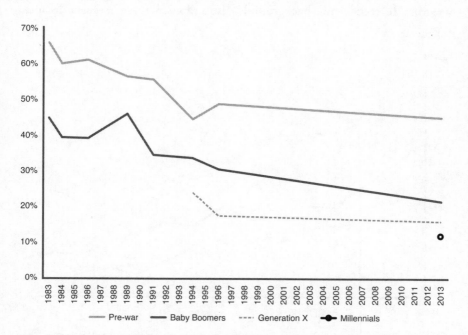

Figure 7.1: Percentage of white British adults who say they would mind if a close relative were to marry a person of Black or West Indian origins. Source: British Social Attitudes (1983–2013).

The decline in concern about interracial marriage in the United States has been much more dramatic than in Britain, and more uniform across generations. The nation started off worse in 1990, with 58 percent of respondents expressing discomfort with interracial relationships (the equivalent figure in Britain was around 50 percent) but ended up better, at around 9 percent in 2018. And this issue is very generational, with a thirty percentage point gap between the Pre-war generation and Millennials and Gen Z. The Pre-war generation have changed their views an awful lot over this period, but being socialized at a different time continues to be a strong influence. There is not, however, much of a gap between other generations.

In both the United States and Britain, it is shocking how recently overtly racist attitudes were widespread, and residual racist preferences persist in significant minorities of white people, including among younger generations. However, more positively, we've come a long way in a relatively short time. These changes in attitudes are also reflected in real-life behaviors; in the United States, interracial couples accounted for 17 percent of marriages by 2015, compared to 3 percent in 1967.[16] In the UK, around one in ten couples are from different ethnic backgrounds, also a rapid increase in recent decades.

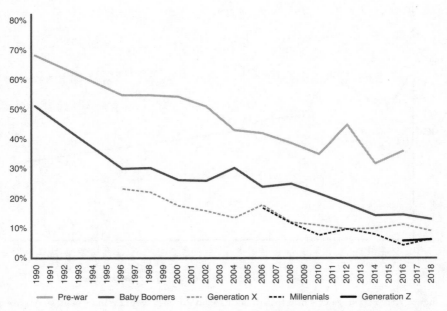

Figure 7.2: Percentage of American adults saying that they would oppose having a close friend or family member marry a Black person. Source: US General Social Survey (1990–2018).

The experience of ethnic minority groups shows how discrimination is hanging on, however. For example, one direct way to understand prejudice in employment is through randomized control trials of job applications. Researchers submit large quantities of resumes with the same qualifications and experience levels that vary one characteristic, often the name, to indicate the candidate's ethnicity across job types. This measures a tiny slice of possible prejudice, but the experimental design removes a lot of the uncertainty of interpretation. And unfortunately, these studies tend to show that racial prejudice in employment practice is widespread and unchanging. One meta-analysis of more than twenty studies in the United States between 1989 and 2015 showed that white candidates were 36 percent more likely to get callbacks than Black candidates with otherwise identical characteristics, and there was no real change over this period.[17]

These underlying judgments of people's capabilities on the basis of race are also visible in the survey data. A different US survey asks people about the characteristics they associate with different racial groups, for example, whether they are hardworking or lazy. There has been an improvement over the past three decades, from around four in ten people believing Black people to be "lazy," to around a quarter now, a shallower decline than prejudicial views on marriage but more consistent across generations. The fact that 23 percent of Millennials and 19 percent of Gen Z still think Black people are lazy is startling. Some suggest that holding on to these stereotypes about work ethic across ethnic groups has allowed racist attitudes among a segment of the population to simply shift focus. This framing, of there being a difference in *application* rather than *abilities* between races, is perhaps more socially acceptable now. It allows people to explain the different outcomes across ethnic groups without acknowledging continued discrimination in an individualistic culture where effort is rewarded.[18] Whatever the explanation, the persistence of these stereotypes in a significant minority of the population, including among the young, is shocking.

The attention that the BLM movement has brought to racial discrimination is the latest in a series of identity-driven divides that have been central to societal tension over the past decade. In particular, major political events and trends have also been driven by divisive debates about immigration: a "nativist" attitude was among the strongest predictors of voting patterns in Donald

Trump's election, immigration control was a core motivation in the Brexit vote, and views on immigration have been linked to the rise of right-wing populist parties across Europe.[19]

As with race, concern about immigration is often deeply generational, and nowhere is this more true than in Britain. Figure 7.3 traces the proportion of each generation for whom immigration is among the most important issues facing the country, and it shows how generationally divisive it became in a short period of time. In the late 1990s, hardly anyone saw immigration as a top concern in Britain—but it shot up as European immigration increased in the early 2000s. It was then often the top issue for the country, peaking just before the EU referendum in 2016 before falling away again. Although the flow of changes during this period was similar across the generations, the levels of concern were utterly different. At the peak of this gap, the Pre-war generation were twice as likely as Gen Z to identify immigration as a top concern. Britain is far from alone in this generational divide: the same hierarchy of concern over this issue is seen in the United States and Europe.

In 2015 and 2016, there was an expectation among some liberal commentators in the UK, the United States, and across Europe that this generational

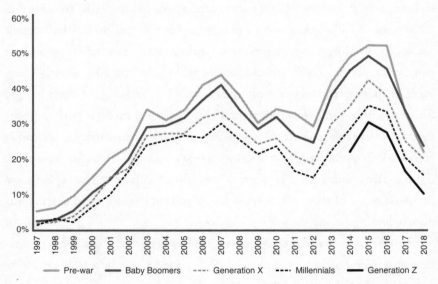

Figure 7.3: Percentage of British adults identifying immigration as a top issue facing the country. Source: Ipsos MORI Issues Index 1997–2018.

difference pointed to a more open future. Indeed, some of my generational analysis was used in a paper called *Britain's Cosmopolitan Future* published in 2015, just before the EU referendum.[20] The paper identified various reasons to believe that Britain was moving toward more outward-facing attitudes: greater diversity, huge increases in university graduates, urban expansion, the decline of traditional institutions like political parties, new communication technologies, and so on. The report ended with a warning that the political parties should embrace "the emerging cosmopolitan majority" or face inevitable electoral decline.

A similar perspective was emerging in the United States. Doug Sosnik, Bill Clinton's former political director, borrowed a phrase from the physicist Freeman Dyson, calling 2016 a "hinge moment" when the trends of urbanization and growing ethnic diversity would result in an acceleration of generational difference. Writing about the 2016 presidential election, Sosnik said, "The candidate running for president in 2016 who best understands how the country is changing and runs a campaign based on the America of the future rather than the America of the past is most likely to be our 45th president."[21]

The reality turned out quite different. We got Brexit in the UK, where some of the most powerful factors in explaining the vote to leave the EU were a concern about the speed of cultural change and a sense of nostalgia.[22] The winning campaign in the United States literally looked backward as it aimed to make the country great "again."

Whether the analysis was wrong or just premature is one of the key debates of our time. One of the risks of looking only at generational trends is that the gaps between cohorts can make the future seem more predictable than it really is. But of course, period and life-cycle effects still matter. The surge in immigration in the UK, and the surge in media and political attention, increased *all* generations' concern about the issue. And we still change as we age, which dampens generational effects. Figure 7.4 traces concern about immigration for Gen X compared with those who were sixteen to twenty-nine years old in each year of the study. In the late 1990s these groups were the same, but as Gen X have aged, their concern about immigration has drifted higher than people who are in that age group today.

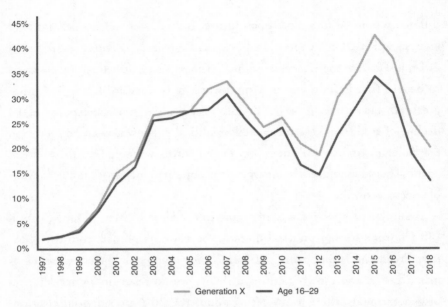

Figure 7.4: Percentage of British adults who consider immigration a top issue facing the country. Source: Ipsos MORI Issues Index 1997–2018.

## THE BATTLE OF THE SEXES—AND THE AGES

Our views of gender roles over the past few decades have played out with similar dynamics, and the overall transformation is equally remarkable. It is hard to imagine that as recently as 1987, 48 percent of the British population believed that "the job of the man is to earn money, the job of the woman is to look after the home and family." Now only 8 percent of people say they hold this view.

If you looked only at this change across the whole population, it would seem like a gradual and consistent shift across British society. However, "generational replacement" effects play a central role. In particular, the Pre-war generation have remained distinct from all other cohorts; a large part of the decline in Britons' agreement that a "woman's place is in the home" is that this generation accounts for a declining proportion of the population.

Many of the Pre-war cohort grew up when women were much less likely to be working: only 24 percent in Britain in 1914, a figure that was still only around 50 percent in the 1960s.[23] More generally, we have lived through what the economics professor Claudia Goldin calls a "grand gender convergence" in the latter half of the twentieth century; there has been a narrowing in the gap between men and women not just in labor-force participation but hours worked, occupation types, education levels, and earnings.[24] Significant gaps remain, but the main point here is that the oldest generations grew up before many of these advances had developed.

This socialization effect means that the generational divide is much stronger than the gender divide. When we split the Pre-war generation into men and women, there is only ever around a five percentage point gap between them throughout the period—much smaller than the twenty percentage point gap between this cohort and the rest. Generation trumps gender on this measure, and Pre-war women are more distinct from their daughters and granddaughters than from their male peers. As one feminist writer put it, progress seemed to falter along a "mother-daughter" divide: "The contemporary women's movement seems fated to fight a war on two fronts: alongside the battle of the sexes rages the battle of the ages."[25] This generational divide in the struggle for gender equality seems set to decline, as all other generations are tightly grouped.

This is also true in the United States; again, only the Pre-war generation stand apart, with Baby Boomers through to Gen Z expressing almost identical views, as we can see in Figure 7.5. The US question asks people whether they agree that "it's much better for everyone involved if the man is the achiever outside the home and the woman takes care of the home and family," which is a slightly softer wording and may partly explain why agreement with the sentiment is higher than in Britain. But it's unlikely to be the full reason—the change over time is also quite distinct.

Over the period as a whole, agreement has dropped steeply, from 66 percent in 1976 to 25 percent by 2018. But this is not nearly as dramatic a decline as in Britain. The difference in end points—25 percent agreeing in the United States but only 8 percent in Britain—is because the decrease in agreement stalled in the United States at the end of the 1980s, and started to slightly rise during the 1990s, before drifting down again in the 2010s.

This coincides with a time in the United States when people were trying to figure out whether women really could "have it all." A 1990 article in *Newsweek* coined the term "mommy wars" to describe the supposed clash between women who stay at home and women who work outside it. These tensions persisted for many years in political and cultural debate: an episode

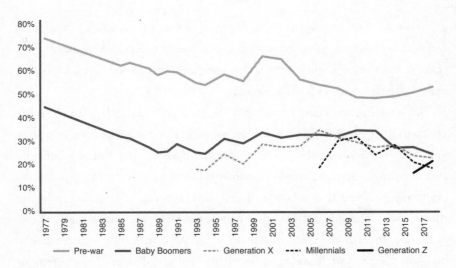

Figure 7.5: Percentage of American adults who agree that it is much better for everyone if the man is the achiever outside the home and the woman takes care of the home and family. Source: US General Social Survey (1977–2018).

of *Dr. Phil*, an American talk show, physically separated the studio audience to literally pit working and stay-at-home mothers against each other in November 2003, reinforcing the simplistic polarization common in the media and commentary.[26]

A much deeper and more consistent polarization is seen in long-term generational trends on attitudes to abortion in the United States, as shown in Figure 7.6. As far back as the 1970s, half or more of Americans have consistently said that a married woman should *not* be able to get a legal abortion just because she does not want more children. Gen Z is slightly less likely to hold this view, but over 40 percent of this youngest group still do. The issue splits the country down the middle, regardless of generation. This is an extraordinary level of consistency on a social issue over a long period. It is also entirely different from Britain, where public opinion has moved a long way: in the early 1980s, two-thirds of the population believed that a woman should not be allowed to have an abortion if she did not wish to have the child, a figure that had fallen to around a quarter for all except the Pre-war generation by 2016. There are no obvious distinctions between the other British generations: all except the oldest have changed their views similarly.

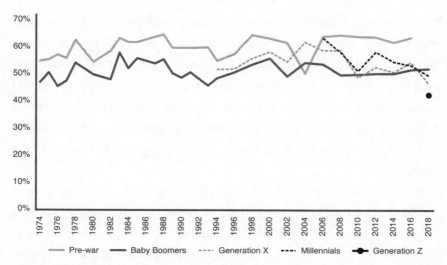

Figure 7.6: Percentage of American adults who believe it should not be possible for a pregnant married woman who does not want more children to get a legal abortion. Source: US General Social Survey (1974–2018).

The explanation for this difference between the two countries is again tied to the much higher connection to religion in the United States than in the UK and how it interacts with political identities. Attitudes toward abortion are a clear dividing line between Republicans and Democrats in the United States, with 82 percent of the latter believing that abortion should be legal in most cases, compared with 36 percent of the former. The issue forms a key plank in the early development of the US "culture wars," a term first popularized by the sociologist James Davison Hunter, who proposed that American politics had experienced prolonged and intense polarization between orthodox, conservative values and progressive, liberal values. The gulf between these two ideological worldviews, Davison Hunter argued, created two irreconcilable tribes. This idea remains disputed, and as with many elements of the culture wars, we need to be careful not to exaggerate the depth of division on abortion in the United States—there is more nuance among and less distance between Americans than you may expect.[27] For example, one poll that allowed people the option to say whether they were pro-life, pro-choice, neither, or both found that around four in ten said "neither" or "both."[28] For a large chunk of the population, it's a complex and contingent issue, and we risk talking up divisions by caricaturing perceptions.

## BEYOND BINARY

If abortion was one of the earliest fronts of the culture wars in the United States, sexual orientation and particularly gender identity have become the most contentious areas in recent years across several countries. Attitudes toward same-sex relationships have, however, evolved over a much longer period and are now less divisive in many countries. We can see the extent of this change in Figures 7.7 and 7.8, which show how people responded to similar questions in Britain and the United States, going back to the 1970s and 1980s.

A number of things stand out from this comparison. First, the proportions of all generations who think homosexuality is "not wrong at all" have increased dramatically in both Britain and the United States. This is a significant period effect—we've all shifted, starting from around 1990 in both countries. It seems quite extraordinary that as recently as 1987, only 11 percent of Brits thought homosexuality was not wrong at all, compared with 69 percent in 2018. I was a teenager in the late 1980s, and that's not how I remember the general attitude at the time, which shows the strength of our tendency to rewrite history based on our values today.

We can also see that the United States started in an almost identical position to Britain, with very similar figures for both Baby Boomers and the Pre-war generation. But although the direction of the trend has been

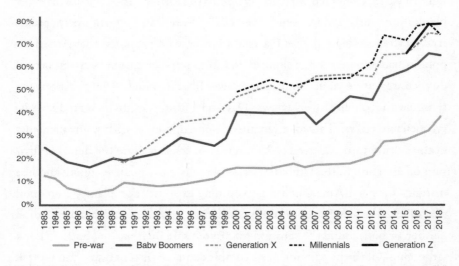

Figure 7.7: Percentage of British adults who view same-sex relations as "not wrong at all." Source: British Social Attitudes (1983–2018).

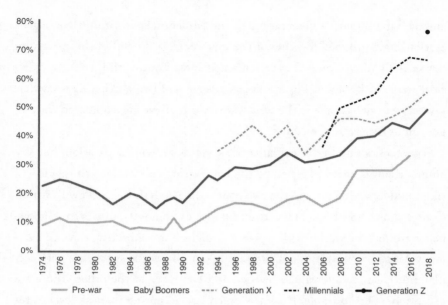

Figure 7.8: Percentage of US adults who view same-sex relations as "not wrong at all." Source: US General Social Survey (1974–2018).

the same, the United States has not moved quite as far; by 2018, 58 percent thought homosexuality was not wrong, compared with 69 percent in Britain.

Distinct generational patterns in the United States and Britain are the key to explaining this difference. When you were socialized has a lasting impact on your attitudes, as is seen most clearly in the Pre-war generations in each country. Their views on homosexuality have not shifted nearly as much as those of other generations, reflecting the fact that their formative experiences came at a time when active discrimination was embedded in many laws and institutions. Homosexual sex was a criminal act in the UK until 1967, when it was only partially decriminalized, and there was a similarly incremental change in the recognition of homosexuality in the United States over the same period. It's no surprise then that the views of the Pre-war generations in Britain and the United States have remained remarkably similar. The same is true at the other end of the generational spectrum; British and American Gen Z also have practically identical views: 80 percent think homosexuality is not at all wrong.

The two countries, then, have drifted apart over the past couple of decades as a result of differences in attitudes in the middle of the generational range, among Baby Boomers, Generation X, and Millennials. In Britain, these generations have grouped together at the more permissive end of the spectrum, but in the United States they've remained spread out, with Gen X tracking closer to Baby Boomers. For example, 75 percent of British Gen Xers say that sex between two people of the same sex is not at all wrong, compared with 57 percent of American Gen Xers.

There are a number of explanations for this growing separation, but key among them is again likely to be the contrasting connections to religion of those middle age cohorts in the two countries. Analysis by the Pew Research Center shows how highly related acceptance of homosexuality is to religious belief around the world, with a pretty straight line connecting the two. Majority Muslim countries like Egypt are at one end of the spectrum, with secular European countries like Sweden and Denmark at the other. There are exceptions—for example, Russia is much less accepting than its level of religious belief would suggest, and Brazil is much more tolerant. The United States is actually more accepting than you'd predict from looking at religiosity levels alone, but the strength of religious connection in these middle generations keeps it much less open than much of Europe.[29]

This international analysis is also an important reminder of how varied attitudes toward homosexuality are around the world. The range is extraordinary, from around 5 percent in countries like Denmark and Norway thinking homosexuality is "morally unacceptable," up to 93 percent in Indonesia. There are many countries where large proportions morally object, from Russia and Turkey at around 70 percent, to Brazil and Mexico at around 40 percent. *Where* you are born is still a much bigger determinant of attitudes toward homosexuality than *when* you were born.

Although trends in attitudes toward different sexual orientations over time and across countries are well documented, it is much more difficult to get consistent and insightful measures of actual sexual identities and behaviors over a long enough period to identify generational differences. However, it is clear that the changes in individual sexual identity have not been nearly as dramatic as our changes in attitudes. The most basic measures of identity, typically collected by official statistics agencies, mostly show a steady upward drift in people identifying as other than heterosexual, from around 1.5 percent to 2.4 percent in the UK in the past decade, and from 2.7 percent in

2008 to 5 percent by 2018 in the United States, with the increase mainly driven by more people identifying as bisexual.[30] There is a clear generational difference in both countries: younger cohorts are more likely to identify as other than heterosexual, up to 10 percent of American Millennials and 4 percent of Gen Z in the UK.

Of course, such binary classifications are very blunt measures of sexual identity, let alone behavior or attraction. Questions that allow people more of a spectrum get a completely different response. For example, one US study by an advertising agency showed that only 48 percent of thirteen- to twenty-year-olds (roughly Generation Z) identified as "completely straight," compared with 65 percent of people aged twenty-one to thirty-four (roughly Millennials).[31] When a similar question was asked in the UK in 2021, the results were almost identical, with just over seven in ten of the general population identifying as exclusively heterosexual but only 54 percent of eighteen to twenty-four-year-olds doing the same.[32]

We should know by now that age-based gaps can only give us limited insight into generational change; only long-term trends can show whether a trend also held with previous generations, but, sadly, these are not available. Unfortunately, this generally does not stop the overreach in the media: one particularly eye-catching headline from *Vice*, drawing on the results of the US study cited above, declared, "Teens These Days Are Queer AF, New Study Says."[33] The presentation of these simple age breakdowns as generational characteristics is part of the problem: comparing reported figures for Baby Boomers with Gen Z looks like an utter revolution in sexual attraction, but we can't tell how Baby Boomers would have responded when they were young, or how Gen Z will when they reach their sixties.

The lack of consistent long-term trends is surprising, because questions that regard sexual orientation as a spectrum rather than a discrete categorization have a long history. Alfred Kinsey, one of the pioneers of sexology in the United States, developed a scale of 0 (completely heterosexual) to 6 (completely homosexual), which he and colleagues used in thousands of interviews exploring men's sexual behaviors, published in his 1948 book *Sexual Behavior in the Human Male*. As Kinsey famously said, "Males do not represent two discrete populations, heterosexual and homosexual. . . . The world is not to be divided into sheep and goats."[34]

Although his survey techniques were unorthodox and less structured than modern approaches, his findings suggest that things may not have changed as much as we might think. His research showed that 37 percent of US males had had some homosexual experience during their lives, that 13 percent were predominantly homosexual for at least three years (as Kinsey correctly recognized, sexual attraction and behavior are not constant states), and that 4 percent were exclusively homosexual throughout their lives.

We are likely seeing important but relatively gradual increases in more diverse sexual identities, attractions, and experiences, combined with a greater willingness to report our attitudes and behaviors—rather than the revolution in sexual fluidity that some suggest. For example, there was a significant rise in women reporting same-sex experience in the UK, from 2 percent to 8 percent between 1990 and 2010.[35] The researchers attempted to discern whether this was a real change or due to women being more willing to report their experiences. Their conclusion was that the change between 1990 and 2000 was partly due to more honest reporting, but the rise between 2000 and 2010 was mostly real.[36]

This shift to viewing sexuality as less binary is reflected in fractious arguments about gender identity and fluidity. Early discussion of attitudes toward gender identity focused on transgender equality. A 2014 *Time* magazine cover story with the headline "The Transgender Tipping Point: America's Next Civil Rights Frontier" emphasized its generational nature.[37] A trans woman interviewed for the article, who didn't begin her transition until middle age, "is certain she could have had a completely different life if she had been born later."

The discussion has quickly developed from a focus on transgender rights to broader issues around gender identification, and the generational framing has become even more prominent. Gen Z in particular is often picked out as the "gender-fluid generation," and for some good reasons, when you consider how much more direct contact they have with people who identify as nonbinary than other generations.[38] Only 27 percent of British Gen Z say they've never met anyone who uses nonbinary pronouns, compared with 68 percent of Baby Boomers.[39]

Some attitudes follow similarly steep age gradients—but it's not always as clear-cut as the generational framing suggests. Roughly twice as many young people as older people in Britain think that "a person should be able to identify as a different gender to the one they were born in," and there's a similar split on whether passports should include a category for people who do not identify as male or female.[40] Support is higher in the United States: half of women and four in ten men agree that there is a spectrum of gender identities, but there are no strong age differences on this question.[41] Indeed, political party is a more reliable indication of attitude toward gender identity among Americans than age; 64 percent of Democrats agree that whether a person is a man or a woman can differ from their sex at birth, while only 19 percent of Republicans do.[42]

The rapidity with which this new front has emerged and is changing makes even current opinion difficult to ascertain, so predicting future generational trends is impossible. However, it seems clear that it isn't a fad among youth, as some argue.[43] I am naturally suspicious when older generations respond to any emergent trend in this way: we have seen a similar tendency with some of the biggest social shifts of modern times. H. G. Wells said some of his contemporaries believed "the vote for women was an isolated fad, and the agitation an epidemic of madness that would presently pass."[44]

Equally, the trajectory of attitudes toward gender identity is far from set or entirely generationally driven. The issue raises complex questions that are still only emerging, which each generation is still working through, including the youngest. Drawing on the Pew survey results outlined above, one American sexology commentator suggested that twenty years from now, our current "bickering over bathrooms will seem quaint."[45] This is too dismissive of some real debates that are playing out and too simplistic a reading of how cultural change both ebbs and flows.

## RISE OF THE NONES?

The continued power of religion to shape a wider set of cultural beliefs has been clear in many of the issues we've already covered in this chapter. It is, then, vitally important to understand how general attachment to religion is changing—particularly as it is one of the most clear-cut generational traits that we'll see. Of course, individuals fall in and out of religious belief all the time, but not a lot changes within each generation as a whole, as we can see in

Figure 7.9, which shows how many of each cohort in Britain say they have no religion.

The generational gaps are enormous: 70 percent of Gen Z report no religious affiliation compared with under 30 percent of the Pre-war generation, and each line is pretty flat. The challenge facing organized religion in Britain is almost entirely generational, which makes the decline slow; it mostly changes as one cohort dies out and is replaced with another that is less devout. But this also makes its decline inevitable. You can't stop these sort of generational tides without an event of "second coming" scale.

As frightening as this picture is for religious institutions, it hides an even greater challenge facing Christian faiths in a number of Western countries, including Britain. The figures for religious identification among younger generations would be even worse without the increase in non-Christian faiths among the British young, largely due to immigration. When we look at association with the Church of England in Britain, the dire situation is clearer. Only 2 percent of the youngest generations identify as Anglicans, compared with nearly 40 percent of the Pre-war generation. And to add to the woe, even the older generational lines show signs of decline, with the Pre-war generation, Baby Boomers, and Gen X each drifting down over time.

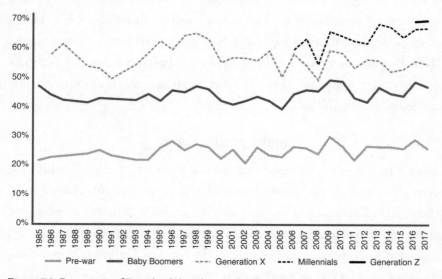

Figure 7.9: Percentage of British adults who say they have no religion. Source: British Social Attitudes (1984–2017).

But the generationally driven death of organized religion is not quite as certain as this pattern suggests. Although "cultural" Christians (those who identify but don't practice) might be dying out, those who remain are much more consistently committed. This is a process that the sociologist Grace Davie has likened to the shift from a "conscript army" to a "professional force."[46] She explains how Christianity in countries like Britain has moved from having "large numbers of people involved whether they liked it or not, to a professional army which people join voluntarily. . . . Broadly speaking, I contend that the professionals are rather more committed than conscripts."

This is largely supported by the generational data: the changes in regular attendance levels in Britain are not nearly as varied between generations and are not collapsing nearly as much. Even on this most generational of issues, different cohorts are not as far apart as they may at first seem. British Baby Boomers have always been lax churchgoers and continue to be, with only around 10 percent attending services weekly, while Millennials have settled at a similar level. Gen X, however, have seen a significant increase in regular churchgoing, tripling to around 15 percent. As the parent of a child nearing secondary school age, I suspect that has something to do with the continued role of religion in school selection in the UK, requiring parents and children to attend services to qualify for places in many schools. Of course, a more important driver of the overall relative stability of these trends is that they cover all faiths and are bolstered by the growth of non-Christian adherents, among whom attendance tends to be more regular.

The United States has an *entirely* different relationship with religion than Britain, where each American generation is twice as likely to identify with a religion than their British counterparts, as Figure 7.10 shows. There is a generational hierarchy similar to that in Britain, but even among the most godless US generation, only 34 percent of Millennials claim no religion, compared with 68 percent in Britain. Even so, the fixation on the "rise of nones" in America is understandable: levels of religious identification may be much higher than in Britain, but it is still experiencing a powerful mix of significant generational and period effects.

There is, of course, a lot of "conscript" rather than "professional" religious attachment among Americans. Although eight in ten report a religious affiliation, only around a quarter attend a weekly religious service. However,

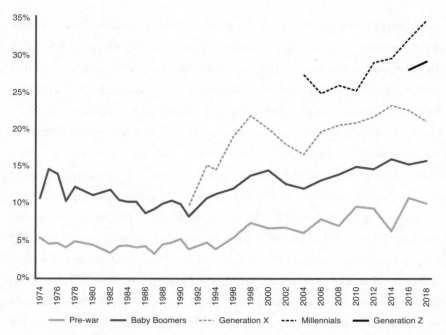

Figure 7.10: Percentage of American adults who say they have no religion. Source: US General Social Survey (1974–2018).

this is significantly higher than in Britain, particularly among Baby Boomers; 10 percent of that cohort in Britain attend weekly services, compared to 30 percent in the United States. But again, the differences between generations *within* the United States is much lower.

Looking beyond anglophone and northern European countries turns the narrative of religious decline on its head. As the Archbishop of Canterbury Justin Welby, the most senior bishop in the Anglican Church, points out, the domestic decline in Britain masks a very different picture elsewhere: "In global terms, a typical Anglican Christian is an African woman just over the age of thirty living on less than $4 per day."[47] Overall, Pew projects that Christians will account for 31 percent of the global population in 2050—the same level as now, due to population growth in developing Christian countries. The Muslim population, 23 percent in 2010, will reach 30 percent by 2050. The proportion of religiously unaffiliated people will fall from 16 percent to 13 percent of the world's population, as Europe's global population share also declines.[48]

These patterns can be seen playing out in the question of whether people see themselves as religious. Germany has a pattern similar to Britain's, with a clear generational hierarchy: older cohorts are more religious than younger cohorts, and only half of Germans as a whole see themselves as religious. But in other Christian countries, such as Italy and Brazil, around seven in ten see themselves as religious, across all generations. The picture is the same in non-Christian countries such as India and Turkey. Northern Europe is not the norm in an increasingly religiously diverse world.

## THE GENERATIONAL CULTURE WARS

It is startling to observe how far our attitudes toward race, gender, and sexuality have shifted in the past few decades. That they have moved so much so quickly should be celebrated, particularly as it is not something we foresaw thirty or forty years ago. That these issues remain a source of conflict is more predictable. A generational perspective helps to explain why such conflict is built in to the constant arrival of new participants in society—it may be a natural part of our societal "metabolism," but we will always fear the young "barbarians." This longer-term perspective also shows that we *always* think that things are changing too fast for us to keep up. In 1914, the US commentator Walter Lippmann wrote, "We are unsettled to the very root of our being. . . . We have changed our environment more quickly than we know how to change ourselves."[49]

The overall impression we get is not of a sudden shift with the latest generation of young people but rather a remarkable change among most generations over the past three or four decades. Generational effects are essential to understanding culture change, but the gaps between today's youth and most other generations are not as large or unusual as they are often portrayed. Of course, we shouldn't downplay the differences entirely; there are important distinctions, and they show up most on emergent issues, as we would expect. For example, support for the BLM protests is roughly twice as high among the youngest compared with the oldest age groups, and in the UK, the young are roughly twice as likely to be "ashamed" of our imperial past than older groups. But these gaps are no different in scale from those between the Prewar generation and Baby Boomers on race. Even on gender identity, the "cultural warrior" label is a poor fit for large sections of the young, and other characteristics have a stronger effect on their views.

Once again, our tendency to focus on one explanation for change hides a richer and more complex reality. Life cycles are important, and we do seem to shift our position on issues like immigration as we age. Period effects also have a say, for example, in moving all generations' views of women's roles in the United States in the 1990s against what looked like a solid generational tide.

Perhaps most importantly, greater division across society as a whole, driven by polarizing politics and social media environments, has sensitized us to high-profile but unrepresentative examples of "woke" and "unwoke" behavior. People of all generations are identifying more with their own group and differentiating themselves more from "other" groups, which leads us to focus on behaviors that attracted less attention in the past. The "war on woke" seems to be more driven by this change in the general environment than by a distinct break in the attitudes of our current generation of young people. By exaggerating differences, we are in danger of falling into a behavior that we claim young people today are guilty of: "catastrophizing."

Overly simplistic generational analysis is part of the problem. Generational replacement is a key driver of cultural change, with older generations being replaced by cohorts socialized in very different times. However, this can give a false sense of certainty; we need to remember the power of shocks that can change our trajectory and life-cycle effects that return younger generations to well-worn paths. Generational trends are also sometimes wrongly translated as "mission accomplished," which skirts the fact that less liberal attitudes persist in significant minorities of younger generations and that inequalities persist.

For example, the writer Douglas Murray shows a palpable frustration about new expressions of inequality, such as a focus on "toxic masculinity": "Why would the . . . rhetoric become so heated when the standards of equality have so much improved? Is it because the stakes are so low? Because people are bored and want to assume the heroic posture amid a life of relative safety and comfort?"[50] It is perfectly reasonable to question the usefulness of such concepts, but doing so should not lead to a dismissal of continuing injustice.

The persistence of discriminatory attitudes and the gaps in outcomes on the basis of gender, race, and sexuality deserve more attention than that.

There is a further risk in emphasizing generational framing, in particular in ascribing so much responsibility to emerging generations. Barack Obama, for example, has repeatedly outlined his particularly strong faith in the "next generation," whose "conviction in the equal worth of all people seems to come as second nature," while implying that their parents and teachers never truly believed the same.[51] This is no doubt intended as encouragement, but it brings its own risks. The trends in our attitudes don't suggest that current generations represent a real break with the recent past on issues including gender, race, and sexuality. Lionizing coming generations not only misrepresents reality but also encourages a false sense of separation.

# CHAPTER 8

# CONSTANT CRISES

"**E**vents, dear boy, events." This was the British prime minister Harold Macmillan's reported response when he was asked what he thought would blow his government off course.[1] The reply succinctly captures the tendency of politicians to view their actions as moment-to-moment survival in the face of the unpredictable. In 1886, the British politician Joseph Chamberlain wrote, "In politics, it's no use looking beyond the next fortnight." Today, two weeks seems positively luxurious, with the advent of twenty-four-hour news and social media. As the former Australian PM Malcolm Turnbull suggested, "It's a 60-second news cycle now, it's instantaneous."[2]

Of all the areas examined in this book, politics is the most obviously determined by sudden, unexpected period effects, but that does not mean that events are all that matters. Indeed, it is important to fight that perception, not least because it reinforces the sense that we are constantly teetering on the edge of crises, whether of trust in politics or even support for democracy. In fact, there is significant continuity and resilience in Western democratic political systems, partly because many of the most important patterns in our political behavior are driven by a combination of slower cohort effects and our own predictable life cycles.

Each of the powerful generational trends we've seen in previous chapters ends up expressed in our political views: the changing attitudes between cohorts shifts the political debate and helps determine individuals' connection to particular political parties. Clearly this is not a one-way relationship, with politicians responding to the will of new generations—politics also shapes our views. "Thatcher's children," those who came of age in the 1980s in the UK and show a greater tendency to be right-leaning than neighboring cohorts, are an example of a generation carrying with them some imprint of the political context they grew up in.[3] Similar patterns have been identified in the United States, including some that work in the opposite direction: those who turned eighteen during the Nixon presidency were more likely to vote Democratic than the average American in elections decades later.[4]

We also change as we age. Numerous versions of the saying "If you're not a liberal when you're twenty-five, you have no heart. And if you're not a conservative by the time you're thirty-five, you have no brain" have come down through the decades. This is about as clear an assertion of the importance of life-cycle effects as you'll see. Our generational data show that the effect is not nearly as absolute as the saying suggests, but it is still an important fact of political life.

In recent years a number of political predictions from pundits and commentators have been confounded, and our tendency to focus on just one of cohort, life-cycle, or period effects is part of the reason for these misses. Age and generation are increasingly important in understanding our politics, but we need to avoid the temptation of looking for one simple explanation.

## GRAY VOTES VERSUS YOUTHQUAKES

The importance of a generational perspective doesn't just apply to the electorate—it's also helpful in understanding the changing profile of political leadership. In particular, the United States stands out among Western democracies for its current drift toward "gerontocracy." Donald Trump was the oldest president to be inaugurated, at seventy years old—until Joe Biden, at seventy-eight. President Biden joins Nancy Pelosi, the eighty-year-old House Speaker, and Chuck Schumer, the seventy-one-year-old Senate majority leader, at the top of the US political hierarchy. As an article in the *Atlantic* put it, most of these individuals "came into the world before the International

Monetary Fund and the CIA; before the invention of the transistor and the Polaroid camera."[5]

An aging political class may seem like a natural consequence of increased longevity and health in later life, but the United States is in fact an outlier; since 1950, the average age of heads of government in OECD nations has steadily declined, from over sixty years old to around fifty-four today, a quarter century younger than Biden.[6] This is largely because of the unusual presidential system in the United States, where the enormous resources and political capital required to run for office take much longer to build. The particularly large US baby boom and the good fortune of this generation in the growth years has made them difficult to dislodge by subsequent smaller cohorts, but this is starting to shift. The slow but relentless force of generational replacement saw a jump—38 percent—in both Gen X and Millennial members of the 116th Congress, but that progress seems to have stalled with the 117th, as Baby Boomers made up almost 70 percent of the incoming Congress.[7] We're still waiting for a generational "hinge moment" in the balance of US political leadership.

However, we need to be mindful of the implied agism and bias in discussions of "gerontocracies." It is not the case that older representatives are bound to act in or appeal to the interests of their own generation: the popularity of Bernie Sanders (seventy-eight) and Jeremy Corbyn (seventy-one) among young people in the United States and the UK was undeniable. More generally, the idea that older leaders are not interested in young people or future-focused issues such as climate change is, as we'll see, patently false. Joe Biden made an explicit cross-generational appeal to young Americans during his campaign: "I view myself as a transitional president. . . . It's a transition to your generation. The future is yours and I'm counting on you."[8]

Simplistic interpretations that leaders or electorates consistently act in their generational self-interest are, therefore, deeply flawed. But, in the end, politics is a "numbers game," and the greater your electoral weight, the more likely it is that political agendas and outcomes will bend toward your interests.

This is a simple function of just two factors: how many of you there are and how many turn out. The first of these factors has clearly worked against younger generations in recent decades in many countries. The demographic bulge that followed the Second World War was significant in a large number of nations, including the United States, the UK, Canada, Australia, New Zealand, France, and most other Western European countries.[9] Increased longevity has also helped to "gray" the electorate. Taken together, these effects have resulted in potential voting power moving steadily up the age range, and this is set to continue: for example, in the UK the median potential voter was forty-six in 2010, but it will be fifty by 2041.[10]

This demographic advantage is multiplied because older groups are also more likely to vote than younger ones. Figure 8.1 compares reported turnout rates of voters under thirty with those aged sixty-five or over, showing a particular imbalance in the UK, Ireland, and the United States, while the gap is much less marked in Spain and is actually reversed in Belgium (the only country in the chart where voting is compulsory). When we combine this unbalanced turnout with the aging profile of the UK, the median actual voter was forty-nine in 2010 and fifty-two in 2019. This results in millions of extra votes for older cohorts in elections, which is best seen when we compare single-year birth cohorts within generations. For example, at the 2015 UK general election, each Millennial who voted was joined by an average of 400,000 people

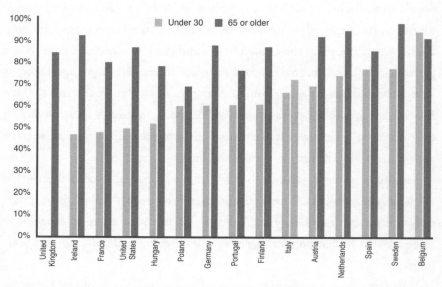

Figure 8.1: Percentage of voters under thirty versus sixty-five or over who report voting in the most recent national election. Source: European Social Survey and US General Social Survey.

born in the same year, while each member of Gen X and each Baby Boomer was joined by 485,000 and 530,000, respectively.[11]

The electoral dominance of older generations may feel like a constant, but in generational terms it's relatively new in countries like the UK. It is true that Baby Boomers were less likely to vote in their youth than the Pre-war generation, but the gap was relatively small. The real break came with Gen X in the 1990s, when a 25 percent gap in claimed turnout opened up between them and the oldest group. It continued to grow with Millennials; by 2015, there was a 40 percent gap between the oldest and the youngest cohort.[12]

We are equally sensitive to any sign that this generation gap is reversing. For example, during the 2017 UK general election, there was much discussion of a "youthquake," where the Labour leader Jeremy Corbyn seemed to mobilize younger generations: he was, for example, greeted like a rock star as he strode onto the Pyramid Stage at the Glastonbury Festival. Detailed analysis following the election showed the impact was not so earthshaking: there *was* a significant increase in turnout of younger groups, but it was most marked among those in their thirties and not of the order suggested by some breathless articles at the time.[13] However, the trend in the past few elections has been toward higher claimed turnout among younger generations, particularly from the dire levels seen in the 2000s.

This is mirrored in generational trends in considering voting as a duty. In 2010, only 40 percent of British Millennials thought voting was a "civic duty," compared with 80 percent of the oldest generation. But by 2017, following two fractious referendums and two general elections, Millennial commitment to voting had increased to 65 percent. Plenty of political scientists had been extremely worried about the health of the electoral system—and rightly so—but a few short years changed that picture significantly.[14] This is likely at least partly related to the tumultuous experience of so many vital political contests in the space of a few years: voting is a habit that younger generations in the UK have had an unprecedented opportunity to develop recently. Events really do matter in politics.

In the United States, Bernie Sanders is a similar left-leaning political figure with strong appeal for younger voters. Sanders lost in the primaries to Joe Biden in 2020, despite huge leads among young Americans in some states—up to fifty-two percentage points in Arizona, for example.[15] But turnout worked against him, with voting rates among young people falling from the 2016 primaries.[16] Even if he had been successful and become the Democratic candidate, the challenge of relying on this youth advantage would have followed him into the presidential race. Analysis by the political scientists David Broockman and Joshua Kalla showed that Sanders would have required an 11 percent rise in the youth vote, over and above any general increase in turnout, just to match the other Democratic candidates' showing against Trump.[17] This sort of increase is unprecedented in US presidential elections.

As in the UK, the reason why the support of the young is riskier to rely on in the United States is the marked gap in voting levels between generations, as shown in Figure 8.2. However, the pattern is quite different, with US generations showing more movement as they age. For example, only around 50 percent of US Baby Boomers claimed to vote in the late 1970s, but this is now 80 percent. In the UK, this trend has been much less dramatic, with Baby Boomers starting out at around 75 percent and ending up at 88 percent. This powerful life-cycle effect helps explain the relative stability of US turnout, which has bobbled around the mid-50s to low-60s since the 1970s (with the

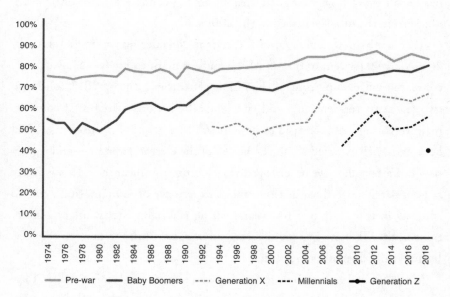

Figure 8.2: Percentage of American adults claiming they voted in the previous presidential election. Source: US General Social Survey (1974–2018).

66 percent turnout at the 2020 presidential election representing a level not seen since 1900). In contrast, UK turnout has fallen from a peak of 84 percent in 1950 to 67 percent in 2019, mostly due to growing gaps between the generations. Although youth turnout is a problem in both countries, in the United States the electorate seems to grow out of it.

## THE SLOW DEATH OF POLITICAL PARTIES?

The United States does, however, face more of a generational challenge regarding connection to political parties. As Figure 8.3 shows, there are worrying long-term trends for the two main parties, with only around four in ten American Millennials identifying as either a Republican or a Democrat, compared with six in ten in the Baby Boomer and Pre-war generations. This is a significant shift, but a longer-term perspective shows that it's not entirely new: in the mid-1970s, when Baby Boomers were young, there was nearly as large a gap between them and the Pre-war generations. It has been this oldest Pre-war generation that has maintained party loyalty, until a steep decline in the latest measure in 2018. The loss of that bulwark Pre-war generation

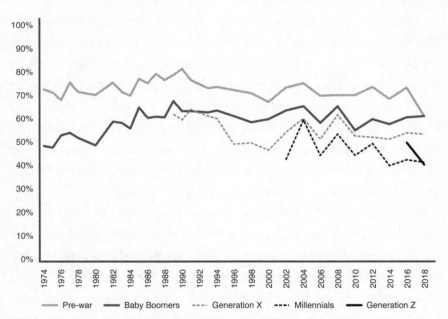

Figure 8.3: Percentage of American adults identifying as either Republican or Democrat. Source: US General Social Survey (1974–2018).

has shifted overall levels of political affiliation in the United States: the slow but relentless process of generational replacement means that identification with the two main parties has fallen from 63 percent to 51 percent in the past forty-four years.

A similar question in a European survey asks whether people feel close to one particular party. This only goes back fourteen years, but the pattern is similar. The generational lines are very flat, with each successive generation sticking at progressively lower levels of party attachment. The overall impact on party identification over this shorter period is less dramatic, but it is also drifting downward, from 52 percent in 2002 to 45 percent by 2018.

There are a number of structural reasons for this decline, including the weakening of religious attachments and labor organizations that previously delivered large numbers of party supporters.[18] It also seems likely related to the cultural changes we've already seen: the rise in individualism makes buying wholesale into one political party for life less likely.

But it's also clear that the outright rejection of political parties is a long way off. And, as with so many aspects of politics, generational trends can be reversed by events. Figure 8.4 tracks the proportion of people in Britain who see themselves as a supporter of a particular party. In the 2000s, it seemed like there was a generationally driven collapse of party loyalty, to a *much* greater degree than seen in the United States or across Europe as a whole. In 2009, for example, fewer than one in ten Millennials supported a particular party; the Pre-war generation five times as likely. Overall, we went from 51 percent of the population reporting party affiliation to *just 29 percent* in two decades. As one political scientist put it: "Millennials . . . regard it as the duty of politicians to woo them. They see parties not as movements deserving of loyalty, but as brands they can choose between or ignore."[19]

But in the frenzied political period between 2014 and 2017, just as turnout and the feeling that voting was a duty increased, party attachment also started to grow for all British generations, including Millennials. In a few eventful years, party support rebounded to 40 percent across the population. This is still a very low level of party identification, historically and internationally, but it illustrates the dangers of prediction in politics based on apparently settled generational trends.

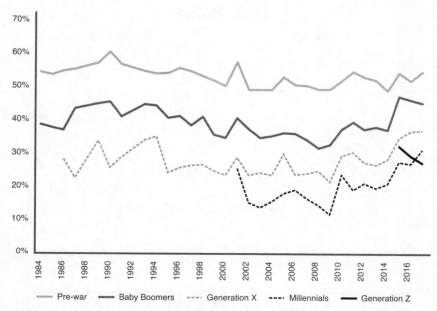

Figure 8.4: Percentage of British adults who consider themselves supporters of any one political party. Source: British Social Attitudes (1984–2017).

## DEMOGRAPHY AND DESTINY

Although the political turbulence of the past few years has been positive for party engagement in the UK, I suspect few people would recommend it as a strategy to reconnect people to politics, not least because it has come with the emergence of age as a clear electoral dividing line. The 2017 general election produced the biggest age gap in party support ever measured in the UK. This fell slightly in the 2019 election, but it still produced an incredible age gradient. Only 21 percent of eighteen- to twenty-four-year-olds voted for the Conservatives, and only 14 percent of those aged seventy or over voted for Labour. Conversely, two-thirds of the oldest group voted Conservative, and over half of the youngest went with Labour.

Looking at long-term generational support for the two main parties shows just how rapid and unusual the shift has been. As Figure 8.5 indicates, there had been little generational basis to Labour Party support since at least the 1980s, with the lines for each generation tracking closely—until a generational explosion in 2017, when over half of Gen Z identified with Labour, compared with barely 20 percent of the Pre-war generation.

## CONSERVATIVE

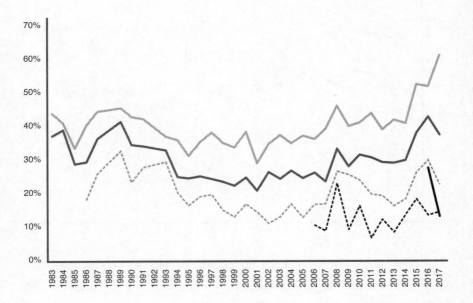

## LABOUR

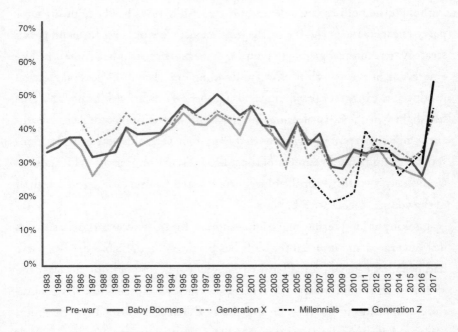

Figure 8.5: Percentage of British adults identifying as Conservative and Labour Party supporters. Conservative (1); Labour (2). Source: British Social Attitudes (1983–2017).

The Conservative vote has always been more related to age, but the generational range in support has also expanded hugely in recent years. This has not been due to a collapse among the young so much as an increasingly fervent level of support from the oldest cohorts, who are now three times more likely to back the Conservatives than are the youngest generations.

The reasons for such dramatic swings are related to short-term political events as much as generational tides. The Labour Party gained its younger vote partly from the collapse of the Liberal Democrats, while the Conservatives gained from the demise of the UK Independence Party. The age gradient of party support was reinforced by the result of the referendum to leave the EU. The Leave-Remain divide between the generations is massive, and it has grown over time: in 2019, 67 percent of Gen Z preferred to remain in the EU, compared with 29 percent of the Pre-war generation.

Whatever the short-term cause, our generational chart suggests the long-term future of the Conservative Party looks bleak, with a support base that is skewed toward generations that are leaving the voting pool and away from those who are arriving in it. However, the death of the Tories has been predicted many times before, and there are reasons to be skeptical.

First, as we've just seen, these patterns can change quickly thanks to the period effect of events. Second, the graying of the electorate and generational gaps in turnout have made the older lines in these charts more valuable over time—and, as we've seen in the predicted increase in the median voter age, this is set to continue.

Third, there is significant truth in that much-mimicked saying about conservatism growing with age. Figure 8.6 compares the proportions of two groups who planned to vote Conservative: Gen X and those aged between eighteen and twenty-nine. In the late 1990s, these groups were exactly the same, but Gen X has aged, while the other group has been constantly refreshed with new members. As a result, and as we saw with concern about immigration in the previous chapter, the two lines have grown apart, with Conservative support rising more among the aging Gen X than eighteen- to twenty-nine-year-olds. This could, of course, be a cohort effect as much as an age effect. But statistical analysis by political scientists James Tilley and Geoffrey Evans suggests that aging in itself is important. They found that the aging effect was worth around 0.35 percent to the Conservatives each year,

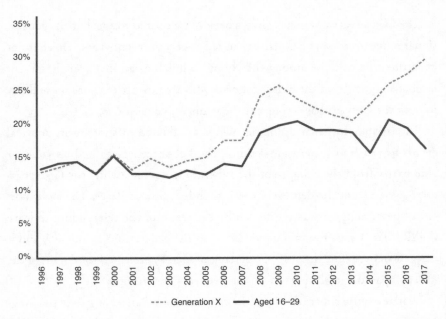

Figure 8.6: Percentage of British adults aged eighteen to twenty-nine and in Generation X who would vote for the Conservative Party if there were a general election tomorrow. Source: Ipsos MORI Political Monitor (1996–2017).

which may not sound like a lot, but it is very valuable over the course of a political lifetime.[20]

Looking internationally can help put your problems in context—and the generational patterns for the Conservative Party should provide some relief to the US Republican Party. Articles on "the GOP generational time bomb" abound, and yet more claim to explain "why Millennials hate us" or even suggest that "Darwin is coming for the GOP."[21] Niall Ferguson and Eyck Freymann argued in an essay titled "The Coming Generation War" that a generational framing is the best way to understand the future trajectories of the two parties, and that the mid to-late 2020s may be the point at which the Democrats' demographic advantage will tell.[22]

However, comparison with the UK Conservative Party suggests that this is far from a certainty. It is true that only 36 percent of eighteen- to twenty-nine-year-olds voted for Trump in 2020, but this is a *significantly* better showing among the young than achieved by the UK's Conservative Party.[23] More generally, the Republican candidate's support was not as skewed toward the oldest groups: 46 percent of those aged between thirty and forty-four voted for Trump, compared with 52 percent of those sixty-five and over, a much flatter gradient than in the UK. This age pattern is, if anything, less skewed by age than the 2016 election.[24]

Figure 8.7 shows a clear generational hierarchy in Republican affiliation, but at its largest the gap between oldest and youngest was around fifteen percentage points. In the UK, that gap is twice as large. Not to dismiss the demographic challenge facing the Republican Party: this is a new generational pattern, and, in a finely balanced two-party system, even a relatively small structural change in the balance of votes could prove decisive. But it's good to maintain perspective.

More generally, Ferguson and Freymann are right to highlight that a generational framing is becoming increasingly prominent in political contests—and not just in the UK and the United States. For example, the 2019 Australian federal election brought generational differences to the fore. The election unexpectedly returned a Liberal-National Coalition to power, dividing the population by age to an extent not seen before: less than a quarter of under-thirty-fives voted for the Liberal Party, and only 29 percent of over-sixty-fives voted Labour, both historic lows.[25] The campaign and its slogans

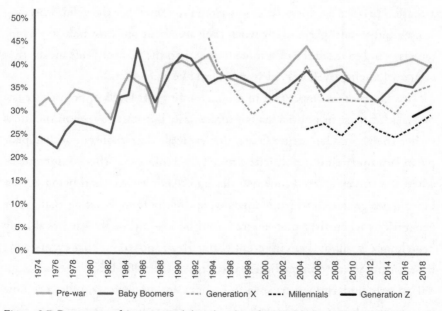

Figure 8.7: Percentage of American adults who identify as Republican. Source: US General Social Survey (1974–2018).

included overt generational pitches: for example, in his 2019 response to the budget, Labour leader Bill Shorten said that "the intergenerational bias that the tax system has against young people must be called out."[26] A stronger generational focus in elections is starting to look like an international trend.

## A NEW CRISIS OF TRUST?

This new age-based division is often framed as being driven by a loss of trust among younger generations, who are rejecting a political system that has let them down. Indeed, a "new crisis of trust" is an almost constant feature of political reporting and commentary. A series of global studies by Edelman, an international PR firm, that tracks trust annually almost always declares yet another dramatic decline: "Trust in Government Plunges to Historic Low," "Global Implosion of Trust," "Record-Breaking Drop in Trust in the US."[27] And nearly as often, headlines blame younger generations: "Millennials Have Stopped Trusting the Government."[28]

I am often invited to give talks on these new crises of trust, whether in religion, banking, business, social media, charities, the police, universities, or, of course, politics. In just about every case, the evidence I present is not as bad as the audience expects. Our natural human tendency is to pay more attention to negative information—we tend to remember the vivid, worrying stories and trends, particularly when they are about our own industry or interests—and to recall the past more fondly than the present. This means that even unchanging levels of criticism can feel like a new trend.

This last point is important to understanding our levels of political trust: our lack of trust in politicians is problematic, but it's a *long-term condition* rather than a sudden, acute crisis. For example, less than one in five people in Britain trust our politicians to tell the truth—but this is the same as when the survey started four decades ago. And, rather than being driven by younger generations, Millennials were slightly more trusting than older generations when they first entered adulthood—although this has mostly been knocked out of them in recent years. This is not to say that events don't have the potential to immediately affect trust: the 2009 UK "expenses scandal" clearly undermined trust in politicians for a few years, but we're now back at exactly the same (very low) level of trust that we saw prior to this. Britain is far from alone in its rampant mistrust of political leaders. The overall pattern and level of trust in politicians is similar across a collection of around twenty countries in Europe, with consistently low levels over the past sixteen years and not much difference between generations.

The truth is that we've been disappointed in our politicians for a long time. The philosopher Onora O'Neill makes the vital distinction between trust and trustworthiness, pointing out that "nobody sensible simply wants more trust. Sensible people want to place their trust where it is deserved. They also want to place their mistrust where it is deserved. They want well-directed trust and mistrust."[29] We have long thought that mistrust is well directed at politicians, a case powerfully made by Nick Clarke and his coauthors in *The Good Politician*, which reviewed long-term surveys and Mass Observation (an archive of essays from a cross section of the public) from as far back as the 1940s.[30] As they point out, even in August 1944, with the Second World War reaching a climax, only 36 percent of respondents to the question "Do you think that British politicians are out merely for themselves, for their party or to do their best for their country?" chose the latter option. This view is backed up by their detailed analysis of how people have thought about politicians through the ages, with common narratives in the mid-twentieth century describing politicians as "out for themselves" and "good talkers" (which was not a compliment).

It is a growing discontent with governments' ability to deliver that stands out, rather than a new crisis of trust. As Figure 8.8 shows, the proportion of Americans saying they have "hardly any" confidence in the people running their government increased to 45 percent in 2018, three times the level seen in 1977. This is a record high, although this long-term view shows that it was nearly as bad in the mid-1990s and early 1970s (the American public's response to the September 11 attacks makes the short-term trend look much worse than it is). This is not driven by younger generations, however. Quite the opposite: the most striking generational pattern is that Millennials and Gen Z enter adulthood with a higher level of confidence than older generations had, although it has quickly eroded, for Millennials in particular. The tendency is for confidence in government to be lost through repeated disappointments.

Does this lack of confidence in governments reflect a threat to democracy as a whole? Many recent books have questioned the long-held assumption

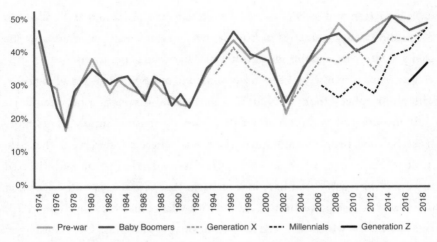

Figure 8.8: Percentage of American adults who say they have "hardly any" confidence in people running the executive branch of the federal government. Source: US General Social Survey (1974–2018).

that once "democratic consolidation" has taken hold and countries have developed democratic institutions, a robust civil society, and a certain level of wealth, their democracy is secure.[31] Instead, these analyses outline how democratic "backsliding" can creep up on us slowly. The Economist Democracy Index rates 167 countries across factors such as electoral processes, civil liberties, and political cultures, and in 2019 it found the lowest rating for the health of democracy since starting in 2006.[32] In the United States, Barack Obama mentioned the word "democracy" eighteen times in his short address to the 2020 Democratic National Convention, highlighting the sense of threat he felt: "Because that's what's at stake right now. Our democracy."[33]

Although the danger is real, it's important that we challenge some of the eye-catching claims that suggest that the public is suddenly and uniquely losing faith in democracy today.[34] We get a rather different perspective when we look at the long-term generational picture. Figure 8.9 tracks satisfaction with the way democracy is working in three countries across many decades. First, this confirms that it really matters which country you are looking at. Satisfaction with democracy is extremely high and increasing in Sweden, but the situation could hardly be more different in Spain, where it collapsed following the 2008 financial crisis. This highlights another of the repeated themes in this chapter: major events really matter. This sensitivity to crises may seem

to indicate a fragile attachment to democracy, but the trends also show a remarkable longer-term resilience to deep shocks. For example, German faith
in democracy recovered markedly from extremely low levels in the mid-1990s,
following reunification. Although we shouldn't downplay the risks we face today, long-term trends show that things have been at least this bad before. Our

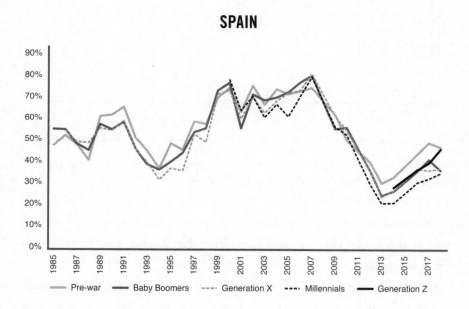

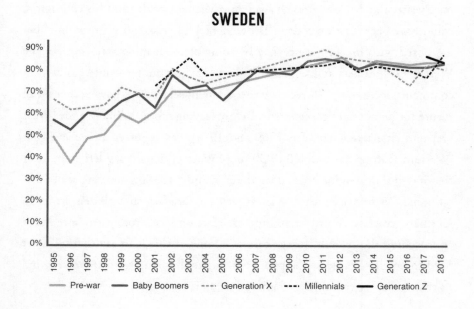

# GERMANY

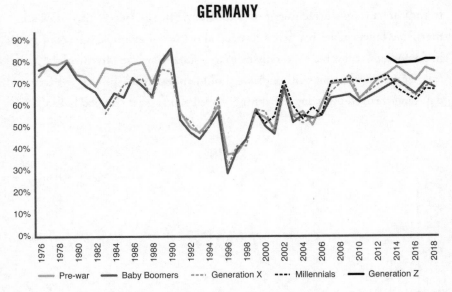

Figure 8.9: Percentage of adults satisfied with how democracy works in their country: Spain, Sweden, Germany. Source: Eurobarometer (1975–2018).

generational perspective also shows that younger cohorts today tend to be *more* satisfied than older cohorts, contrary to claims that it's the young who lose faith quickest.

Previous lows in public faith also coincided with deep concerns from politicians and commentators. The introductory remarks in *The Crisis of Democracy*, written in 1975 by French academic Michel Crozier and his colleagues, could have been written today: "Is democracy in crisis? This question is being posed with increasing urgency by some of the leading statesmen of the West, by columnists and scholars."[35] Some of their quotes would easily fit in comment pieces now: "In recent years, acute observers . . . have seen a bleak future for democratic government. Before leaving office, Willy Brandt [West German chancellor between 1969 and 1974] was reported to believe that 'Western Europe has only 20 or 30 more years of democracy left in it; after that it will slide, engineless and rudderless, under the surrounding sea of dictatorship.'" A few years after this was written, satisfaction with democracy in Germany reached record highs, and satisfaction levels today are once again approaching those levels, forty years on. None of this is to say that we don't need to bolster democratic support but rather that long-term trends remind us that we can be too quick to believe that all is lost.

## MILLENNIALS RISING . . .

Strauss and Howe predicted that Millennials would ride to American politics' rescue. They expected that generation to come of age "so willing and energised" that they would deliver on their belief in politics as a "tool for turning collegial purpose into civic progress." According to Strauss and Howe, Millennials' high level of civic commitment would bring risks, as their "youthful hunger for social discipline and centralised authority could lead Millennial youth brigades to lend mass to dangerous demagogues," but their political power was not in question because they would "confound pundits with their huge turnouts."[36] I doubt many Millennials will recognize this portrait of their generation.

This may be an extreme example of inaccurate political prediction, but it illustrates the pointlessness of long-term fortune-telling in politics using simplistic generational caricatures. A key conclusion from the data presented in this chapter is that political trends are a complex blend of cohort, life-cycle, and period effects. Political punditry often ignores this fact, preferring grand schemes or themes, and this helps explain why so many political pundits make so many bad predictions.

By separating these effects more carefully and taking a long-term generational view, we can get better answers to some of the big questions in politics. The death of political parties is slow and exaggerated, and it can be turned around by events. Support for democracy is not a generational characteristic; although we may see differences in how groups feel about specific leaders or policies, our support for the fundamental aspects of our political system remains strong. As for our mistrust in political leaders, this is a chronic condition, and one that young generations grow into rather than instigate.

Age and generation are undoubtedly more important dividing lines in a number of countries than they were in the past. However, this isn't just due to demographic or cultural trends—political parties and leaders have played a role in shaping this trend. As Ferguson and Freymann point out, it makes complete sense for the Republican Party to take "campus politics national" by accusing their opponents of an obsession with "safe spaces, trigger warnings and gender-neutral pronouns" that are an "alien parallel world" to many older voters.[37] Likewise, it's understandable that Biden, following Obama's lead, should place such emphasis on appealing to the next generation.

The trend of parties becoming more reliant on particular age groups for support brings risks not just to parties but to politics more generally. When one side thinks it has demography on its side, the other will respond by exaggerating the extremism of its opponents in order to pull waverers back to its shrinking base. And as this generational caricaturing grows, each party will find it increasingly difficult to ask its supporters to engage in the trade-offs that avoid further polarization. This is the root of the growing generational aspect to the culture wars in both the United States and the UK: as the Resolution Foundation points out, "generational locks" are emerging in political support, and they're difficult to shift once they're in place.[38]

This may seem like normal political tactics, but the scale of the generational divisions it could create would be a significant barrier to a collective vision for the future. Setting old against young, even if on the basis of a dubious reading of actual divisions, is a dangerous path. All the evidence we've seen suggests that generational differences on the actual issues are not nearly as great as they're often made out to be—but a concerted political effort could change that.

# CHAPTER 9

# CONSUMING THE PLANET

In a speech to political and business leaders, the legendary conservationist David Attenborough captured the unique challenge of addressing climate change: "What happens now and in these next few years will profoundly affect the next few thousand years."[1] Unfortunately, our political and economic systems are particularly ill suited to addressing threats that require urgent action to avoid long-term consequences. This is not a new shortcoming, caused by twenty-four-hour news, Twitter streams, and financial markets that crash in seconds. Rather, our pathological short-termism is more fundamental, driven by how humans struggle to focus on the future.

The Australian philosopher Roman Krznaric neatly summarizes the problem in *The Good Ancestor*: "We treat the future like a distant colonial outpost devoid of people, where we can freely dump ecological degradation, technological risk and nuclear waste, and which we can plunder as we please."[2] He draws a parallel with the British colonization of Australia, which built on the legal concept *terra nullius*—"nobody's land"—to justify its actions. Krznaric suggests that we currently see the future as *tempus nullius*—"nobody's time"—to allow us to ignore the effect of today's actions on tomorrow's world.

This is not to say that we are incapable of taking a longer view. In fact, one of the defining characteristics of humans is our ability to envision the future and the many alternatives it brings. As the psychologist Daniel Gilbert has described, "Our brains, unlike the brains of almost every other species, are prepared to treat the future as if it were present." We are the "ape that learned to look forward."[3] But simply because we can think about the future does not mean that we always do. As Krznaric suggests, there is a tension between our ability to think "short and long"—and short tends to win out. In evolutionary terms, longer-term thinking is something that we're still learning how to do. This idea is supported by studies in which people record whether they are thinking about the past, present, or future during the course of a day: while we spend 14 percent of our time thinking about the future, 80 percent of these thoughts are about the same or the next day. Other studies show that beyond the next fifteen to twenty years, our futures seem blank.[4]

Of course, one obvious reason we don't spend so much time trying to plan for the distant future is that it is really hard to control. John Maynard Keynes wrote, "It is not wise to look too far ahead; our powers of prediction are slight, our command over results infinitesimal. It is therefore the happiness of our own contemporaries that is our main concern; we should be very chary of sacrificing large numbers of people for the sake of a contingent end, however advantageous that may appear."[5]

There is also an emotional aspect to our reluctance to plan too far in advance, as the writer Nathaniel Rich outlines: "If human beings really were able to take the long view . . . we would be forced to grapple with the transience of all we know and love in the great sweep of time. So we have trained ourselves, whether culturally or evolutionarily, to obsess over the present, worry about the medium term and cast the long term out of our minds, as we might spit out a poison."

Although it is understandable to avoid this long view as individuals, our political systems are *required* to confront it. The Irish philosopher Edmund Burke saw governments as custodians of the contract between generations. For him, society is a partnership in science, art, and "every virtue," "not only between those who are living, but between those who are living, those who are dead and those who are to be born."[6]

The multiple challenges facing our planet are the clearest illustration of our struggle to match this Burkean ideal. Instead, our short-term consumer culture reinforces our natural tendency to "think short" and distracts us from long-term challenges. These are powerful effects, so it shouldn't be surprising that they also shape younger generations, but that's not what we're led to believe by endless commentary. Two of the most destructive generational myths are that young people are rejecting consumer culture for more sustainable alternatives and that older people don't care about our planet's future. The former gives a false sense of comfort that there is a coming behavioral sea change that will halt climate change, and the latter carelessly discards the current and potential support of vast swathes of the population.

You can understand why the simplistic "battle of the age groups" framing has taken hold, not least because this is a theme emphasized by Greta Thunberg herself. There have also been some remarkable instances of youth action, most notably the global climate strikes that involved over 1.6 million young students in more than three hundred cities, but the highest-profile environmental campaigners span as wide an age range as you can get. Even at a cursory glance at climate change marches, it is far from a universally young movement: at one Extinction Rebellion event in London, people charged with offenses by the Metropolitan Police were aged between nineteen and seventy-seven.[7] Our generational analysis of attitudes and behaviors shows that although there are clear differences between generations on some measures, they are frequently wildly overblown.

Climate change is the most obviously generational issue we'll see in this book—not because it's a source of division between young and old, but because our response requires a truly generational perspective.

## WE STILL THINK SHORT

Starting with the fundamental question of whether people recognize that the world's climate is changing, a major European survey has shown that there is no real age divide in the recognition of climate change. Around half of the Pre-war generation think the world's climate is definitely changing. That figure rises to around six in ten among Gen X, the generation most likely to hold this view, with the youngest generations slightly less certain.

The picture changes, however, when Europeans are asked whether climate change is natural or caused by humans. There is a clearer generational hierarchy here: just over half of Gen Z think it is man-made, compared with around a third of the Pre-war generation. In contrast to much of the rhetoric, we are a long way from a universal acceptance of anthropogenic climate change among the young, or universal denial among older generations. More generally, large proportions of all age groups, including the young, remain unconvinced. This is despite the overwhelming evidence—twenty of the hottest years on record since 1880 have occurred since 1998—and near-unanimous consensus—97 percent of climate scientists—that human activity is the dominant cause.[8]

Longer-term surveys paint a picture of gradually increasing concern and relatively small generational difference. For example, Figure 9.1 shows that the proportion of people in the United States who think a rise in world temperatures caused by the greenhouse effect is either "very" or "extremely" dangerous has increased from 47 percent to 61 percent over the past twenty-five years. There is a generational hierarchy, with younger cohorts feeling a greater sense of threat—but the differences aren't large, with levels of concern among Baby Boomers catching up in recent years and only the Pre-war generation lagging behind.

A similar pattern emerged in a survey that asks people to select the most important issues facing their country from a list that includes everything

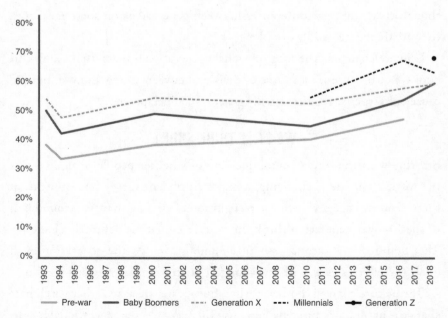

Figure 9.1: Percentage of American adults who consider the rise in world temperature caused by the greenhouse effect "extremely" or "very" dangerous. Source: US General Social Survey (1993–2018).

from the economy and crime to health services. In Britain, environmental issues have featured relatively far down the list for most of the past twenty years, with less than 10 percent of the population mentioning them. In contrast, the top issues, whether the economy, health services, immigration, or Brexit, were regularly picked by 60 to 70 percent of people as most important. The issue dominating our lives in 2020, COVID-19, was chosen as a top issue by over 80 percent of Brits at its peak.

These questions of "salience" illustrate the power of our "present bias" in how we respond to threats: longer-term issues tend to be swamped by more immediate challenges. For example, when the pandemic hit, the reported salience of all other issues, including environmental concerns, plummeted. Prior to the COVID-19 crisis, there had been signs that worries about environmental issues were growing. As Figure 9.2 shows, concern peaked in Britain in 2018, because of a rise among all generations except the Pre-war generation. However, it was still a relatively low priority, and similar to the level of concern seen in 2007, before the financial crisis shifted our attention to more immediate worries.

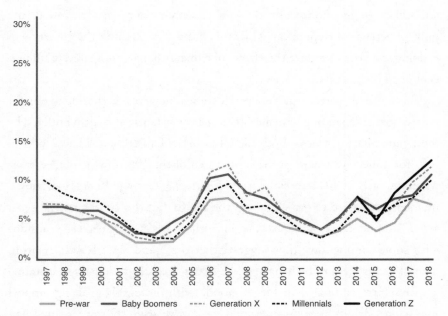

Figure 9.2: Percentage of British adults who say that "pollution / the environment" is one of the most important issues facing Britain today. Source: Ipsos MORI Issues Index (1997–2018).

A different international study has since 2010 asked a similar question on top worries, and some countries show slightly more marked generational gaps than Britain. In Canada, Australia, and the United States, Gen Z were the most concerned generational group, followed by Millennials: around three in ten of the youngest generation select climate change as a top concern, compared with around 15 percent of Baby Boomers. But again, this is not a clear generational break.

This is also clear in longer-term British and American surveys that ask whether governments should spend "more" or "much more" on protecting the environment (the UK) and whether the government is currently spending too little (the United States). Again, younger cohorts in both countries tend to want governments to do more. For example, in Britain, 54 percent of Gen Z want spending to increase, compared to 32 percent of the Pre-war generation. In the United States, Millennials are the generation most likely to think the government is spending too little. However, excluding the Pre-war generation, the gaps are not that dramatic, partly reflecting the degree to which climate change division in the United States is political. Despite some signs that younger Republicans are pulling away from older Republicans, party gaps still outweigh age. For example, a Pew Research Center study showed that only 52 percent of Republican Millennials and Gen Z think the government is doing too little to reduce the effects of climate change, compared to 90 percent of *all* Democrats.[9]

The standout pattern in the overall trends, however, is that demands for environmental spending have not increased consistently and seem buffeted by more immediate concerns. Both the UK and the United States saw a spike in calls for more investment in the second half of the 1980s, which faded away when the early 1990s recession hit. As Figure 9.3, tracing US opinion, shows, momentum started to grow again in the 2000s, but the 2008 financial crisis set environmental spending back as a priority. This cyclical pattern is at odds with some commentary that suggests that the "good news is that environmental issues seem to be behaving like issues such as gay marriage, criminal justice reform and marijuana legalisation," with inexorably growing support for change, driven by younger people.[10] As we've seen, the generational patterns on support for gay marriage and the legalization of marijuana are *utterly*

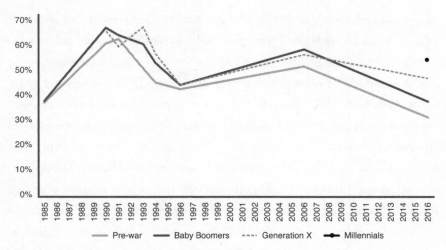

Figure 9.3: Percentage of American adults who say that the country spends too little on protecting the environment. Source: US General Social Survey (1974–2018).

different from the endorsement of environmental spending: we are a lot less certain about the future than this interpretation suggests.

Of course, tackling climate change is not just about government spending; as awareness of our myriad effects on the planet has grown, endless news articles and comment pieces have suggested that younger generations in particular are expressing their environmental concern in more direct ways, shifting their own behavior and consumption patterns to reduce their impact on the planet.[11]

## THE END OF CAR CULTURE?

One of the most effective environmental actions we can take as individuals is to stop using our cars. According to a Swedish study, this would save 2.4 tons of $CO_2$ per driver per year, significantly more than, for example, shifting to a meat-free diet (which saves 0.8 tons of $CO_2$ per person per year).[12] So it seemed to be good news when, for a number of years in the late 2000s and early 2010s, young people appeared to shun cars. For example, in 2010, adults aged between twenty-one and thirty-four bought just 27 percent of all new vehicles sold in America, down from a peak of 38 percent in 1985.[13] Understandably, this caused concern among car manufacturers and a flurry of opinion pieces on its possible implications: it was "the end of car culture," as the

*New York Times* put it in 2013.[14] The evidence seemed stark in just about all well-off countries: compared with previous generations, younger cohorts delayed getting a driving license, were less likely to own a car, drove fewer miles, and in some countries used public transport more.[15] Two separate articles in the *Atlantic* in 2012 offered two groups of reasons for the drop: economic factors—young people could no longer afford to own cars in the wake of the financial crisis—and wider cultural factors—a preference for city living, less interest in the status of car ownership, a comfort with sharing rather than owning, greater use of technology to connect with others, delayed marriage and child-rearing, a greater concern for the environment.[16]

However, as we've seen previously, patterns that look like permanent cohort shifts can be due to delay rather than rejection and are often tied to broader changes in how generations live. For example, a 2019 paper showed that US Millennials owned 0.4 percent fewer vehicles per household than Baby Boomers did at the same age—but after controlling for a range of variables including income levels, educational attainment, geography, and family formation, this difference disappeared.[17] The same pattern is seen with car use: when the researchers control for the same economic and life stage factors, "vehicle miles traveled" data show that American Millennials are, if anything, *more* active car users than older generations. As the paper concludes, "While Millennial vehicle ownership and use may be lower early on in life, these differences are only temporary and, in fact, lifetime vehicle use is likely to be greater."

Similar studies in other countries have found the same pattern—changes in car ownership and use are not as dramatic as they first seem, and shifting lifestyles and delayed life cycles are important explanations.[18] Figure 9.4 bears this pattern out. Irish Millennials' car ownership, for example, continued to increase throughout their twenties and thirties, until, in 2018, they almost matched Gen X levels when the latter were a similar age in 2005.

Analyses that point to delay rather than rejection have not stopped the accusation that Gen Z are taking their turn at "killing the car industry," but such claims mostly result from the same pattern of younger generations postponing vehicle ownership. It's definitely the case that our relationship with cars is changing, but the death of car culture is exaggerated partly as a result of confusing period, life-cycle, and cohort effects.

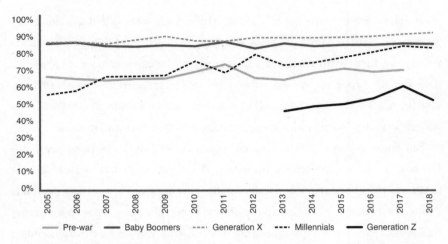

Figure 9.4: Percentage of Irish adults owning a car. Source: Eurobarometer (2005–2018).

COVID-19 and its economic fallout have already caused further swings. The car industry was one of the harder-hit sectors in the early stages of the pandemic, with global sales of just over 70 million new vehicles in 2020, 18.5 million lower than estimates at the start of the year—roughly equivalent to all new car sales in the United Kingdom, Japan, and the United States combined.[19] The medium-term effects of the pandemic are still emerging, but early signs from China pointed to a sharp recovery in car use, as commuters shunned public transport. By the middle of April 2020, congestion in major Chinese cities was 90 percent of pre-lockdown levels, while subway use was at just 50 percent.[20] Auto companies wasted no time capitalizing on anxiety regarding public transportation; a newspaper ad in Germany showed a massive face mask across the front of a VW Tiguan, an ear loop stretched over each side mirror, with the tagline "safety first." We may see some lasting decreases in traffic, as remote work seems likely to settle at a higher level than pre-COVID, but it seems unlikely that a long-term effect of the pandemic will be greater use of public transportation.

## ON PURPOSE

The exaggeration of generational difference regarding sustainable consumption extends way beyond car use. In recent years, headlines and opinion pieces have painted a vivid picture of how young people's focus on environmental and social purpose has changed their patterns of consumption and affected their relationships with brands. First, Millennials were billed as "the green generation": "sustainability is their shopping priority," and they "make efforts to buy products from companies that support the causes they care about."[21] This swiftly moved on to Gen Z: we were told that "purpose-driven, sustainable brands are the ones who will capture the hearts, minds, and wallets" of a generation who "wants to know about your values, ethics and mission."[22]

But there is just about no evidence that these assertions reflect real differences in those generations' priorities. A British study has covered a wide range of ethical behaviors since the 1990s, ranging from boycotting products due to the behavior of the company behind them, choosing a product because of the company's principles, seeking out information on how responsible a company is, and paying more for ethically sourced products.[23] Each behavior shows a similar pattern: younger generations are no more likely to say they have behaved in these ways than older generations, and in some cases they are less likely. For example, a fifth of Baby Boomers report having boycotted a product because a company had not behaved responsibly, compared with 16 percent of Millennials. And Generation X are more likely than Millennials to pay more for products that are ethically sourced.

Of course, these patterns may be a feature of age rather than cohort: we may be more prepared to act on our principles as we get older, or perhaps we get richer and more willing to spend on the right sort of products. However, the length of this study allows us to compare cohorts at the same age and get a generational view. For example, in 1999, when Generation X were a similar age to Millennials in 2015, Gen X were actually slightly *more* likely to choose a product or service because of the behavior of a company (17 percent versus 12 percent for Millennials).

The pattern appears to be similar in other countries. A European study that began in 2004 confirms that product boycotts are more prevalent in middle age. Germany is typical of the European pattern; as Figure 9.5 shows, Gen X and Baby Boomers are most likely to have boycotted a product in the previous twelve months. Gen Z currently lag a long way behind—but as the line for Millennials suggests, this behavior seems to increase with age. Although the claims that this trend is driven by new waves of young activists seem wrong, we shouldn't downplay how much more common this behavior is becoming in some countries: Germany has seen a significant increase among all except the oldest cohorts over the past decade. Brands should be increasingly mindful of direct consumer action, but they should also recognize that it is not solely, or even mainly, driven by younger generations. On this measure, "cancel culture" seems to be more of a middle-age thing.

However, the differences between countries on these measures are often bigger than those between generations, both in levels of boycotting and the trends—yet another example of "country before cohort." For example, there is wide variation in reported boycotting behavior among Gen X across countries, as well as disparate trajectories. Nearly 60 percent of Gen X in Sweden have boycotted a product in the previous year, following a steep increase over the past fourteen years, compared to under 10 percent of Gen X in Poland, a figure that has barely changed. In the UK, Generation X are closer to Poles than Swedes on this behavior, with one in five having boycotted a product and a pretty flat trend.

The overblown claims for young people's "brand activism" reflects the influence marketing agencies have on the creation and dissemination of generational myths. Endless reports and press releases create a sense of change that's not justified by the facts, but they consistently attract significant

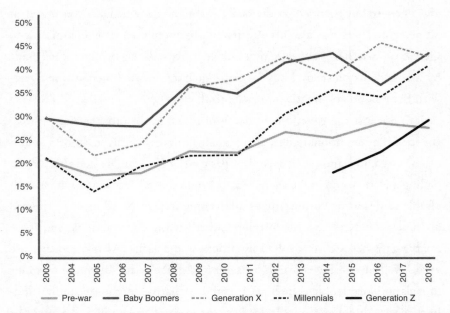

Figure 9.5: Percentage of German adults who say they have boycotted certain products in the prior twelve months. Source: European Social Survey (2002–2018).

attention. In a chapter that began with the existential threat to our planet, it may seem strange to examine such spurious trends, but in many ways that's the point: our consumer culture reflects and reinforces our natural tendency to emphasize the short term and the novel at the expense of the distant but more meaningful. The assertion that younger generations are escaping consumer culture and rejecting brands and advertising is not just wrong, it's dangerous. Younger generations are perhaps even more entwined in modern brand-driven consumerism than are older generations, which means a generationally driven sustainable future is much less certain than peddled myths suggest.

Generational marketing exists less to discover true social trends and more to help sell marketers' value to companies, so they often end up finding problems that don't really exist. Articles claiming that brand loyalty is "not such a biggie for Millennials" offer various advice on how to advertise to a generation that is "notoriously fickle."[24] One challenge in identifying truly generational consumer insight is that the data on long-term trends required to isolate cohort effects don't really exist—but even snapshot surveys show that there is no evidence to support such claims. According to the Ipsos Global Trends Survey in 2019, for example, 43 percent of Millennials and Gen Z said they always try to buy branded products. Baby Boomers seemed less concerned, at 32 percent. There was also little difference between Gen X, Millennials, and Gen Z on whether they were "more likely to trust a new product if it's made by a brand they already know"—three-quarters of each generation agree, with Baby Boomers slightly more skeptical.

It is not just the generational death of brand loyalty that is exaggerated; the idea that traditional advertising fails to impress younger cohorts is also often raised, in claims such as "only 1 per cent of Millennials said that a compelling advert would make them trust a brand more."[25] Of course, it isn't advisable to draw conclusions about advertising impact based on self-reported attitudes—we're poor at identifying and reporting our reactions, and there are big gaps between our stated intentions and actions. As is often the case with headline-chasing research, this study also looks at Millennial opinions in isolation, overlooking the high probability that we might see similar findings across all generations. Indeed, when research is conducted across the whole population, Gen Z and Millennials say they pay *more* attention to advertising than other cohorts. The age gradient is pretty straightforward across various types of media tested, with younger generations saying they pay more heed. For example, 52 percent of Gen Z said they paid at least a little attention to movie theater ads, compared with 48 percent of Millennials, 41 percent of Generation X, and just 31 percent of Baby Boomers. And it is not just that younger generations are more likely to notice ads on a wider variety of media types—they are more likely to say they *like* them: 35 percent of Gen Z, compared with 19 percent of Baby Boomers.

A similar commonplace assertion is that personal recommendations rather than advertising are key to Millennials' purchasing decisions. Typical headlines include bold statements like "Millennials trust People over Brands" and declare the generation "leaders in word-of-mouth recommendations."[26] At first glance, this seems to correspond with the research—Millennials do say they are more influenced by social media, known peers, opinion leaders, and experts than other generations.[27] But, again, it's a misdirection: younger people tend to report they are more influenced by *all* sources—including traditional advertising. Data from the United States, for example, show that Millennials claim to draw on a more varied pool of resources before they make decisions about brands. It's true that American Millennials are more likely to claim they are influenced by experts, family, and friends than Generation X and Baby Boomers, but they're also more likely to say they are influenced by communications from businesses, whether through traditional media or online.[28] The underlying theme here seems to be a greater use of multiple sources, rather than personal recommendations replacing traditional communications and advertising. Younger generations are very much *not* rejecting these key tools of consumerism.

## A LONGTIME PROJECT

Our consumer culture is inextricably linked to both our reliance on short-term thinking and our slow and partial recognition of the severity of the environmental emergency facing the planet. Most obviously, as Al Gore has argued, "Governing institutions have been suborned by vested interests obsessed with short-term gain rather than long-term sustainability."[29] As George Monbiot, British environmental writer, suggests, this creates a "cannibal economy" that undermines the future.

Underlying this, however, is the more general human tendency to be drawn to immediate circumstances and our corresponding struggle to focus on the longer term. As Monbiot writes, "It was easier [for people] to pretend that the science was wrong and their lives were right than to accept that the science was right and their lives were wrong."[30] We *can* think "long," but we don't find it easy, and we're surrounded by an economic and political context that discourages it.

Given these powerful forces, it should be no surprise that younger generations haven't entirely broken free. It's true that the young show greater concern about the environment according to some measures, but the differences are not huge, and they have not translated into more markedly sustainable behaviors. The impression given by endless articles and analyses is of a clean generational break. This is not just misleading but dangerous, as it suggests that we can rely on young people to both demand action from governments and take direct action themselves.

The focus on the young also grossly exaggerates the lack of concern felt by the old. I feel the same unease as the sociologist and writer Anne Karpf about the "unthinking ageism" that has crept into some corners of the environmental movement. The Gen Z singer Billie Eilish said in an interview, "Hopefully the adults and the old people start listening to us [about climate change]. Old people are gonna die and don't really care if we die, but we don't wanna die yet."[31] This particularly blunt way of putting it reflects a more general attitude that caricatures whole cohorts of the older population as indifferent to the environment or future generations. This is not just wrong—it also ignores the growing demographic weight and financial power of this cohort. Support for a greener future depends on uniting the generations, rather than dividing them. There are clear ways to do that, starting with including older people in the conversation about climate change and appealing to the greater focus on "legacy thinking" that we develop as we age. As gerontologists Elizabeth Hunter and Graham Rowles suggest, "Few of us are comfortable with the idea that we live, we die, and that is it. We want to believe that there is a purpose in life and that we will make a mark of some kind. . . . This is the fertile ground from which the desire for legacy sprouts."[32]

We will need all the help we can get to keep the focus on climate change in the aftermath of the COVID-19 pandemic. In the early stages of our response, scientists were hopeful that lockdowns around the world would significantly reduce $CO_2$ emissions. This initially seemed justified, with global emissions in April 2020 down by 17 percent on the previous year. But that optimism was short lived, as even a partial return to normality increased emissions significantly—they were only 5 percent down on the previous year by June, and were predicted to between 4 and 7 percent down over 2020 as a whole.[33] Given the incredible changes in our lives, as Bill Gates said, "What is remarkable is not how much emissions will go down because of the pandemic, but how little."[34]

Of course, the most important effects of COVID-19 will be seen over the longer term, and there are some encouraging signs. Investment in more sustainable growth is a core element of a number of the emerging Build Back Better plans across countries and institutions: for example, the European Union's Next Generation recovery fund sets aside 25 percent of EU spending for climate-friendly expenditure.[35] However, such plans certainly shouldn't be taken for granted; a further theme of our long-term analysis is how easily environmental concerns are derailed by more immediate priorities, particularly during economic downturns that increase our focus on the here and now.[36] It's about to get even harder to think long.

# CHAPTER 10

# US AND THEM

**G**enerational thinking, as we understand it today, is a relatively new way of explaining social change. Many of the foundational works were written during the turbulent years following the First World War, an event that "dug a chasm between the generations."[1] It's no surprise, then, that conflict is at its very heart. It is clear in the irreversible rage in Wilfred Owen's preface to his *Poems* at "the willingness of the old to sacrifice the young":[2]

> My subject is War, and the pity of War. The Poetry is in the pity. Yet these elegies are to this generation in no sense consolatory. They may be to the next. All a poet can do today is warn.[3]

This same sentiment also deeply affected sociologists and philosophers who were trying to make sense of the First World War's consequences for relationships between generations. The Spanish philosopher José Ortega y Gasset, for example, conceptualized history as a series of epochs, with each new generation considering itself either heir to a valuable heritage or born to destroy it.[4] Karl Mannheim also saw conflict as central to how generations are formed and act. First, he said, a generation needs to have common experiences and a shared identity that create some sort of affinity. Mirroring ideas on class formation and conflict, he suggested that this sense of identity will tend to lead to competition with others: a generation is a coherent social identity not just "in itself" but "for itself."[5]

This framing also infects a lot of recent discussion of generational relationships, where futures have been "stolen" by one generation and need to be forcibly taken back by another. As we've seen throughout this book, this attitude doesn't reflect how most of the public see intergenerational relations. And there is at least one obvious reason for the discrepancy between theory and observation. Our familial connections up and down the generations remain much stronger than our connections to our peer groups. This may seem blindingly obvious, but it is often strangely absent from the type of generational commentary that pits one generation against another. It leads to rather absurd analysis, such as a piece in the German magazine *Der Spiegel* that presented the conflict between old and young as a major issue in the financial crisis, with older people living at the expense of the young, and proclaimed, "It's high time the next generation took to the streets to confront their parents."[6]

Other obstacles tend to limit generational conflict, too. In particular, age is a unique characteristic to base such divisions on, compared with class, gender, or ethnicity—as we *all* inevitably pass through the different age categories. We know, for instance, that the support afforded to older people is an indicator of what we'll receive when we are old, so we'll probably be a little more cautious in going to war against it. Of course, our generational membership is a characteristic that *doesn't* change; as we've seen, many in the current generations of older people have likely had a better deal than future generations will in their old age—but our own unstoppable life cycles are still likely to give us reason to pause.

The view that serious generational conflict is either imminent or justified reflects our tendency to explain phenomena as being caused by a single factor, in this case a generational effect. But as we've seen, we gain a better understanding of our changing societies when we take into account generational, life-cycle, and period effects. Our analysis of the nature, scope, and potential of generational conflict is richer when we recognize each element: generational self-interest is real but also moderated by our love for our grandparents, parents, children, and grandchildren; the inevitability of our life cycles connects us to older age groups based on a self-interest absent across other societal divisions; and period effects can alter the relationship between generations in significant ways. On the last of these, we've already outlined the unprecedented separation of the generations into increasingly distinct communities. In this chapter, we'll see this change mirrored in a separation of our digital lives. Mannheim recognized the potential of rapid technological change to increase the importance and difficulty of maintaining intergenerational connections, and it's no less relevant today.

If we look at these effects together, we can see that it's not intergenerational warfare we should be most worried about, but a drifting apart of age groups. This powers the stereotypes that exaggerate the division between generations and leads us to miss out on a host of positive benefits from generational connections.

## OUR GENERATION?

But let's start with Mannheim's first generational question—whether we identify as part of "our generation." The Pew Research Center asked this question in the United States in 2015 and found that lots of Americans do, although it depends on which generation they're in. At one end of the spectrum, only 40 percent of Millennials say they identify with that label, compared with 58 percent of Gen X and 79 percent of Baby Boomers (this survey was too early to test Gen Z identification). Given these results, it's no surprise that many people, particularly Millennials, see themselves as belonging to different generations than the one dictated by their birth year: a third of US Millennials see themselves as Gen X (we may be a forgotten generation, but, for many people, it's still better than being a Millennial). I particularly admire the chutzpah of the 8 percent of Millennials who think they're part of the "Greatest Generation," the label used in the United States for those born in the 1920s or before. I'm sure this is not an attempt to claim credit for fighting in the Second World War or living through the Great Depression—if you're asked to pick a generational label, why not pick the one called "Greatest"?

The Pew survey goes on to ask people how well they think the term applies to them personally, and the pattern is similar: 70 percent of Baby Boomers think it describes them well, 38 percent of Gen X think the same about their label, as do 30 percent of Millennials. So, although it varies across groups, generational identity, even as summed up in simple labels, is not trivial. When a British study asked people what they would say was most important to their identity (not including their family or job) when introducing themselves, the top answers were their interests, values, and opinions. But the next important thing was their "age or generation," ahead of nationality and way ahead of social class, ethnicity, and religion. Although this question combines age and generation in a single category, it suggests that we see when we were born as an important indicator of our identity.[7]

At first glance, we also seem to have strong images of the key characteristics of other generations. In a survey across thirty countries conducted for this book by Ipsos, the top and bottom five traits associated and not associated with each generation are shown in Figure 10.1. And it isn't great news for Gen Z. On the plus side, half of the public say Gen Z are tech savvy, but that's the only positive in a top five that includes materialistic, selfish, lazy, and arrogant. It's true that Gen Z are not well-off financially, and it may even be fair to say they're not yet work oriented—after all, lots of them are still in school—but, more damningly, very few people see them as community oriented, respectful, or ethical.

Perhaps surprisingly, given the "Generation Me" and "snowflake" images that are thrust on them, Millennials suffer less of a character assassination. Like Gen Z, they are also seen as tech savvy and materialistic—but next come more positive characteristics: they're work centric, well educated, and ambitious. Again, like Gen Z, they're not widely seen as ethical—but neither are they seen as narcissistic, agist, lazy, or sheltered.

However, even this positive report card can't compete with the praise showered on Baby Boomers—for being respectful, work centric, community oriented, tolerant, and well educated, with hardly anyone considering them selfish, narcissistic, or lazy. Sure, they're not seen as tech savvy or trendsetting, but that's a small price to pay for such a positive picture. This may come as a surprise to Baby Boomers who have seen the social media portrayals of them "ruining everything." It does, however, fit with how they see themselves, at least in the United States. A different study asked generations whether they had a favorable view of their own and other generations, and Baby Boomers were by far the most positive: 83 percent said they were favorable

## Gen Z

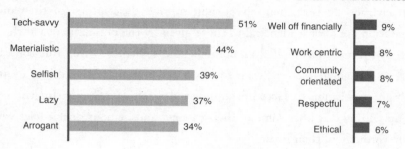

**Top 5 Characteristics**

| | |
|---|---|
| Tech-savvy | 51% |
| Materialistic | 44% |
| Selfish | 39% |
| Lazy | 37% |
| Arrogant | 34% |

**Bottom 5 Characteristics**

| | |
|---|---|
| Well off financially | 9% |
| Work centric | 8% |
| Community orientated | 8% |
| Respectful | 7% |
| Ethical | 6% |

## Millennials

**Top 5 Characteristics**

| | |
|---|---|
| Work centric | 37% |
| Tech-savvy | 37% |
| Well educated | 35% |
| Ambitious | 33% |
| Materialistic | 31% |

**Bottom 5 Characteristics**

| | |
|---|---|
| Ethical | 14% |
| Narcissistic | 12% |
| Ageist | 11% |
| Lazy | 11% |
| Sheltered | 10% |

## Baby Boomers

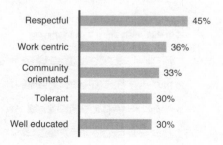

**Top 5 Characteristics**

| | |
|---|---|
| Respectful | 45% |
| Work centric | 36% |
| Community orientated | 33% |
| Tolerant | 30% |
| Well educated | 30% |

**Bottom 5 Characteristics**

| | |
|---|---|
| Selfish | 8% |
| Tech-savvy | 6% |
| Trendsetters | 6% |
| Narcissistic | 5% |
| Lazy | 4% |

Figure 10.1: Perceived characteristics of Generations. Source: Ipsos Global Trends Survey (2019).

toward their own generation, compared with 53 percent of Gen X and 57 percent of Millennials.[8]

Gen Z are, then, clearly the generational weak link. They even agree with that characterization themselves: their top five descriptors for their own generation are almost identical to those given by the population as a whole: tech savvy, materialistic, lazy, ambitious, and selfish. So given this contrast in generational characteristics, is society set to plummet downhill, as a venal younger generation replaces upstanding older cohorts? Surely this younger group will take at least some of their distinct and heinous deficiencies with them throughout their lives?

Millennials, by contrast, seem to have completely turned around their image. We asked the same questions about Millennials and Baby Boomers in 2017, and Figure 10.2 compares opinions about Millennials then and two years later. Millennials had already established their tech-savvy credentials in 2017, but in contrast with their current image as work centric, well educated, and ambitious, at that point they were regarded as materialistic, selfish, lazy, and arrogant. Although only two years separated these studies, they show a remarkable transformation in the perceived character of a generation.

Of course, this is no more a "generational rebirth" of Millennials than Gen Z are destined to be the worst-regarded generation ever. Both patterns are nothing but a reflection of our timeless denigration of young people. It was a little too early in 2017 to ask about Gen Z, as they were still coming up as a recognizable cohort and label. Millennials, then, were the newest generation identified, and shorthand for "youth." As soon as Gen Z became available,

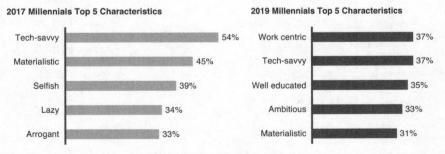

**Millennials in 2017 versus 2019**

2017 Millennials Top 5 Characteristics

| | |
|---|---|
| Tech-savvy | 54% |
| Materialistic | 45% |
| Selfish | 39% |
| Lazy | 34% |
| Arrogant | 33% |

2019 Millennials Top 5 Characteristics

| | |
|---|---|
| Work centric | 37% |
| Tech-savvy | 37% |
| Well educated | 35% |
| Ambitious | 33% |
| Materialistic | 31% |

Figure 10.2: Perceived characteristics of Millennials in 2017 and 2019. Source: Ipsos Global Trends Survey (2017 and 2019).

we transferred our negative stereotypes about youth to them—in an almost identical way, if you look back to Figure 10.1. Our apparent generational splits in how we see each other are nothing of the sort—they are age-based clichés that don't stick over time. Beyond our tendency to negatively judge the young, we mostly see each other as pretty decent. Even Millennials.

This is not as trivial and obvious as it seems. First, generations are very often thought to embody a particular characteristic and expected to take that label with them through life. For example, according to some high-profile generational analysis, Millennials were supposed to be either "narcissistic" or "civic minded," depending on who you listened to. Second, even though we've seen in this book that Millennials are often generally very similar to previous young cohorts, I genuinely expected the negative image to stick to the "Millennial" label. I've always felt sympathy for them for the double whammy of tough circumstances combined with denigration on a scale never seen before. When I saw the results, I was surprised that their bad reputation hadn't followed them.

This is good news, as it suggests that the public doesn't actually buy into the simplistic view that whole generations can be summed up for the rest of their life in just one or two words. The bad news is that we can expect the "Generation Me" headlines to continue for each new cohort of young people *forever*—we're incredibly susceptible to believing that today's youth are worse than any previous versions. A 1969 US newspaper article talked about the (now sainted) Baby Boomer generation in similar terms: "With all this smuggery, self-righteousness and self-pity, there is a temptation to tell the young pups off. But as a matter of fact, current American youth has indeed had a great crime committed against it. It is the worst-raised generation in our history."[9] Expect to see a similar piece in 2069.

## DISCONNECTING COHORTS

One of the key reasons that Millennials have been piled on so much is that they grew up just as our lives turned digital. The explosion of social media gave us a new outlet for sharing shallow stereotypes in memes and 140 characters or fewer. These technologies have not just made it easier to complain about each other—they also mean that different generations live in increasingly separate digital spaces.

A signal of how central to our lives these new technologies, particularly the smartphone, have become is seen in the endless surveys that ask what we'd rather give up: "One in Ten Millennials Would Rather Lose a Finger Than Give Up Their Smartphone," according to one headline.[10] Four in ten Americans say they would give up their dog or their partner for a month before their phone, two in ten say they would give up their toothbrush (urgh) or shoes (?) for a week, and, depending on which dubious survey you pick, between a third and half of respondents would forgo sex for between one week and three months.[11] Less speculative and more meaningful questions about our actual behavior with our phones also illustrate our attachment: four in ten Americans sleep with their phones right next to their bed, and a similar proportion say they always or often browse the internet or use apps within ten minutes of waking up.[12]

The speed with which smartphones have become central to our lives is clear from Figure 10.3. Hardly anyone had access to smartphones in Britain in 2008; today there is near universal ownership among Gen Z, Millennials, and Gen X. Gen Z have known little else, while Millennials' experiences over the course of their adult lives have been varied. Around seven in ten British

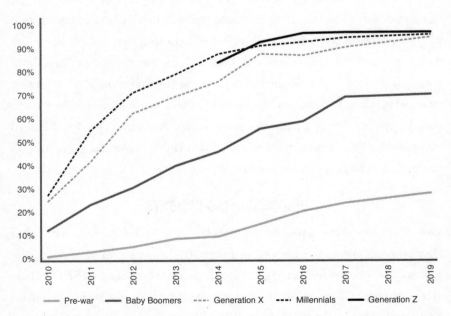

Figure 10.3: Percentage of British adults who own a smartphone. Source: Ipsos MORI Tech Tracker (2010–2019).

Baby Boomers own a smartphone, while the Pre-war generation continue to nudge upward, to 30 percent. This is as likely to be driven by how increasingly difficult it is to get "dumb" phones these days than the attraction of smart-phones' functionality.

This doesn't look like a significant separation between the generations—but the gaps in how different cohorts *use* their smartphones are much greater than blunt ownership measures suggest. For example, a technology time-use diary survey run by Ofcom, the UK communications regulator, showed that in 2016, Millennials spent an average of nearly 1,500 minutes (around twenty-five hours) on their smartphones each week, compared with less than half that for Gen X. The oldest group, aged fifty-five and over, spent half as much time as Gen X, at around 300 minutes. So although British Gen Z and Millennials may be only around 30 percent more likely to own a smart-phone than their parents and grandparents, they spend five times as long us-ing them.[13]

It's not just the intensity of use that varies between generations, it's also what we do online. In particular, social media use diverges more by genera-tion than anything we'll look at in this book. Taking France as an example,

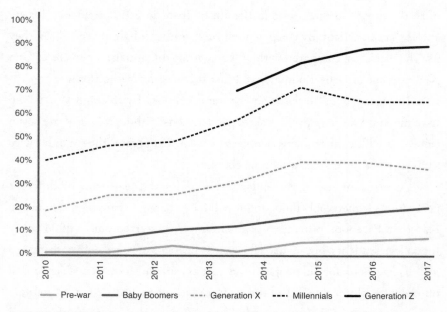

Figure 10.4: Percentage of French adults using online social networks every day. Source: Eu-robarometer (2010–2017).

Figure 10.4 shows that nine in ten Gen Zers use social media every day—while only 7 percent of the Pre-war generation do. Millennials are a fair way behind Gen Z, and Gen X are a further big step down. And unlike smartphone ownership, social media use among Baby Boomers is much closer to the Pre-war generation than the youngest cohorts.

The different ways young and old interact through technology is the source of a key disconnect in real life. When Italian academics interviewed older people as part of a study on age-based stereotypes in mobile phone use, one seventy-nine-year-old respondent said of her thirteen-year-old great-nephew: "I meet them, they say 'Hello aunt!,' I greet them and . . . down! They bend over the phone and then there is no more conversation."[14] But, of course, there is a decent chance the thirteen-year-old *is* still in a conversation—it's just not with his great aunt. This ability to be physically present but constantly connected elsewhere is new: it's an ability older generations may have wished for during their own boring visits to relatives—but it has consequences for intergenerational connection.

It's not just that different generations use social media at different levels—they're also on different networks. Each platform has its own distinct generational profile, as we can see in Figure 10.5, based on analysis of a data set of thirty thousand interviews in Britain by Ipsos in 2019. Snapchat, for example, has a particularly steep generational gradient: half of Gen Z say they use the platform, compared with 16 percent of Millennials, 5 percent of Gen X, 1 percent of Baby Boomers, and just 0.1 percent of the Pre-war generation. Instagram use also skews young, but Facebook, Twitter, and WhatsApp have much flatter user profiles across generations: although Gen Z are seven times more likely than Baby Boomers to be on Instagram, they're only twice as likely to be on WhatsApp or Facebook.

Of course, the use of particular technologies and platforms by different generations is incredibly fluid, and it will have changed again by the time you read this. Facebook provides a prime example. It started out in 2004 solely for college students, but in just a few years the focus of commentary shifted to ask, "Is Facebook for old people?" and, just as quickly, to answer, "Facebook is officially for old people."[15] On the surface, this seems just wrong, as younger generations are still the most likely to ever use the platform. However,

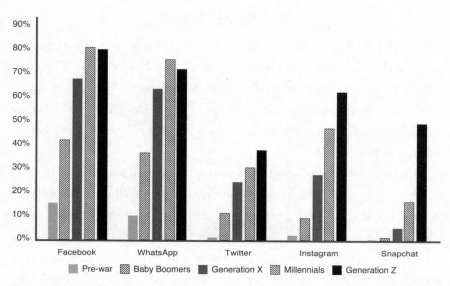

Figure 10.5: Use of social media platforms among British adults. Source: Ipsos MORI Tech Tracker (2019).

younger generations' intensity of Facebook use has declined substantially. This is hardly surprising: at a time when digital spaces are vital for young people to explore their individual and group identities, it makes sense to gravitate away from platforms where their parents' generation are increasingly posting embarrassing photos and messages. The graying of the "blue app" has inevitably led to mockery from young people, with two American twenty-year-olds setting up a Facebook "group where we all pretend to be boomers," which has nearly three hundred thousand members.[16] The content is a mix of all-caps political rants ("MY GRANDSON FORGOT TO CALL ME ON MY BIRTHDAY. THANKS OBAMA"), disgusting medical queries ("Good home remedies for anal tremors?"), inappropriate use of graphics ("TOM IS DIVORCING ME" above an image of party balloons), and Minions gifs. Although it's mostly good, satirical fun, it's also a case study in how quickly darker stereotypes can appear in our segmented digital world. The group administrators have admitted they sometimes struggle to moderate the strong homophobic and racist posts credited to Baby Boomers. Although there may be elements of truth in these sorts of portrayals, they exaggerate the real-world degree of cultural separation between the generations and show how easily extreme stereotyping can take hold online.

## "CORONIALS" RISING

The COVID-19 crisis has provided an unwelcome boost to these generational clichés, whether that meant memes of Baby Boomers hoarding toilet rolls or refusing to wear face masks, or the selfishness of "Generation Me" in continuing to party and complain. As one clickbait *Daily Telegraph* headline put it, "The Self-Pitying 'Woke' Generation Needed a War—and in Coronavirus They've Got One."[17]

However, the potential for the pandemic to increase generational division reaches way beyond sensationalist comment pieces. Of all the possible types of global crises, it is hard to think of a constellation of characteristics that would pose a greater challenge to intergenerational connection. This starts with literal separation, through lockdowns and restrictions that have kept generations apart. We've learned a new language of "shielding," "cocooning," "self-quarantining," and "bubbles." Given the much greater risk that the disease poses to the old, this group has had to be particularly cautious, accentuating the trend toward separation. As the British actress Joan Collins tweeted, a particularly harmful aspect of this is "bolstering the existing belief among the general public . . . that the old should keep out of everyone's way."

It is the young, however, who will be more affected by the long-term impact of these extraordinary restrictions on how we've had to live, from the disruption to their education to the coming economic effects. In Ireland, more than half of people aged between eighteen and twenty-four who were working before the coronavirus pandemic claimed the pandemic unemployment payment in the summer of 2020, compared to just over 20 percent of workers aged between twenty-five and thirty-four.[18] In Britain, people aged between sixteen and twenty-five were more than twice as likely as older workers to have lost their job, while six in ten saw their earnings fall.[19] And this is before the long-term economic "scarring" of career and economic progression that we know will affect the young more than the old.[20]

The differential effects on generations reach way beyond education and employment into social relations and mental health, partly because of the different physical living conditions between age groups. For example, as we saw earlier, older groups have risen up the housing ladder more easily than younger generations, so much so that one report on English living conditions during the pandemic found that older people's homes are twice as spacious:

those sixty-five and over live in fifty square meters per person, compared with twenty-six square meters for sixteen to twenty-four-year-olds. The report also found that young people in England are three times more likely to live in a damp home than older people, and more than one and a half times as likely to have no yard or to live in a run-down or congested neighborhood.

But despite these very real differences in experiences, none of the niche caricatures of intergenerational conflict have reflected the actual generational behavior during the lockdowns. As the journalist James Ball neatly summed up in a tweet: "Millennials and Gen Z are supportive of lockdown largely to protect *others*: their parents, grandparents, vulnerable people their age, etc. Lockdown has a high cost on them, and they're willingly bearing it. Mocking them as scared for their own sake is a cheap shot that misses."[21] Likewise, Dorothy Byrne, editor-at-large at Channel 4 and a sixty-seven-year-old with underlying medical conditions, wrote in the *Guardian*:

> Over the past weeks, I've been deeply moved by the sacrifices younger people are making. . . . [S]ociety is taking part in a remarkable exercise to keep those like me alive. In my own street, many people have lost their jobs. . . . Three of my lovely young neighbours were immediately told they would be evicted. One might expect people facing hardship to turn inwards; instead, they came round and asked me if they could do my shopping. You often hear about Britain's intergenerational divide. Indeed, one constantly reads that the young resent the old. . . . But I've never bought the narrative that pits one age group against another. Younger people resent a political class that has failed them, yes, but they don't resent me.[22]

Others made the point that older people were also deeply concerned about the young—and that the actions we all took to protect older groups was the result not just of love but also of respect for the value they bring to society, as outlined in a letter to the *Times*:

> Sir, Help! I opened the paper today to find a letter from my 81-year-old mum . . . announcing she would prefer a younger person to take her ventilator should she become seriously ill with Covid-19. Although I am in favour of living wills and sensible decisions about life and death, may I remind my mother

that she still tutors maths, runs her residents' association, provides emergency care for dogs and grandchildren and makes unbeatable Christmas cakes. The over-80s have become very noble in the face of the coronavirus, underestimating their value to society. We are not just protecting them out of love—we need them.

These individual stories and perspectives are important in countering some of the stereotypes that have taken hold. We will see an avalanche of reports, evaluations, and inquiries on what exactly happened during the pandemic in the months and years to come, but in the meantime we need to resist a fake sense of generational division. As Alex Evans, author of *The Myth Gap*, says, "This is a moment when early drafts . . . count for a lot. . . . [S]tories *create* our reality as much as they describe it, and can all too easily become self-fulfilling prophecies, especially in conditions of high uncertainty. So it matters a great deal that we nurture stories right now about how generations are coming together . . . and rally around a new, hopeful, shared agenda."[23] This is especially important because it may set the tone for what comes next and how we might plot our way back to recovery.

The generational perspective on the crisis and its aftermath will and should be crucial, but it's currently being set out in a very simplistic way. Completely unsurprisingly, the race to attach generational labels to the pandemic has already begun. We've had the "Coronials," the "Illenials" (which doesn't make much sense, given that young people are largely unaffected by the disease), the "Quaranteens" (I quite like that one), and, inevitably, the tech-related "Generation Zoom." Of course, this is a ludicrous game to play so early in a crisis that will undoubtedly shape generations in ways that we can't yet see.

I am very suspicious of this sort of generational naming. However, I completely disagree with the suggestion that COVID-19, far from a generational event, is "as close to a homogenous and constant period effect as we could ever observe."[24] One of the defining features of the pandemic has been how differently the consequences have been experienced by different groups, with age a key factor. In fact, this is *the* most generational event in just about all our lifetimes, because when we were born has played a key role in shaping how we've been affected so far, and this will continue to be the case for years to come.

This characterization of the pandemic as a uniform period effect completely misses the point of how generational effects work.

Throughout all the focus on generations during the COVID-19 pandemic, you may have noticed that, as usual, the middle generations have been *almost entirely* left out. We are, of course, in the thick of it, juggling kids, parents, and working from home, but we're not the primary focus of either the short-term health threat or the long-term implications. It's not surprising, then, that some of us tried to take advantage of that "forgotten middle child" position to focus on our real passions, as one tweet outlined: "I would open pubs for 35 to 45-year-olds exclusively first. The youth can't be trusted not to go silly and the elderly are at risk if they catch the lurgy. Clear sweet spot of age which can be trusted. Rest of you stay safe at home please, give us a month to check it's safe out."[25]

## BUILDING CONNECTION IN A DISCONNECTED AGE

As I write this, vaccines to protect against COVID-19 are being rolled out across the world. Although the signs are encouraging, I am unsure what the world will look like in even a few months' time. But for all our sakes, I hope the vaccines and treatments we've developed at breakneck pace allow generations to mix freely again soon. Maintaining personal connections across age groups has been shown time and again to be incredibly important, both at the personal and the societal level. Anthropological studies looking at age mixing among children and adults show older kids who spend time with younger ones learn to be nurturing, while the younger ones learn how to be less dominant, and both groups benefit from spending time with adults outside their family. Kids who play with only their exact peers, on the contrary, are more likely to be competitive.[26]

As part of his eight stages of adult development, Erik Erickson coined the term "generativity" to describe the concern older people feel about their responsibility for establishing and guiding the next generation.[27] Marc Freedman suggests that our focus on legacy may come initially from our drive to pass on our genes, but "as we move through and beyond midlife, generativity ripens into a broader concern for the next generation, for all the children who will outlive us." Erikson contrasts generativity with self-concern, a narcissism that denies our own mortality and prevents us from seeing ourselves as part of something greater. David Brooks talks about how we similarly shift from a focus on "resume virtues," the "skills you bring to the marketplace," to "eulogy virtues," the ones we want to be remembered for: "whether you were kind, brave, honest or faithful. Were you capable of deep love?"[28]

We outlined in an earlier chapter the importance of reversing generational segregation in where we live and the small steps already being taken to bring us back together. Many other initiatives attempt to increase meaningful contact between age groups while also providing commercial services, including schemes that find spare rooms in older people's homes for young people in university towns: Nesterly in Boston is one.[29] John W. Gardner, the former US secretary of health, education, and welfare developed the idea for an "Experience Corps" to connect older people to public elementary schools. It was launched in the 1990s by collaborators Marc Freedman and Linda Fried, and it focuses on helping students read by the time they get to the third grade. Freedman says he often gets asked, "Was it a corps designed to bring the *experience* of older people . . . to benefit young people or was it a corps designed to provide older people useful and meaningful *experiences?* To which I'd say yes and yes."

The Cares Family is a group of community networks in the UK that represents another take on this same balance of benefits, with a mission to "find connection in a disconnected age." Its founder, Alex Smith, describes how the idea came to him in 2010. He was running in the local council elections, and when he was out canvassing he met Fred, an eighty-four-year-old neighbor who hadn't left his house in three months. Alex pushed Fred in his wheelchair to the polling station and the next day returned to help him get a haircut. As the pair became friends, it was clear that this was a truly mutual relationship: Fred felt less lonely through his interactions with Alex, who in turn felt more connected to his community. The Cares Family started in North London, before opening branches in South London, Manchester, Liverpool, and East London. Altogether the initiatives have connected twenty-two thousand people in programs that reduce isolation, improve relations across the generations, and help people feel happier, closer to their community, and supported in times of need. These careful, thoughtful initiatives are inspiring—but not enough, in the face of the powerful trend pushing us apart. They deserve more support, and governments need to take more of a lead, by starting to see generational connection as a core objective.

The efforts of these social entrepreneurs stand in stark contrast to the opportunistic promotion of narratives of generational conflict to sow division. Steve Bannon's 2010 documentary *Generation Zero* provides a prime example of the latter. It is a bizarre film that is often literally painful to watch, with loud, dramatic music and rapidly interspersed videos of setting suns, butterflies emerging from cocoons, riots, and statues of Christ on the cross. The core message, which focuses on the lack of responsibility and foresight that led to the 2008 financial crisis, is reasonable if unsurprising.

But the film goes on to connect the causes and consequences of the crash to the thesis in Strauss and Howe's *The Fourth Turning*, in order to blame the crisis on the liberalism of the Baby Boomers during the 1960s and signal an inevitable reckoning to come. It builds a sense of impending decline and doom through the heavy caricaturing of generations and eras: the 1990s was apparently a time of "bad manners" and "cynicism." The documentary is the culmination of a long line of thought beginning with the "pulse rate hypothesis" of history developed by a number of philosophers and sociologists at the turn of the twentieth century, which "sought the regularities of the universal rhythm of generations."[30] This has been considered an outlier in generational thinking in its attempt to "impose biological rhythms on socio-historical phenomena."[31] But Strauss and Howe turned it into a prophecy of inevitable unraveling, on which Bannon hung his unnerving documentary.

The problem with this framing is not just the crass stereotyping of whole generations or even the selective reading of history to fit a narrative. The real issue is the supposed looming inevitability of crisis, which removes any sense of agency in changing course. We risk falling victim to our propensity to always believe we're on the verge of chaos: as the British author and academic Noel Annan once wrote, "All generationalists believe their own generation is lost."[32]

The reality is that generational change is an inevitable mix of harmony and tension, where conflict of some sort is built in. Ortega suggested that "the concept of the generation is the most important one in the whole of history," precisely because it constitutes the mechanism by which "history moves, changes, wheels and flows."[33]

In practice, the lack of real resentment between generations is partly due to the strength of love between them. The Harvard Study of Adult Development, launched in 1938, followed men from a wide variety of backgrounds for over three-quarters of a century. One finding stands out above all others: relationships are the crucial ingredient in well-being, particularly as we age. As George Vaillant, the Harvard professor who led the study for four decades, wrote, "Happiness is love. Full stop." And this is particularly the case where love spans the generations: those in middle age and beyond who care for the next generation are three times as likely to be happy as those who don't. This may seem like just another cozy idea, but the importance of these roles in our society is getting increasing attention, which will only be accentuated by the COVID-19 crisis. Bill Gates, for example, suggested that we introduce a "tax on robots," to fund the training and employment of people to "let us do a better job of reaching out to the elderly, having smaller class sizes, helping kids with special needs. You know, all of those are things where human empathy and understanding are still very, very unique. And we still deal with an immense shortage of people to help out there."[34]

Marc Freedman has outlined how activities that bring the generations together result in every dollar being "spent twice," because both generations benefit. But as he says, "In the long run, the love may well be what matters most. . . . [E]very emotion is also felt twice." Our forced separation during the pandemic has made it even clearer what we're missing—contact, not conflict.

# CHAPTER 11

# THE END OF THE LINE?

For such a famously warm-hearted Christmas movie, Frank Capra's *It's a Wonderful Life* addresses some very dark themes. Much of the first half of the film focuses on the suffocation of small-town life, with George Bailey's attempts to escape thwarted by his sense of obligation. George seems to be from a different era than his carefree younger brother. He is an archetype of the "civic-minded generation" brought up in pre-war America (he was "born older," his father tells him). Inevitably, as he grinds along this single-track life, he hits a midlife crisis that only divine intervention (or a major hallucinatory breakdown, depending on your view) can snap him out of. By the end of the film, he has come to terms with his lot, shaped by the age and circumstances he was born into.

The spur for George's revelation is seeing how Bedford Falls would have changed without him. In the end, *It's a Wonderful Life* is compelling because this vision of an alternative reality raises big questions, before answering them in a reassuringly Christmassy way. How is our own character and life course shaped by our formative experiences? And what do we add to the world before we're gone for good?

It turns out that George's presence changed a lot. He saved his brother's life, who in turn saved a whole platoon during the war. He stopped a grief-stricken pharmacist (who'd just received word that his son had died in the Spanish flu pandemic) from inadvertently poisoning a customer. He saved the soul of his town by preventing a run on the bank.

George's story embodies the three key mechanisms of change that we've seen in this book: how our lives and attitudes shift as we age, how individual events can change everything for whole populations, and how the circumstances we grew up in shape us throughout our lives. George's life, like all of ours, is a blend of these life-cycle, period, and cohort effects. His struggles mirror the tension we all face between cutting our own path and falling into line with existing ways of doing things, and they demonstrate how confronting our mortality sharpens our thinking on what's important and the difference we can make.

We can't all be George, with such clear-cut evidence that we matter as individuals. But we can hold on to a greater sense of the collective legacy of our generation. You can see how we strive for that in how quickly our thoughts are drawn to what our generation "gave the world" or what it might achieve. We aspire to be in the "generation to end world poverty."[1] We want future generations to look back on how we've responded to COVID-19 and, as Queen Elizabeth II suggested in her address to the Commonwealth at the start of the crisis, recognize that our generation was "as strong as any."[2] We also sometimes call on other generations to make a difference, as when Greta Thunberg argues that it is the responsibility of today's adults to save the planet from a climate change disaster that may determine her future.

## WHY GENERATIONS MATTER

Generational perspectives are powerful because they are interwoven with the fundamentals of human existence and societal change; while individuals are born, live, and die, society flows on, changed a little or a lot by our cohort's presence and then its absence. We've seen throughout this book how great thinkers have focused on this as *the* mechanism of social progress. August Comte identified the generation as a key factor in "the basic speed of human development." He insisted that "we should not hide the fact that our social progress rests essentially upon death; which is to say that the successive steps of humanity necessarily require a continuous renovation . . . from one generation to the next."[3]

Yet not everything is determined by this process of generational renewal. All the great generational thinkers have recognized the power of events in shaping our future and the role that life cycles play in creating intergenerational tension. Unlike other generational analysis, my aim in this book has not been to prove that generational difference is *all* that matters in understanding how societies change—the truth usually resists such simplicity. Societies actually change through the interplay of cohort, life-cycle, and period effects: each is powerful, and none is automatically more important than the others. Thinking more carefully about each aids our understanding of how we as individuals are shaped and how societies change. It helps us bust myths about individual generations and separate exaggerated claims and stereotypes from hugely significant shifts. And it suggests what we should do to build the future we want to see.

A generational perspective is not a substitute for socioeconomic perspectives like class or race—they are all useful in understanding the world and how it's changing. However, studying the interaction between when you were born and the circumstances you were born into highlights new patterns, including some of the most important changes in our societies. It would not be possible to identify the changing impact of inequality on life chances without a generational perspective, for example. Ultimately, a truly generational perspective—carefully separating cohort, life-cycle, and period effects, rather than subscribing to simplistic clichés—provides us with new insights into some of the biggest issues we're facing today and points to how we should react. Looking back across the book, seven key themes stand out.

## PHONY GENERATIONAL STEREOTYPES ARE FEEDING A PHONY GENERATIONAL WAR

Our susceptibility to stereotypes is the most common trap we fall into when discussing generational difference. Lurid examples of young people behaving badly during the pandemic may get clicks, but they misrepresent the incredible compliance of both young and old with difficult restrictions. Generational thinking helps us understand why we naturally see the young as more likely to behave badly: the latest generation will *always* be an "invasion of barbarians" in our cultures and practices. Merely recognizing this thinking helps us guard against falling for the clichés of a mini-industry of generational consultants, marketing headlines, and sensationalist books. They may seem trivial individually, but together they are destructive.

Similarly, a generational perspective teaches us that we should be wary of moral panics about new technologies: whenever an innovation we didn't grow up with is identified as the cause of an emergent problem, we should be skeptical until we see solid evidence. For example, accepting the simple answer that smartphones and social media are responsible for increased mental disorders among young people leads us to look in the wrong place for answers and miss taking more effective—if less straightforward—action.

Although the overwhelming tendency is to attach negative stereotypes to young people, it's equally important to resist overly positive ones. The way Strauss and Howe lionize a coming wave of super-civic Millennials is an obvious example, but there are a number of other more consequential ones. The myth that our current younger generations are more focused on acting sustainably or with social purpose than previous generations is risky, as it leads to complacency among the rest of us, built on the assumption that there will be an inevitable rise in environmental concern and action as they make up greater proportions of the overall population. It also erases the concern older people have about future generations and the planet.

This tendency to stereotype includes characterizing younger generations as "woke." Although they are undoubtedly continuing the liberalizing trend in key cultural debates, there is nothing in the data to suggest a sudden break into a different cultural tribe: in fact, we've seen just as rapid generational changes in the recent past. Remembering that cohort effects are only one way societies change will help us to correctly identify why this "culture war" rhetoric is happening now: it is largely a period effect of the polarization of politics and social media creating a stronger sense of difference than is justified.

Such exaggerated differences often appear purely as clickbait, but they are encouraged on both sides of the political divide. It makes sense that those with increasingly older voter bases would want to take "campus politics national" and that those on the other side would exaggerate the virtue of the young. But both strategies fuel the overblown sense of generational difference, skirt the significant minorities of young people who don't hold these views, and give a false sense that our cultural attitudes evolve in only one direction between generations. Instead, as we've seen, there are ebbs and flows over time, in response to events and life-cycle changes.

## A LOSS OF CONNECTION, NOT CONFLICT, IS OUR BIGGEST RISK

Increased stereotyping and tension are no doubt partly a result of how we have allowed the generations to drift apart, both physically and digitally, to a degree not seen in our history. This not only adds to these negative trends but deprives us of the significant benefits of interacting with different age groups.

For these reasons, we should have a greater focus on encouraging intergenerational connection than can be achieved through piecemeal initiatives of inspired entrepreneurs. We've drifted apart partly by choice but also through inattention in government and planning. The separation imposed by the necessary response to the COVID-19 pandemic has only emphasized what we're missing, as well as providing endless examples of how the generations have instinctively supported each other. Reestablishing and bolstering intergenerational connection should form a key element of our recovery plans.

This may sound like a tall order, given the power of the trends pushing us apart, but some governments have started to take up the challenge. In 2014 and 2015, Singapore conducted a huge consultation exercise on creating an "action plan for successful ageing."[4] This culminated in a $3 billion plan, one of the key strands of which is to create a "Kampong [village] for all ages," an effort to build "a cohesive society with intergenerational harmony." The program covers much more than just intergenerational contact, including transportation, education, employment, and much more, but its strong focus is on bringing the ages together. Singapore's experience to date shows that it won't be easy to get right and will take time to pay off—but also that it is possible to make a difference.

In the meantime, we also need to establish stronger connections between the generations to address shared societal challenges. There is increasing interest around the world in deliberative democracy techniques that bring the whole population together, through methods such as citizens' assemblies, to debate and decide on key issues. These tools can be highly effective ways to bridge generational divides and even to encourage us to connect to future generations. For example, Saijo Tatsuyoshi and his colleagues at the Kochi

University of Technology have developed a simple but effective approach called "future design," which asks citizens to role-play future generations in deliberative discussions on all sorts of policy challenges, from water supplies to public housing. The impact is clear: simply imagining ourselves as future generations reduces our focus on immediate priorities.[5]

## DELAYED LIFE CYCLES ARE CHANGING THE LIFE COURSE FOR NEW GENERATIONS

Life-cycle effects are easy to miss in the generational narratives we're fed, but they exert an extraordinarily powerful force over our attitudes and behavior. Time and again, cohorts that start off moving in a distinctive direction from previous generations are pulled back toward a well-worn life course. But these life-cycle transitions have shifted to later in life for recent generations of young people, thanks to a "delayed adulthood" effect. This is one of the big changes of our time, and it is a result of all sorts of significant shifts: extended education, wage stagnation, precarious employment, increased debt, and soaring housing costs. The delay in key life stages is more the result of difficult circumstances than either a new age of exploration or the active choices of a "coddled" generation.

Delayed adulthood is also responsible for a lot of the misperceptions about emerging generations on everything from car ownership to sex lives and smoking habits. Many of these trends come back into line with those of previous cohorts—just later. This is a result of changed circumstances, rather than innate characteristics within the generation. Younger generations are coming to adult life with less experience of independence and in need of more support, but that doesn't make them a "snowflake generation."

## "MUGGING GRANDMA" IS NOT THE SOLUTION

Despite the tough circumstances facing recent generations of young people, they have little desire to improve their lot by taking from the old. The reasons for this are both multiple and deeply personal. We love our parents and grandparents and don't want to see them penalized, maybe in part because the burden would shift to us. We also know that we'll be old one day, and how we treat older people now is one of the only indicators we have of how we'll be treated in the future. More generally, we have a strong sense that we should recognize people who have contributed, and older people have contributed the most.

Our main focus, then, should *not* be on a crude redistribution of resources between existing generations. It is right to look at the balance between generations, but poorer generational outcomes are more a result of wage stagnation and increasing barriers to building wealth. Shuffling the burden between the age groups is not what people really want, and it won't do a lot to help. This will be even more the case when the balance of our societies tip toward older generations.

Instead, people want better jobs, economic growth that benefits them, and a solution to the broken housing market. Of course, such things are hugely difficult to achieve, but that's the nature of the generational problem: there is no short-term fix to restore faith in a better future for ourselves and our children.

From the evidence we've seen, it's clear that a better solution on housing needs to be a key element of this brighter future. The aspiration to own property is constant across generations, but it is increasingly unmet. Governments need to close this expectation gap, either by supporting home ownership or by shifting aspirations through improving the alternatives, by providing more high-quality social housing or better regulation of private renting. We have become incredibly stuck in countries like the UK, but the longer we are, the more our individual futures will be determined by the resources we can draw on from our family, and the more support private renters will need in retirement. A comprehensive housing plan should be a cornerstone of any plan to "build back better."

## INEQUALITY IS AN INCREASINGLY INTERGENERATIONAL ISSUE

It is not just housing opportunities that are increasingly linked to our family background—we're seeing new generational patterns across issues including health inequality and family stability. Childhood obesity, for example, has become related to social class in recent generations. More generally, the extraordinary growth of wealth and its concentration in a section of older age groups is one of the key economic stories of our time. Future inequalities between generations are being "baked in" as advantage and disadvantage is increasingly handed down through an incipient caste system.

It used to be that "today" would always be the right answer to the question of when you would like to have been born. This was testament to the incredible progress we've made and how everyone has moved, even if the better-off were progressing more quickly. But we are now seeing actual reversals for those with fewer resources in richer countries, with shocking declines in life expectancies among the left and kept behind. These groups are currently exceptions, but increasing proportions of the population will get pulled in as the concentration of advantage continues.

Changing this increasingly intergenerational inequality is an almighty task, and one that has had little political focus, partly as a result of complacency from the public. As we've seen, this absence of anger, particularly from young people, is partly due to being at the end of a trend toward greater individualism. The sense of personal responsibility and belief in meritocracy may be strong, but they have limits. Growing resentment and dwindling faith in a better future, even if they don't lead to revolution, will continue to undermine social and political stability.

Recognition of the need for governments to act with greater "social imagination" to address these challenges is growing, particularly following the COVID-19 crisis.[6] As the economist Mariana Mazzucato suggests, governments have been "tinkering not leading."[7] This needs to change, as "only government has the capacity to steer the transformation necessary," to recast how economic organizations are governed and how economic actors, civil society, and citizens relate to each other. This is a long-term, intergenerational project.

## CRISES AND DECLINE ARE *NOT* INEVITABLE

One of the key risks of looking *only* at generational change is that it gives a greater sense of certainty about the future than is justified. This includes the attempt by Strauss and Howe to overlay a rhythm on generational types and the resultant eras they produce. This type of thinking points to unavoidable crises, and, though a politically useful tool for some, it is based on a spurious reading of history and is a bad guide to the future.

More than this, it adds a feeling that there is nothing we can do to avert these crises. There is a parallel doom-mongering in every "new crisis of trust," while the longer-term trends show that trust levels were never that high and, at worst, have seen a long, slow decline. These long trends also show that things have often been as bad, or worse. The large fluctuations in satisfaction with democracy that we've seen in past decades should be seen as a sign of resilience rather than weakness.

This long view also reveals that current outcomes were not nearly as certain as they may now appear. Hindsight bias makes us think our fate was foreordained, including the relative good fortune of older generations and the tougher times current younger generations face. In fact both result from the interplay among circumstance, decisions, and actions.

Together, these facts suggest that we are more in control than it sometimes appears. We need to remember that we have agency, even when the challenges facing us are vast, complex, and interconnected. We have pulled ourselves up from similar lows before; it doesn't happen through a single "New Deal" but over the long term, through myriad bottom-up and top-down actions.

## WE NEED A MINISTRY FOR THE FUTURE

*The Ministry for the Future*, a novel by Kim Stanley Robinson, paints a frighteningly realistic picture of a dystopian near future, where governments are failing to reduce carbon emissions and climate change is killing millions. In response, the parties to the Paris Agreement create a "Subsidiary Body for Implementation of the Agreement," which is nicknamed "The Ministry for the Future." The ministry's role is "to advocate for the world's future generations of citizens, whose rights, as defined in the Universal Declaration of Human Rights, are as valid as our own . . . [and it is] charged with defending all living creatures present and future who cannot speak for themselves, by promoting their legal standing and physical protection."[8]

The novel raises all sorts of moral dilemmas around what a future-focused, generation-spanning agenda would look like. As one activist tells the head of the ministry, "There are about a hundred people walking this Earth, who if you judge from the angle of the future like you're supposed to do, they are mass murderers. . . . If you really were *from* the future, so that you knew for sure there were people walking the Earth today fighting change, so that they were killing your children and all their children, you'd defend your people. In defence of your home, your life, your people, you would kill an intruder."

In the novel, which is more hopeful than this sounds, the ministry helps to rework complex, interconnected social and economic processes and incentives to direct power and money away from the production of fossil fuels and consumption, and toward more sustainable alternatives. Admittedly, it takes some significant interventions to achieve this goal, including a new carbon currency and the type of "black ops" you'd associate with a terrorist group or intelligence agency.

Somewhere between this imagined extreme and our governments' weak attempts to think and act generationally, there is a middle ground of how we might formalize our responsibility to consider the future.

There are some early signs of a rebalancing toward this longer perspective, both in how we frame issues and how institutions react. In an encyclical in 2015, Pope Francis affirmed his view that "intergenerational solidarity is not optional, but rather a basic question of justice, since the world we have received also belongs to those who will follow us."[9] National governments have also started to act: the United Arab Emirates has a Ministry of Cabinet Affairs and the Future, and Hungary has an ombudsman for future generations.[10]

One particularly important example is the Future Generations Act in Wales. As Jane Davidson, the minister who proposed it, said, "It is revolutionary because it enshrines into law that the well-being of the current and future people of Wales is explicitly the core purpose of the government in Wales."[11] The act was the first to do this anywhere in the world, and it required public bodies to "think about the long-term impact of their decisions . . . to prevent persistent problems such as poverty, health inequalities and climate change." It also established the role of future generations commissioner to oversee its implementation. The commissioner does not have the power to stop or change policy and can only make recommendations, "naming and shaming" public bodies falling short of the objectives of the act. Even so, this approach has already produced results, as several decisions to go ahead or block activity have explicitly cited the act, including the first minister's refusal to approve a new six-lane highway. As Davidson suggests, it is an early step toward the ultimate goal of changing the culture of governance. Although this is not the full answer, it is an exciting base to build on.

Of course, such innovations are dwarfed by the scale of the challenge involved in embedding a longer-term perspective, when consumer culture and economic and political systems push us in the other direction. As we respond to COVID-19, it is vital that we test how much further we can take this, partly because it feels like real change is more possible now, given how much our lives have already shifted and the scale of the rebuilding task to come, but also to guard against our natural tendency to focus on the here and now when crises hit. It's the right time to institutionalize some longer-term thinking.

## . . . X, Y, Z

I believe that generational thinking tells us something unique and valuable about our future that can help us shape it—but there are many people who would like to see an end to all discussions of generations. I can understand why, given what we are so often fed as generational analysis. I've written a book that explains why a lot of what you've been told is generational in fact isn't. This is not because I don't see any value in generational thinking but the opposite: it's too important, particularly right now, to be left to these misdirections. Its importance is not because I see an impending, inevitable crisis or all-out generational war, but because we seem to have lost faith in a better future for our current and future generations of young people. That's risky, and in many ways, it sums up the challenge of our world in the wake of COVID-19. An understanding of generations, including what brings us together as much as what separates us, is vital to our response.

Regardless of my own view, I think it is very unlikely that Gen Z will be the last generational line I'll be plotting in my charts. In the end, the key reason why generational stories will continue to be important is the simplest: they help us figure out who we are. Just like George Bailey, we need to understand how we fit into this overall picture, even if it's not a completely truthful vision. We also just find it *irresistible* to ridicule the young, blame the old—and forget about those in the middle.

☐ ■ ☐

The lives of family members I currently have memories of will span two hundred years, which will stretch from my grandparents, born in the 1910s, to my children, who have a good chance of living to the 2110s. People I know and love will have lived in incredibly different times, from grandads who worked in coal mines and steel works, to who knows what my children will be doing. On the one hand, it makes my own slice of time seem incredibly small—but on the other, it connects me to a vast range of human experience. The "200-year present" is a term coined by the sociologist Elise Boulding to describe a way of thinking about the present with full awareness of both the effects of past actions on us now and of our present actions on the future. It encourages a long-term perspective, acknowledging that the past is still with us in its effects and that today's actions will determine the future. We need more two-hundred-year thinking.

# ACKNOWLEDGMENTS

With many thanks to Louise, Bridget, and Martha for their incredible support and patience, to Mike Harpley and Eric Henney for brilliant editing, and to Michele Scotto di Vettimo, Nick Humphrey, Hermione Fricker, Robin Dennis, and Sarah Chatwin for their excellent editing and research. Thanks also to the team at Ipsos MORI for their work on the generational studies that started this: Ben Page, Hannah Shrimpton, Michael Clemence, Gideon Skinner, Suzanne Hall, Matt Walliams, K. D. Hasler, Fintan O'Connor, Darrell Bricker, and Kelly Beaver for support on the studies. I am also very grateful to the past and present teams at the National Centre for Social Research (NatCen) for their generous sharing of data when I first started examining generational change, particularly Alison Park, Nancy Kelley, and Peter Dangerfield, who also helped set up the initial analysis. Thanks also go to the team at King's who've been understanding of my distraction and generous in comments, including Jonathan Grant, and George Murkin for his design help, and to the many people who've been working to better understand generational dynamics and connections who have helped inform the book. These include Robert D. Putnam, Jean Twenge, Laura Gardiner and David Willetts at the Resolution Foundation's Intergenerational Centre, Alex Smith at the Cares Family, and Beatrice Pembroke at King's.

# NOTES

## INTRODUCTION: THE QUESTION OF OUR GENERATION

1. Van Elsland, S. L. (2020). COVID-19 Deaths: Infection Fatality Ratio Is About 1% Says New Report. Imperial College London. October 29. www.imperial.ac.uk/news/207273 /covid-19-deaths-infection-fatality-ratio-about/.

2. Pancevski, B., S. Meichtry, and X. Fontdegloria (2020). A Generational War Is Brewing over Coronavirus. *Wall Street Journal*. March 19. www.wsj.com/articles/a-generational -war-is-brewing-over-coronavirus-11584437401.

3. Sparks, H. (2020). Morbid "Boomer Remover" Coronavirus Meme Only Makes Millennials Seem More Awful. *New York Post*. March 19. https://nypost.com/2020/03 /19/morbid-boomer-remover-coronavirus-meme-only-makes-millennials-seem-more-awful/.

4. BBC News (2020). Coronavirus: Under-25s and Women Financially Worst-Hit. April 6. www.bbc.co.uk/news/business-52176666.

5. Portes, J. (2020). The Lasting Scars of the Covid-19 Crisis: Channels and Impacts. *Vox EU CEPR*. June 1. https://voxeu.org/article/lasting-scars-covid-19-crisis.

6. Mannheim, K. (1952). The Problem of Generations. In *Essays on the Sociology of Knowledge*. Ed. P. Kecskemeti. New York, Routledge. 5: 276–332.

7. Comin, D., and M. Mestieri (2013). Technology Diffusion: Measurement, Causes, and Consequences. NBER working paper no. 19052. Cambridge, MA, National Bureau of Economic Research. www.nber.org/papers/w19052.

8. Rosa, H. (2013). *Social Acceleration: A New Theory of Modernity*. Trans. J. Treejo-Mathys. New York, Columbia University Press.

9. I have deliberately used a simple graphical approach rather than complicated statistical models to make the analysis as accessible as possible. But there is no way around what statisticians call the "identification problem" when trying to separate the effects of age, period, and cohort. They are exactly "colinear"—that is, if we know someone's age and the year we're taking our measurement, we automatically know when they were born. This makes it literally impossible to fully disentangle which of the effects is causing changes. There are statistical techniques that try to get around this, but all of them rely on assumptions that attempt to fix or strip out one of the three effects to measure the others. While what we've done in this

book is much simpler, the point remains that we need to be cautious in claiming the effects are completely separable.

10. Freeman, K. J. (1908). *Schools of Hellas: An Essay on the Practice and Theory of Ancient Greek Education from 600 to 300 BC.* New York, Macmillan. 74.

11. Seder, J. (2016). 15 Historical Complaints About Young People Ruining Everything. Mental Floss. www.mentalfloss.com/article/77445/15-historical-complaints-about-young-people-ruining-everything.

12. *Dawson Daily News* (1906). Boys are Ruined: Dime Novels Cause Lads to Murder.

13. Thompson, C. (2014). Why Chess Will Destroy Your Mind. Message. May 22. https://medium.com/message/why-chess-will-destroy-your-mind-78ad1034521f.

14. Taylor, K. (2019). Millennials and Their Spending Habits Are Wreaking Havoc on These 18 Industries. *Business Insider.* February 1. www.businessinsider.com/millennials-hurt-industries-sales-2018-10?r=US&IR=T.

15. Dobson, R. (2017). *Millennial Problems: Everyday Struggles of a Generation.* London, Square Peg. 12.

16. Hummert, M. L. (1999). A Social Cognitive Perspective on Age Stereotypes. In *Social Cognition and Aging.* Ed. Hess, T. M., and F. Blanchard-Fields. San Diego, CA, Academic. 175–196; Popham, L., and T. Hess (2015). Theories of Age Stereotyping and Views of Aging. In *Encyclopedia of Geropsychology.* Ed. Pachana, N. A. Singapore, Springer Science+Business Media. 1–10. www.researchgate.net/publication/299478040_Theories_of_Age_Stereotyping_and_Views_of_Aging.

17. Gibbs, N. R. (1988). Living: Grays on the Go. *Time* 131(8): 66–75. http://content.time.com/time/subscriber/article/0,33009,966744-9,00.html.

18. Kihlstrom, E. (2018). Shhh! Ageing Is Good Business. Innovate UK. May 14. https://innovateuk.blog.gov.uk/2018/05/14/shhh-ageing-is-good-business/.

19. *Guardian* (2019). OK Boomer: Millennial MP Responds to Heckler in New Zealand Parliament. November 5. www.youtube.com/watch?v=OxJsPXrEqCI.

20. Stone, L. (2019). The Boomers Ruined Everything. *Atlantic.* June 24. www.theatlantic.com/ideas/archive/2019/06/boomers-are-blame-aging-america/592336/.

21. Walker, J. [@jonwalker121] (2019). I am neither a millennial nor a boomer. I come from a generation so irrelevant that people can't even be bothered to hate us. Twitter. November 14. https://twitter.com/jonwalker121/status/1194919236730343424.

22. Fussell, P., quoted in Gordinier, J. (2008). *X Saves the World: How Generation X Got the Shaft but Can Still Keep Everything from Sucking.* London, Penguin. xxi.

23. Seemiller, C., and M. Grace (2018). *Generation Z: A Century in the Making.* Abingdon, Routledge.

24. Gordinier (2008); Hennessey, M. (2018). *Zero Hour for Gen X: How the Last Adult Generation Can Save America from Millennials.* New York, Encounter Books. 58.

25. Coupland, D. (1991). *Generation X: Tales for an Accelerated Culture.* New York, Macmillan.

26. Taleb, N. N. (2010). *The Black Swan: The Impact of the Highly Improbable.* London, Penguin.

27. Worldometer (2020). Countries Where COVID-19 Has Spread. www.worldometers.info/coronavirus/countries-where-coronavirus-has-spread/.

28. Ipsos MORI (2019). Ipsos MORI Global Trends Survey. www.ipsosglobaltrends.com/.

29. Shrimpton, H., G. Skinner, and S. Hall (2017). *The Millennial Bug*. Resolution Foundation and the Intergenerational Commission. www.resolutionfoundation.org /app/uploads/2017/09/The-Millennial-Bug.pdf; Duffy, B., F. Thomas, H. Shrimpton, H. Whyte-Smith, M. Clemence, and T. Abboud (2018). *Beyond Binary: The Lives and Choices of Generation Z*. London, Ipsos MORI. 150. www.ipsos.com/ipsos-mori/en-uk /ipsos-thinks-beyond-binary-lives-and-choices-generation-z.

## CHAPTER 1: STAGNATION GENERATION

1. Willetts, D. (2019). *The Pinch: How the Baby Boomers Took Their Children's Future— and Why They Should Give It Back*. London, Atlantic Books.

2. Rahman, F., and D. Tomlinson (2018). *Cross Countries: International Comparisons of Intergenerational Trends*. Resolution Foundation and the Intergenerational Commission. www .resolutionfoundation.org/app/uploads/2018/02/IC-international.pdf.

3. Rahman and Tomlinson (2018).

4. Bangham, G., S. Clarke, L. Gardiner, L. Judge, F. Rahman, and D. Tomlinson (2019). *An Intergenerational Audit for the UK: 2019*. Resolution Foundation. June. www .resolutionfoundation.org/app/uploads/2019/06/Intergenerational-audit-for-the-UK.pdf.

5. Office for National Statistics (2012). *Pension Trends: Pensioner Income and Expenditure*. https://webarchive.nationalarchives.gov.uk/20160107023853/http://www.ons.gov.uk /ons/rel/pensions/pension-trends/chapter-11--pensioner-income-and-expenditure--2012 -edition-/sum-ch11-2012.html.

6. Willetts (2019).

7. Belot, M., S. Choi, E. Tripodi, E. van den Broek-Altenburg, J. C. Jamison, and N. W. Papageorge (2020). Unequal Consequences of COVID-19 Across Age and Income: Representative Evidence from Six Countries. IZA discussion paper no. 13366. June. http://ftp.iza .org/dp13366.pdf.

8. Barclays (2019). Small "Swaprifices" Could Save Millennials up to £10.5bn a Year. Press release. https://home.barclays/news/press-releases/2019/02/small--swaprifices --could-save-millennials-up-to-p10-5bn-a-year/.

9. Thompson, R. (2019). Millennial Spending Habits Are Being Questioned (Again) and the Internet Isn't Here for It. Mashable. February 20. https://mashable.com/article /millennial-coffee-spending-reaction.

10. Costello, F., and A. Acland (2016). Spending the Kids Inheritance, What It Means for UK Companies. Innovate UK. July 19. https://innovateuk.blog.gov.uk/2016/07/19 /spending-the-kids-inheritance-what-it-means-for-uk-companies/.

11. Best, W. (2016). Gray Is the New Black: Baby Boomers Still Outspend Millennials. VISA Consulting and Analytics. https://usa.visa.com/partner-with-us/visa-consulting -analytics/baby-boomers-still-outspend-millennials.html.

12. Scott, A. (2019). The "Silver Tsunami" Is the Workforce the World Needs Right Now. *Quartz*. May 1. https://qz.com/work/1605206/senior-workers-are-the-key-to -economic-growth/.

13. Twenge, J. M. (2006). *Generation Me: Why Today's Young Americans Are More Confident, Assertive, Entitled—and More Miserable Than Ever Before*. New York, The Free Press.

14. Twenge, J. M. (2018). *iGen: Why Today's Super-connected Kids Are Growing Up Less Rebellious, More Tolerant, Less Happy—and Completely Unprepared for Adulthood*. New York, Atria Books.

15. Twenge (2018); and Twenge (2006).

16. Fell, B., and M. Hewstone (2015). *Psychological Perspectives on Poverty: A Review of Psychological Research into the Causes and Consequences of Poverty*. Joseph Rowntree Foundation. June 4. www.jrf.org.uk/report/psychological-perspectives-poverty; Heshmat, S. (2015). The Scarcity Mindset: How Does Being Poor Change the Way We Feel and Think? *Psychology Today*. April 2. www.psychologytoday.com/gb/blog/science-choice/201504/the-scarcity-mindset.

17. Bangham et al. (2019).

18. Shorrocks, A., J. Davies, and R. Lluberas (2017). *The Global Wealth Report 2017*. www.credit-suisse.com/corporate/en/research/research-institute/global-wealth-report.html.

19. Shorrocks, Davies, and Lluberas (2017).

20. Wiltshire, T., and D. Wood. (2017). Three Charts On: The Great Australian Wealth Gap. *Conversation*. October 1. https://theconversation.com/three-charts-on-the-great-australian-wealth-gap-84515.

21. Josuweit, A. (2018). 5 Money Tips Millennials Can Learn from Their Grandparents. *Forbes*. March 15. www.forbes.com/sites/andrewjosuweit/2018/03/15/5-money-tips-millennials-can-learn-from-their-grandparents.

22. Bangham et al. (2019).

23. Intergenerational Commission (2018). *A New Generational Contract: The Final Report of the Intergenerational Commission*. London. Resolution Foundation. www.resolutionfoundation.org/advanced/a-new-generational-contract/.

24. Willetts (2019).

25. Intergenerational Commission (2018).

26. Intergenerational Commission (2018).

27. Intergenerational Commission (2018).

28. Clark, G., and N. Cummins (2015). Intergenerational Wealth Mobility in England, 1858–2012: Surnames and Social Mobility. *Economic Journal* 125(582): 61–85. https://doi.org/10.1111/ecoj.12165.

29. Howker, E., and S. Malik (2013). *Jilted Generation: How Britain Has Bankrupted Its Youth*. London, Icon Books.

30. Chan, K. K., E. J. Huang, and R. A. Lassu (2017). Understanding Financially Stressed Millennials' Hesitancy to Seek Help: Implications for Organizations. *Journal of Financial Education* 43(1), 141–160. www.jstor.org/stable/90018423.

31. Scanlon, K., F. Blanc, A. Edge, and C. Whitehead (2019). *The Bank of Mum and Dad: How It Really Works*. LSE, the Family Building Society. January. www.lse.ac.uk/business-and-consultancy/consulting/assets/documents/the-bank-of-mum-and-dad.pdf.

32. Intergenerational Commission (2018).

33. Eisenberg, R. (2019). The Distressing Growth of Wealth Inequality of Boomers. *Forbes*. October 16. www.forbes.com/sites/nextavenue/2019/10/16/the-distressing-growth-of-wealth-inequality-of-boomers/.

34. Putnam, R. D. (2016). *Our Kids: The American Dream in Crisis*. New York, Simon and Schuster.

35. Norris, P., and R. Inglehart (2019). *Cultural Backlash*. Cambridge, Cambridge University Press.

36. Hofstede, G. (2001). *Culture's Consequences: Comparing Values, Behaviors, and Organizations Across Nations*. London, Sage; Schwartz, S. H. (1999). A Theory of Cultural Values

and Some Implications for Work. *Applied Psychology: An International Review* 48(1): 23–47. https://doi.org/10.1111/j.1464-0597.1999.tb00047.x; Schwartz, S. H. (2009). Causes of Culture: National Differences in Cultural Embeddedness. In *Quod Erat Demonstrandum: From Herodotus' Ethnographic Journeys to Cross-Cultural Research*. Ed. Gari, A., and K. My-lonas. Athens, Pedio Books. https://scholarworks.gvsu.edu/iaccp_proceedings/5/.

37. Thatcher, M. (1975). Speech to Conservative Party Conference. Blackpool, October 10. www.margaretthatcher.org/document/102777.

38. Reagan, R. (1964). "A Time for Choosing." Televised speech. Los Angeles County, CA, October 27. www.reaganlibrary.gov/reagans/ronald-reagan/time-choosing-speech -october-27-1964.

39. Malik, S. (2014). Adults in Developing Nations More Optimistic Than Those in Rich Countries. *Guardian*. April 14. www.theguardian.com/politics/2014/apr/14 /developing-nations-more-optimistic-richer-countries-survey.

40. Thomson, D. (2015). *Selfish Generations? The Ageing of New Zealand's Welfare State*. Wellington, NZ, Bridget Williams Books.

41. General Social Survey (1984–2016). https://gssdataexplorer.norc.org/.

42. British Social Attitudes Study (2016). www.bsa.natcen.ac.uk/.

43. Duffy. B., S. Hall, D. O'Leary, and S. Pope. *Generation Strains: A Demos and Ipsos MORI Report on Changing Attitudes to Welfare*. Demos. www.demos.co.uk/files/Demos _Ipsos_Generation_Strains_web.pdf?1378677272.

44. Falkingham, J., and J. Hills, eds. (1995). *The Dynamic of Welfare: The Welfare State and The Lifecycle*. New York, Prentice-Hall.

## CHAPTER 2: HOME AFFRONT

1. ITV (1967). At Last the 1948 Show. Monty Python's We Were So Poor. www .youtube.com/watch?v=VAdlkunflRs.

2. Rach, J. (2018). "The Estate Agent Said I'd Caused Mould by Breathing": "Genera-tion Rent" Share Their Horror Stories—Including a Woman Whose Landlord Had Sex in Her Bed. *Daily Mail*. August 23. www.dailymail.co.uk/femail/article-6090591/Generation -rent-share-horror-stories-including-mould-rip-prices-holes-CEILING.html.

3. *Daily Mail* (2014). In the Wealthiest Nation on Earth . . . but More Than 1.6 Mil-lion Americans Do Not Have Indoor Plumbing. April 23. www.dailymail.co.uk/news /article-2611602/In-wealthiest-nation-Earth-1-6-million-Americans-dont-indoor-plumbing .html; Ingraham, C. (2014). 1.6 Million Americans Don't Have Indoor Plumbing. *Wash-ington Post*. April 23. www.washingtonpost.com/news/wonk/wp/2014/04/23/1-6-million -americans-dont-have-indoor-plumbing-heres-where-they-live/; *Daily Mail* (2010). Homes Less Affordable Than 50 Years Ago—but at Least More of Them Have Indoor Toilets! This Is Money. January 20. www.thisismoney.co.uk/money/article-1244777/Homes-affordable -50-years-ago--indoor-toilets.html.

4. Goodman, R. (2020). *The Domestic Revolution*. London, Michael O'Mara Books.

5. Lavelle, D. (2018). "Slugs Came Through the Floorboards": What It's like to Be a Millennial Renting in Britain. *Guardian*. August 5. www.theguardian.com/society/2018 /aug/05/landlord-flat-affordable-rent-millennials-uk-cities-farcical.

6. Ewens, H. (2018). The Real Reason Millennials Complain About Housing. *Vice*. Au-gust 9. www.vice.com/en_uk/article/bjb5kz/the-real-reason-millennials-complain-about -housing.

7. Department for Communities and Local Government (2017). *English Housing Survey: Housing Costs and Affordability, 2015–16.* https://assets.publishing.service.gov.uk /government/uploads/system/uploads/attachment_data/file/627683/Housing_Cost_and _Affordability_Report_2015-16.pdf.

8. Ewens (2018).

9. *Economist* (2019). Global House-Price Index. June 27. www.economist.com/graphic -detail/2019/06/27/global-house-price-index?date=1975-03&index=real_price& places=IRL&places=USA.

10. Madrigal, A. (2019). Why Housing Policy Feels like Generational Warfare. *Atlantic.* June 13. www.theatlantic.com/technology/archive/2019/06/why-millennials-cant-afford -buy-house/591532/.

11. Intergenerational Commission (2018). *A New Generational Contract: The Final Report of the Intergenerational Commission.* Resolution Foundation. May 8. London. www .resolutionfoundation.org/advanced/a-new-generational-contract/.

12. Collinson, P. (2015). The Other Generation Rent: Meet the People Flatsharing in Their 40s. *Guardian.* September 25. www.theguardian.com/money/2015/sep/25 /flatsharing-40s-housing-crisis-lack-homes-renting-london.

13. Kelly, J. (2015). Peep Show and the Stigma of Flat-Sharing in Your 40s. *BBC News Magazine.* November 11. www.bbc.co.uk/news/magazine-34775063.

14. Phillips, M. (2014). Most Germans Don't Buy Their Homes, They Rent: Here's Why. *Quartz.* January 23. https://qz.com/167887/germany-has-one-of-the-worlds-lowest -homeownership-rates/.

15. *Zeit Online* (2019). Weniger junge Leute wohnen in den eigenen vier Wänden. August 9. www.zeit.de/news/2019-08/09/weniger-junge-leute-wohnen-in-den-eigenen-vier -waenden.

16. Kotlikoff, L. J., and S. Burns (2012). *The Clash of Generations: Saving Ourselves, Our Kids, and Our Economy.* Cambridge, MA, MIT Press.

17. Sternberg, J. C. (2019). *The Theft of a Decade: How the Baby Boomers Stole the Millennials' Economic Future.* New York, Public Affairs.

18. Loxton, R. (2019). Housing in Germany: Why Are Fewer Young People Buying Their Own Homes? *Local.* August 9. www.thelocal.de/20190809/housing-in-germany -why-are-fewer-young-people-buying-their-own-homes.

19. Choi, J. H., L. Goodman, B. Ganesh, S. Strochak, and J. Zhu (2018). Millennial Homeownership: Why Is It So Low, and How Can We Increase It? Urban Institute. July 11. www.urban.org/research/publication/millennial-homeownership.

20. Choi et al. (2018).

21. Choi et al. (2018).

22. White, G. B. (2015). Millennials Who Are Thriving Financially Have One Thing in Common . . . Rich Parents. *Atlantic.* July 15. www.theatlantic.com/business/archive /2015/07/millennials-with-rich-parents/398501/.

23. White (2015).

24. Before the pandemic, the Resolution Foundation attempted to predict whether Millennials in the UK will catch up with the home ownership rates of previous generations, applying the best- and worst-case conditions for home ownership from recent history. In the think tank's most optimistic scenario, Millennials may end up just a few percentage points behind. But in the pessimistic scenario, barely half of Millennials will be homeowners by the

time they're forty-five years old, twenty percentage points behind Baby Boomers. Corlett, A., and L. Judge (2017). *Home Affront: Housing Across the Generations*. Resolution Foundation and the Intergenerational Commission. September. www.resolutionfoundation.org/app /uploads/2017/09/Home-Affront.pdf.

25. Morris, A. (2016). *The Australian Dream: Housing Experiences of Older Australians*. Clayton, VIC, Csiro. www.publish.csiro.au/book/7269/.

26. Baum, S., and M. Wulff (2003). *Housing Aspirations of Australian Households*. Australian Housing and Urban Research Institute, Queensland Research Centre. https:// pdfs.semanticscholar.org/eff1/e6c82d6ba380e3611e182741b2ace71b405c.pdf.

27. Kotlikoff and Burns (2012).

28. Kotkin, J. (2019). The End of Aspiration. *Quillette*. April 10. https://quillette .com/2019/04/10/the-end-of-aspiration/.

29. Corlett and Judge (2017).

30. Arnold, M. (2020). Surge in European House Prices Stokes Concerns over Market Resilience. *Financial Times*. November 5. www.ft.com/content/2606dd0d -d009-4fc6-8801-2a089d76bdc5.

31. Marsh, S. (2016). The Boomerang Generation—and the Childhood Bedrooms They Still Inhabit. *Guardian*. March 14. www.theguardian.com/world/commentisfree/2016 /mar/14/the-boomerang-generation-and-the-childhood-bedrooms-they-still-inhabit.

32. Duffy, B. (2018). *The Perils of Perception: Why We're Wrong About Nearly Everything*. London, Atlantic Books.

33. Stein, J. (2013). Millennials: The Me Me Me Generation. *Time*. https://time.com/247 /millennials-the-me-me-me-generation/.

34. Barroso, A., K. Parker, and R. Fry. (2019). Majority of Americans Say Parents Are Doing Too Much for Their Young Adult Children. Pew Research Center. www .pewsocialtrends.org/2019/10/23/majority-of-americans-say-parents-are-doing-too-much -for-their-young-adult-children/.

35. Collinson, P. (2019). Record Numbers of Young Adults in UK Living with Parents. *Guardian*. November 15. www.theguardian.com/uk-news/2019/nov/15 /record-numbers-of-young-adults-in-uk-living-with-parents.

36. Office for National Statistics (2016). Why Are More Young People Living with Their Parents? February 22. www.ons.gov.uk/peoplepopulationandcommunity /birthsdeathsandmarriages/families/articles/whyaremoreyoungpeoplelivingwith theirparents/2016-02-22.

37. Arnett, J. J. (2000). Emerging Adulthood: A Theory of Development from the Late Teens Through the Twenties. *American Psychologist* 55(5): 469-480. www.jeffreyarnett.com /articles/ARNETT_Emerging_Adulthood_theory.pdf.

38. Côté, J. (2000). *Arrested Adulthood: The Changing Nature of Identity-Maturity in the Late-Modern World*. New York, New York University Press.

39. Dey, J. G., and C. R. Pierret (2014). Independence for Young Millennials: Moving Out and Boomeranging Back. *Monthly Labor Review* 137(1). www.jstor.org/stable /monthlylaborrev.2014.12.004.

40. Aspen Institute (2019). The Perils of Age Segregation. April 17. www.aspenideas.org /articles/the-perils-of-age-segregation; Freedman, M., and T. Stamp (2018). The U.S. Isn't Just Getting Older: It's Getting More Segregated by Age. *Harvard Business Review*. June 6. https://hbr.org/2018/06/the-u-s-isnt-just-getting-older-its-getting-more-segregated-by-age.

41. Neyfakh, L. (2014). What "Age Segregation" Does to America. *Boston Globe*. August 31. www.bostonglobe.com/ideas/2014/08/30/what-age-segregation-does-america/o568E8xoAQ7VG6F4grjLxH/story.html.

42. Freedman, M. (2018). *How to Live Forever: The Enduring Power of Connecting the Generations*. New York, Public Affairs.

43. Freedman (2018).

44. McCurdy, C. (2019). *Ageing, Fast and Slow: When Place and Demography Collide*. Resolution Foundation. October 28. www.resolutionfoundation.org/publications/ageing-fast-and-slow/.

45. Warren, I. (2017). The Unequal Distribution of an Aging Population. Centre for Towns. November 20. www.centrefortowns.org/blog/16-the-unequal-distribution-of-an-aging-population.

46. McCurdy (2019).

47. Allport, G. W., K. Clark, and T. Pettigrew (1954). *The Nature of Prejudice*. Reading, MA, Addison-Wesley.

48. Neyfakh (2014).

49. Generations United (2018). *All in Together: Creating Places Where Young and Old Thrive*. Eisner Foundation. www.gu.org/app/uploads/2018/06/SignatureReport-Eisner-All-In-Together.pdf.

50. Tversky, A., and D. Kahneman (1973). Availability: A Heuristic for Judging Frequency and Probability. *Cognitive Psychology* 5(2): 207–232. https://doi.org/10.1016/0010-0285(73)90033-9.

51. *Wikipedia* (n.d.). Hindsight Bias. https://en.wikipedia.org/wiki/Hindsight_bias#Examples.

52. Milligan, B. (2013). Home Ownership: Did Earlier Generations Have It Easier? BBC News. November 29. www.bbc.co.uk/news/business-24660825.

53. TIC Finance (n.d.). How Many Repossessions in UK Year on Year? UK Repossession Statistics, 1969–2019. www.ticfinance.co.uk/stats/.

## CHAPTER 3: REACHING HIGHER, FALLING FLAT

1. Gellman, L. (2016). Helping Bosses Decode Millennials—for $20,000 an Hour. *Wall Street Journal*. May 18. www.wsj.com/articles/helping-bosses-decode-millennialsfor-20-000-an-hour-1463505666.

2. Nolan, H. (2015). Target's Dumb Internal Guide to Millennials (and Other Generations). *Gawker*. January 9. https://gawker.com/targets-dumb-internal-guide-to-millennials-and-other-g-1678496059.

3. Shrimpton, H., G. Skinner, and S. Hall (2017). *The Millennial Bug: Public Attitudes on the Living Standards of Different Generations*. Resolution Foundation and Intergenerational Commission. September. www.resolutionfoundation.org/app/uploads/2017/09/The-Millennial-Bug.pdf.

4. OECD (2016). *Education in China: A Snapshot*. Paris. www.oecd.org/china/Education-in-China-a-snapshot.pdf.

5. Stapleton, K. (2017). Inside the World's Largest Education Boom. *Conversation*. April 10. https://theconversation.com/inside-the-worlds-largest-higher-education-boom-74789.

6. Tomlinson, D., and F. Rahman (2018). *Cross Countries: International Comparisons of Intergenerational Trends*. Resolution Foundation. February 19. www.resolutionfoundation

.org/publications/cross-countries-international-comparisons-of-intergenerational -trends/.

7. Arminio, J., T. K. Grabosky, and J. Lang (2014). *Student Veterans and Service Members in Higher Education*. New York, Routledge.

8. OECD (2019). Health at a Glance 2019: OECD Indicators. Paris. www.oecd-ilibrary .org/sites/6303de6b-en/index.html?itemId=/content/component/6303de6b-en.

9. Rothman, L. (2016). Putting the Rising Cost of College in Perspective. *Time*. August 31. https://time.com/4472261/college-cost-history/.

10. Choi, J. H., L. Goodman, B. Ganesh, S. Strochak, and J. Zhu (2018). Millennial Homeownership: Why Is It So Low, and How Can We Increase It? Urban Institute. July 11. www.urban.org/research/publication/millennial-homeownership; Friedman, Z. (2019). Student Loan Debt Statistics in 2019: A $1.5 Trillion Crisis. *Forbes*. February 25. www.forbes .com/sites/zackfriedman/2019/02/25/student-loan-debt-statistics-2019/#6cac7908133f.

11. Britton, J., L. Dearden, L. van der Erve, and B. Waltmann (2020). *The Impact of Undergraduate Degrees on Lifetime Earnings*. Institute for Financial Studies. February 29. www .ifs.org.uk/publications/14729.

12. Abel, J. R., and R. Deitz (2019). Despite Rising Costs, College Is Still a Good Investment. Federal Reserve Bank of New York. June 9. https://libertystreeteconomics.new yorkfed.org/2019/06/despite-rising-costs-college-is-still-a-good-investment.html.

13. Ma, J., M. Pender, and M. Welch (2019). *Education Pays 2019: The Benefits of Higher Education for Individuals and Society*. Trends in Higher Education Series. College Board. https://research.collegeboard.org/pdf/education-pays-2019-full-report.pdf; Universities New Zealand (2018). Key Facts and Stats. www.universitiesnz.ac.nz/sites/default/files /uni-nz/NZ-Universities-Key-Facts-and-Stats-Sept-2016_0.pdf.

14. Belfield, C., J. Britton, F. Buscha, L. Dearden, M. Dickson, L. van der Erve, L. Sibieta, A. Vignoles, I. Walker, and Y. Zhu (2018). *The Impact of Undergraduate Degrees on Early-Career Earnings*. Institute for Financial Studies. www.ifs.org.uk/uploads/publications /comms/DFE_returnsHE.pdf.

15. Britton et al. (2020).

16. Pascarella, E. T., and P. T. Terenzini (2005). *How College Affects Students: A Third Decade of Research*. Volume 2. Hoboken, NJ, John Wiley & Sons.

17. Goodhart, D. (2020). *Head, Hand, Heart: Why Intelligence Is Over-rewarded, Manual Workers Matter, and Caregivers Deserve More Respect*. New York, Free Press.

18. Ortiz-Ospina, E., S. Tzvetkova, and M. Roser (2018). Women's Employment. Our World in Data. https://ourworldindata.org/female-labor-supply.

19. Intergenerational Commission (2018). *A New Generational Contract: The Final Report of the Intergenerational Commission*. London. Resolution Foundation. www.resolution foundation.org/advanced/a-new-generational-contract/.

20. Scott, A. (2019). The "Silver Tsunami" Is the Workforce the World Needs Right Now. *Quartz*. May 1. https://qz.com/work/1605206/senior-workers-are-the-key-to -economic-growth/.

21. Kochhar, R. (2020). Hispanic Women, Immigrants, Young Adults, Those with Less Education Hit Hardest by COVID-19 Job Losses. Pew Research Center. June 9. www .pewresearch.org/fact-tank/2020/06/09/hispanic-women-immigrants-young-adults-those -with-less-education-hit-hardest-by-covid-19-job-losses/.

22. Rahman and Tomlinson (2018).

23. Rounds, D. (2017). Millennials and the Death of Loyalty. *Forbes*. April 4. www .forbes.com/sites/forbescoachescouncil/2017/04/04/millennials-and-the-death-of -loyalty/#1f0073526745.

24. Brech, A. (2019). Millennials Work Far Fewer Hours Than Our Parents— So Why Are We Much More Stressed? *Stylist*. www.stylist.co.uk/life/millennials -less-hours-more-stressed-parents-study/267863.

25. Duffy, B., H. Shrimpton, and M. Clemence (2017). *Millennial Myths and Realities*. Ipsos MORI. July 15. www.ipsos.com/ipsos-mori/en-uk/millennial-myths-and-realities.

26. Gratton, L., and A. J. Scott (2016). *The 100-Year Life: Living and Working in an Age of Longevity*. London, Bloomsbury.

27. Duffy, Shrimpton, and Clemence (2017).

28. Susskind, D. (2020). *A World Without Work*. London, Allen Lane.

29. Susskind (2020).

30. Pfau, B. N. (2016). What Do Millennials Really Want at Work? The Same Things the Rest of Us Do. *Harvard Business Review*. April 7. https://hbr.org/2016/04/what -do-millennials-really-want-at-work.

31. Seemiller, C., and G. Grace (2018). *Generation Z: A Century in the Making*. London, Routledge.

32. Seemiller and Grace (2018).

33. Montes, J. (2017). *Millennial Workforce: Cracking the Code to Generation Y in Your Company*. Self-published, Lulu.

34. Stillman, D., and J. Stillman (2017). *Gen Z Work: How the Next Generation Is Transforming the Workplace*. New York, Harper Collins.

35. Montes (2017).

36. Microsoft Canada Consumer Insights Team (2015). Attention Spans. https://docs .google.com/viewerng/viewer?url=https://prc.olio.co.za/wp-content/uploads/2016/11 /2015-Attention-Spans-Report-Microsoft.pdf&hl=en.

37. MacLeod, J. W., M. A. Lawrence, M. M. McConnell, G. A. Eskes, R. M. Klein, and D. I. Shore (2010). Appraising the ANT: Psychometric and Theoretical Considerations of the Attention Network Test. *Neuropsychology* 24(5), 637–651. www.ncbi.nlm.nih.gov /pubmed/20804252.

38. Costanza, D. P., and L. M. Finkelstein (2015). Generationally Based Differences in the Workplace: Is There a There There? *Industrial and Organizational Psychology* 8(3), 308–323. https://doi.org/10.1017/iop.2015.15.

39. Costanza, D. P., J. M. Badger, R. L. Fraser, J. B. Severt, and P. A. Gade (2012). Generational Differences in Work-Related Attitudes: A Meta-analysis. *Journal of Business and Psychology* 27(4), 375–394. www.jstor.org/stable/41682990?seq=1#page_scan_tab _contents.

## CHAPTER 4: HAPPY NOW

1. Bryce, E. (2019). The Flawed Era of GDP Is Finally Coming to an End. *Wired*. August 3. www.wired.co.uk/article/countries-gdp-gross-national-happiness.

2. McMahon, D. M. (2017). For Most of History, People Didn't Assume They Deserved to Be Happy. What Changed? *Quartz*. April 18. https://qz.com/958677/happiness-a -history-author-darrin-m-mcmahon-explains-when-the-idea-of-happiness-was-invented/.

3. Stearns, P. N. (2012). The History of Happiness. *Harvard Business Review.* January/February. https://hbr.org/2012/01/the-history-of-happiness.

4. Stearns (2012).

5. Brickman, P., and D. T. Campbell (1971). Hedonic Relativism and Planning the Good Society. In *Adaptation Level Theory.* Ed. M. H. Appley. New York, Academic Press. 287–301.

6. Blanchflower, D. G., and A. J. Oswald (2019). Do Humans Suffer a Psychological Low in Midlife? Two Approaches (with and Without Controls) in Seven Data Sets. NBER Working Paper Series. August. www.nber.org/papers/w23724.pdf.

7. Blanchflower, D. G. (2021). Is Happiness U-Shaped Everywhere? Age and Subjective Well-Being in 145 Countries. *Journal of Population Economics* 34, 575–624. https://link.springer.com/article/10.1007/s00148-020-00797-z.

8. Jordan, J. (2018). Dylan Moran: "Britain Is Sending Itself to Its Room and Not Coming Down." *Guardian.* July 13. www.theguardian.com/books/2018/jul/13/dylan-moran-dr-cosmos-britain-brexit.

9. Rauch, J. (2014). The Real Roots of Midlife Crisis. *Atlantic.* December. www.theatlantic.com/magazine/archive/2014/12/the-real-roots-of-midlife-crisis/382235/.

10. Wunder, C., A. Wiencierz, J. Schwarze, and H. Küchenhoff (2013). Well-Being over the Life Span: Semiparametric Evidence from British and German Longitudinal Data. *Review of Economics and Statistics* 95(1), 154–167. https://papers.ssrn.com/sol3/papers.cfm?abstract_id=1403203.

11. López Ulloa, B. F., V. Møller, and A. Sousa-Poza (2013). How Does Subjective Well-Being Evolve with Age? A Literature Review. *Population Ageing* 6, 227–246. https://doi.org/10.1007/s12062-013-9085-0.

12. Easterlin, R. A. (2006). Lifecycle Happiness and Its Sources: Intersections of Psychology, Economics, and Demography. *Journal of Economic Psychology* 27(4), 463–482.

13. Judd, B. (2020). "Middle Age Misery" Peaks at 47.2 Years of Age—but Do the Statistics Ring True? ABC News. January 14. www.abc.net.au/news/2020-01-15/middle-age-misery-peaks-at-47.2-midlife-crisis/11866110.

14. Blanchflower, D. G., and A. J. Oswald (2008). Is Well-Being U-Shaped over the Life Cycle? *Social Science & Medicine* 66(8), 1733–1749. www.sciencedirect.com/science/article/abs/pii/S0277953608000245.

15. Clark, A. E. (2019). Born to Be Mild? Cohort Effects Don't (Fully) Explain Why Well-Being Is U-Shaped in Age. IZA discussion paper no. 3170. www.econstor.eu/bitstream/10419/34422/1/551074736.pdf.

16. Blanchflower, D. G., and A. J. Oswald (2017). Do Humans Suffer a Psychological Low in Midlife? Two Approaches (with and Without Controls) in Seven Data Sets. IZA Discussion Paper No. 10958. August 31. National Bureau of Economic Research (NBER). https://papers.ssrn.com/sol3/papers.cfm?abstract_id=3029829.

17. Vassilev, G., and M. Hamilton (2020). Personal and Economic Well-Being in Great Britain: May 2020. www.ons.gov.uk/peoplepopulationandcommunity/wellbeing/bulletins/personalandeconomicwellbeingintheuk/may2020#understanding-the-impact-on-personal-and-economic-well-being.

18. Jan-Emmanuel De Neve, M. N. (2014). Busts Hurt More Than Booms Help: New Lessons for Growth Policy from Global Wellbeing Surveys. *Vox EU CEPR.* October 8. https://voxeu.org/article/wellbeing-research-recessions-hurt-more-booms-help.

19. Kahneman, D., and A. Tversky (1979). Prospect Theory: An Analysis of Decision Under Risk. *Econometrica* 47(2), 263–292. www.jstor.org/stable/1914185?origin=crossref& seq=1.

20. Yechiam, E. (2015). The Psychology of Gains and Losses: More Complicated Than Previously Thought. American Psychology Association. January. www.apa.org/science /about/psa/2015/01/gains-losses.

21. Greene, L. (2016). Are Millennials Really the Most Mentally Ill Generation? *Moods Magazine*. June 1. www.moodsmag.com/blog/millennials-really-mentally -ill-generation/; Soeiro, L. (2019). Why Are Millennials So Anxious and Unhappy? *Psychology Today*. July 24. www.psychologytoday.com/gb/blog/i-hear-you/201907 /why-are-millennials-so-anxious-and-unhappy.

22. Thorley, C. (2017). *Not by Degrees: Improving Student Mental Health in the UK's Universities*. London, Institute for Public Policy Research. www.ippr.org/files /2017-09/1504645674_not-by-degrees-170905.pdf.

23. Twenge, J. M., A. B. Cooper, T. E. Joiner, M. E. Duffy, and S. G. Binau (2019). Age, Period, and Cohort Trends in Mood Disorder Indicators and Suicide-Related Outcomes in a Nationally Representative Dataset, 2005–2017. *Journal of Abnormal Psychology* 128(3), 185. www.apa.org/pubs/journals/releases/abn-abn0000410.pdf.

24. Twenge, J. (2017). *iGen: Why Today's Super-Connected Kids Are Growing Up Less Rebellious, More Tolerant, Less Happy—and Completely Unprepared for Adulthood—and What That Means for the Rest of Us*. New York, Atria Books.

25. James, D., J. Yates, and E. Ferguson (2013). Can the 12-Item General Health Questionnaire Be Used to Identify Medical Students Who Might "Struggle" on the Medical Course? A Prospective Study on Two Cohorts. *BMC Medical Education* 13(1), 48. www .ncbi.nlm.nih.gov/pmc/articles/PMC3616988/.

26. Mental Health of Children and Young People Surveys (2018). Mental Health of Children and Young People in England, 2017. https://digital.nhs.uk/data-and -information/publications/statistical/mental-health-of-children-and-young-people-in -england/2017/2017.

27. McManus, S., and E. Fuller (2009). Adult Psychiatric Morbidity in England: Survey of Mental Health and Wellbeing. NatCen. http://natcen.ac.uk/our-research/research /adult-psychiatric-morbidity-survey/.

28. Twenge (2017).

29. World Health Organization (2018). *Adolescent Mental Health in the European Region*. Copenhagen. www.euro.who.int/__data/assets/pdf_file/0005/383891/adolescent -mh-fs-eng.pdf?ua=1.

30. Li, L. Z., and S. Wang (2020). Prevalence and Predictors of General Psychiatric Disorders and Loneliness During COVID-19 in the United Kingdom: Results from the Understanding Society UKHLS. medRxiv. www.medrxiv.org/content/10.1101/2020.06.09 .20120139v1.

31. Sample, I. (2020). Covid Poses "Greatest Threat to Mental Health Since Second World War." *Guardian*. December 27. www.theguardian.com/society/2020/dec/27 /covid-poses-greatest-threat-to-mental-health-since-second-world-war.

32. Gayer, C., R. L. Anderson, C. El Zerbi, L. Strang, V. M. Hall, G. Knowles, S. Marlow, M. Avendano, N. Manning, and J. Das-Munshi (2020). *Impacts of Social Isolation Among Disadvantaged and Vulnerable Groups During Public Health Crises*. Economic and Social Research

Council. June. https://esrc.ukri.org/files/news-events-and-publications/evidence-briefings /impacts-of-social-isolation-among-disadvantaged-and-vulnerable-groups-during-public -health-crises/; Mental Health Foundation (2021). Coronavirus: The Divergence of Mental Health Experiences During the Pandemic. www.mentalhealth.org.uk/coronavirus /divergence-mental-health-experiences-during-pandemic.

33. Rawlinson, K. (2018). Social Media Firms Must Share Child Mental Health Costs. *Guardian.* June 14. www.theguardian.com/society/2018/jun/14/nhs-child-mental -health-costs-social-media-firms-must-share.

34. Duffy, B., H. Shrimpton, and M. Clemence (2017). *Millennial Myths and Realities.* Ipsos MORI. July 15. www.ipsos.com/ipsos-mori/en-uk/millennial-myths-and-realities.

35. Kelly, Y., A. Zilanawala, C. Booker, and A. Sacker (2018). Social Media Use and Adolescent Mental Health: Findings from the UK Millennium Cohort Study. *EClinical Medicine* 6, 59–68. www.thelancet.com/action/showPdf?pii=S2589-5370%2818%2930060-9.

36. Orben, A., and A. K. Przybylski (2019). The Association Between Adolescent Well-Being and Digital Technology Use. *Nature Human Behaviour* 3(2), 173–182. www .gwern.net/docs/psychology/2019-orben.pdf.

37. Orben, A., T. Dienlin, and A. K. Przybylski (2019). Social Media's Enduring Effect on Adolescent Life Satisfaction. *Proceedings of the National Academy of Sciences* 116(21), 10226–10228. www.pnas.org/content/116/21/10226. Although this paper looked at technology use in general, similar papers by the same authors found the same lack of relationship with social media use specifically.

38. Viner, R. M., A. Gireesh, N. Stiglic, L. D. Hudson, A.-L. Goddings, J. L. Ward, and D. E. Nicholls (2019). Roles of Cyberbullying, Sleep, and Physical Activity in Mediating the Effects of Social Media Use on Mental Health and Wellbeing Among Young People in England: A Secondary Analysis of Longitudinal Data. *Lancet Child & Adolescent Health* 3(10), 685–696. www.thelancet.com/journals/lanchi/article/PIIS2352-4642(19)30186-5 /fulltext.

39. Department for Education (2019). *State of the Nation 2019: Children and Young People's Wellbeing.* https://assets.publishing.service.gov.uk/government/uploads/system /uploads/attachment_data/file/838022/State_of_the_Nation_2019_young_people _children_wellbeing.pdf.

40. Markey, P. M., and C. J. Ferguson (2017). Teaching Us to Fear: The Violent Video Game Moral Panic and the Politics of Game Research. *American Journal of Play* 10(1), 99– 115. https://files.eric.ed.gov/fulltext/EJ1166785.pdf.

41. Markey and Ferguson (2017).

42. Howe, N. (2019). Millennials and the Loneliness Epidemic. *Forbes.* May 3. www.forbes .com/sites/neilhowe/2019/05/03/millennials-and-the-loneliness-epidemic/#e5951b57676a; CBC Radio (2016). Loneliness in Canadian Seniors an Epidemic, Says Psychologist. September 20. www.cbc.ca/radio/thecurrent/the-current-for-september-20-2016-1.3770103 /loneliness-in-canadian-seniors-an-epidemic-says-psychologist-1.3770208.

43. Hawkley, L. C., K. Wroblewski, T. Kaiser, M. Luhmann, and L. P. Schumm (2019). Are US Older Adults Getting Lonelier? Age, Period, and Cohort Differences. *Psychology and Aging* 34(8), 1144. www.ncbi.nlm.nih.gov/pubmed/31804118.

44. Nyqvist, F., M. Cattan, M. Conradsson, M. Näsman, and Y. Gustafsson (2017). Prevalence of Loneliness over Ten Years Among the Oldest Old. *Scandinavian Journal of Public Health* 45(4), 411–418.

45. Hawkley et al. (2019).

46. Clark, D. M. T., N. J. Loxton, and S. J. Tobin (2015). Declining Loneliness over Time: Evidence from American Colleges and High Schools. *Personality and Social Psychology Bulletin* 41(1), 78–89. https://journals.sagepub.com/doi/abs/10.1177/0146167214557007?journalCode=pspc.

47. DiJulio, B., L. Hamel, C. Muñana, and M. Brodie (2018). Loneliness and Social Isolation in the United States, the United Kingdom, and Japan: An International Survey. *Economist* and Kaiser Family Foundation. http://files.kff.org/attachment/Report-Loneliness-and-Social-Isolation-in-the-United-States-the-United-Kingdom-and-Japan-An-International-Survey.

48. Klinenberg, E. (2013). *Going Solo: The Extraordinary Rise and Surprising Appeal of Living Alone*. New York, Penguin.

49. Dubner, S. J. (2020). Is There Really a "Loneliness Epidemic"? *Freakonomics*. Ep. 407. Podcast. February 26. https://freakonomics.com/podcast/loneliness/.

50. Lepore, J. (2020). The History of Loneliness. *New Yorker*. April 6. www.newyorker.com/magazine/2020/04/06/the-history-of-loneliness.

51. Scheimer, D., and M. Chakrabarti (2020). Former Surgeon General Vivek Murthy: Loneliness Is a Public Health Crisis. *On Point*. March 23. www.wbur.org/onpoint/2020/03/23/vivek-murthy-loneliness.

52. Holt-Lunstad, J., T. B. Smith, and J. B. Layton (2010). Social Relationships and Mortality Risk: A Meta-analytic Review. *PLoS medicine* 7(7), e1000316. https://doi.org/10.1371/journal.pmed.1000316.

53. Chivers, T. (2019). Is the "Epidemic of Loneliness" Fake News? *UnHerd*. May 8. https://unherd.com/2019/05/is-the-epidemic-of-loneliness-fake-news/.

54. Chivers, T. (2019). Do We Really Have a "Suicidal Generation"? *UnHerd*. February 4. https://unherd.com/2019/02/do-we-really-have-a-suicidal-generation/.

55. Office for National Statistics (2018). Suicides in the UK: 2018 Registrations. www.ons.gov.uk/peoplepopulationandcommunity/birthsdeathsandmarriages/deaths/bulletins/suicidesintheunitedkingdom/2018registrations. When the ONS looks at trends, it groups the data in wider age ranges, because of the volatility of such rare events, to avoid precisely the overinterpretation you so often see in the media.

56. Office for National Statistics (2019). Middle-Aged Generation Most Likely to Die by Suicide and Drug Poisoning. August 13. www.ons.gov.uk/peoplepopulationandcommunity/healthandsocialcare/healthandwellbeing/articles/middleagedgenerationmostlikelytodiebysuicideanddrugpoisoning/2019-08-13.

57. Office for National Statistics (2019).

58. Dougall, N., C. Stark, T. Agnew, R. Henderson, M. Maxwell, and P. Lambert (2017). An Analysis of Suicide Trends in Scotland 1950–2014: Comparison with England & Wales. *BMC Public Health* 17(1), 970. www.ncbi.nlm.nih.gov/pmc/articles/PMC5738808/.

59. BBC News (2019). Deaths by Suicide and Drugs Highest Among Generation X. August 13. www.bbc.co.uk/news/health-49329595.

60. John, E., and A. Butt (2020). Deaths Related to Drug Poisoning by Selected Substances. Office for National Statistics. October 14. www.ons.gov.uk/peoplepopulationandcommunity/birthsdeathsandmarriages/deaths/datasets/deathsrelatedtodrugpoisoningbyselectedsubstances.

61. Case, A., and A. Deaton (2020). *Deaths of Despair and the Future of Capitalism*. Princeton, NJ, Princeton University Press.

62. *Psychology Wiki* (n.d.). Clustering Illusion. https://psychology.wikia.org/wiki /Clustering_illusion.

63. *Wikipedia* (n.d.). Correlation Does Not Imply Causation. https://en.wikipedia.org /wiki/Correlation_does_not_imply_causation.

64. O'Boyle, C. G. (2014). *History of Psychology: A Cultural Perspective*. London, Psychology Press.

## CHAPTER 5: A HEALTHY FUTURE?

1. Case, A., and A. Deaton (2020). *Deaths of Despair and the Future of Capitalism*. Princeton, NJ, Princeton University Press.

2. Case and Deaton (2020).

3. Roser, M. (2020). The Spanish Flu (1918–20): The Global Impact of the Largest Influenza Pandemic in History. Our World in Data. March 4. https://ourworldindata .org/spanish-flu-largest-influenza-pandemic-in-history.

4. Morens, D. M., J. K. Taubenberger, and A. S. Fauci (2008). Predominant Role of Bacterial Pneumonia as a Cause of Death in Pandemic Influenza: Implications for Pandemic Influenza Preparedness. *Journal of Infectious Diseases* 198(7), 962–970. www.ncbi.nlm.nih .gov/pmc/articles/PMC2599911/.

5. Roser (2020).

6. Jha, P. (2009). Avoidable Global Cancer Deaths and Total Deaths from Smoking. *Nature Reviews Cancer* 9(9), 655–664. www.nature.com/articles/nrc2703.

7. Centers for Disease Control and Prevention (2016). Current Cigarette Smoking Among Adults in the United States. Smoking & Tobacco Use. www.cdc.gov/tobacco/data_statistics /fact_sheets/adult_data/cig_smoking/.

8. NHS (2019). Around 1.8m Fewer Adult Smokers in England in 2018 Compared with Seven Years Ago. https://digital.nhs.uk/news-and-events/around-1.8m-fewer-adult -smokers-in-england-in-2018-compared-with-seven-years-ago; NHS (2016). Statistics on Smoking, England. https://digital.nhs.uk/data-and-information/publications/statistical /statistics-on-smoking/statistics-on-smoking-england-2016.

9. Centers for Disease Control and Prevention (2016).

10. *The Tobacco Atlas* (2020). Consumption. https://tobaccoatlas.org/topic /consumption/.

11. Saad, L. (2008). U.S. Smoking Rate Still Coming Down. Gallup. July 24. https:// news.gallup.com/poll/109048/us-smoking-rate-still-coming-down.aspx.

12. Schaeffer, K. (2019). Before Recent Outbreak, Vaping Was on the Rise in U.S., Especially Among Young People. September 26. Pew Research Center. www .pewresearch.org/fact-tank/2019/09/26/vaping-survey-data-roundup/.

13. Public Health England (2015). E-cigarettes Around 95% Less Harmful Than Tobacco Estimates Landmark Review. Press release. August 19. www.gov.uk/government /news/e-cigarettes-around-95-less-harmful-than-tobacco-estimates-landmark-review.

14. Harris, R., and C. Wroth (2019). FDA to Banish Flavored E-cigarettes to Combat Youth Vaping. NPR. September 11. www.npr.org/sections/health -shots/2019/09/11/759851853/fda-to-banish-flavored-e-cigarettes-to-combat-youth-vaping? t=1588112377545&t=1588799163720.

15. Nilsen, E. (2019). The FDA Has Officially Raised the Age to Buy Tobacco Products to 21. *Vox*. December 27. www.vox.com/2019/12/27/21039149/fda-officially-raised -age-to-buy-tobacco-from-18-to-21.

16. Belluz, J. (2016). Cigarette Packs Are Being Stripped of Advertising Around the World: But Not in the US. *Vox*. June 2. www.vox.com/2016/6/2/11818692/plain-packaging-policy-us-australia.

17. Duffy, B., H. Shrimpton, and M. Clemence (2017). *Millennial Myths and Realities*. Ipsos MORI. July 15. www.ipsos.com/ipsos-mori/en-uk/millennial-myths-and-realities.

18. Borrud, G. (2011). German Teenagers Are Drinking Less Alcohol, but More Irresponsibly. *DW*. February 4. www.dw.com/en/german-teenagers-are-drinking-less-alcohol-but-more-irresponsibly/a-14818251; Livingston, M., J. Raninen, T. Slade, W. Swift, B. Lloyd, and P. Dietze (2016). Understanding Trends in Australian Alcohol Consumption—an Age–Period–Cohort Model. *Addiction* 111(9), 1590–1598. https://onlinelibrary.wiley.com/doi/epdf/10.1111/add.13396.

19. Bhattacharya, A. (2016). *Youthful Abandon: Why Are Young People Drinking Less?* Institute of Alcohol Studies. July. www.ias.org.uk/uploads/pdf/IAS%20reports/rp22072016.pdf.

20. World Health Organization (2018). *Global Status Report on Alcohol and Health 2018*. September 27. www.who.int/publications/i/item/9789241565639.

21. Johnston, L. D., R. A. Miech, P. M. O'Malley, J. E. Bachman, and M. E. Patrick (2020). *Monitoring the Future National: Survey Results on Drug Use, 1975–2019; Overview, Key Findings on Adolescent Drug Use*. Ann Arbor, Institute for Social Research, University of Michigan. www.monitoringthefuture.org/pubs/monographs/mtf-overview2019.pdf.

22. Smith, R. A. (2020). The Effects of Medical Marijuana Dispensaries on Adverse Opioid Outcomes. *Economic Inquiry* 58(2), 569–588. https://onlinelibrary.wiley.com/doi/pdf/10.1111/ecin.12825; Grinspoon, P. (2019). Access to Medical Marijuana Reduces Opioid. Harvard Health Blog. May 9. www.health.harvard.edu/blog/access-to-medical-marijuana-reduces-opioid-prescriptions-2018050914509.

23. Duffy, B. (2020). How Britain Became Socially Liberal. Policy Institute, King's College London. www.kcl.ac.uk/policy-institute/research-analysis/moral-attitudes.

24. Johnston et al. (2020).

25. Ball, J. (2020). Teen Use of Cannabis Has Dropped in New Zealand, but Legalisation Could Make Access Easier. *Conversation*. February 20. https://theconversation.com/teen-use-of-cannabis-has-dropped-in-new-zealand-but-legalisation-could-make-access-easier-132165.

26. Menayang, A. (2017). Millennials Are "the Most Health-Conscious Generation Ever," Says Report by the Halo Group. *Food Navigator*. March 26. www.foodnavigator-usa.com/Article/2017/03/27/Millennials-scrutinize-health-claims-more-than-other-generations#.

27. Goldman Sachs (2020). Millennials Coming of Age. www.goldmansachs.com/our-thinking/pages/millennials/.

28. World Health Organization (2020). Obesity and Overweight. April 1. www.who.int/news-room/fact-sheets/detail/obesity-and-overweight

29. World Health Organization (2020). Commission on Ending Childhood Obesity. www.who.int/end-childhood-obesity/en/.

30. Bann, D., W. Johnson, L. Li, D. Kuh, and R. Hardy (2017). Socioeconomic Inequalities in Body Mass Index Across Adulthood: Coordinated Analyses of Individual Participant Data from Three British Birth Cohort Studies Initiated in 1946, 1958 and 1970. *PLoS Medicine* 14(1), e1002214. doi:10.1371/journal. pmed.1002214.

31. Elgar, F. J., T.-K. Pförtner, I. Moor, B. De Clercq, G. W. Stevens, and C. Currie (2015). Socioeconomic Inequalities in Adolescent Health 2002–2010: A Time-Series Analysis of 34 Countries Participating in the Health Behaviour in School-Aged Children Study. *Lancet* 385(9982), 2088–2095. www.researchgate.net/publication/271207089 _Socioeconomic_inequalities_in_adolescent_health_2002-2010_A_time-series_analysis _of_34_countries_participating_in_the_Health_Behaviour_in_School-aged_Children _study.

32. Johnson, W., L. Li, D. Kuh, and R. Hardy (2015). How Has the Age-Related Process of Overweight or Obesity Development Changed over Time? Co-ordinated Analyses of Individual Participant Data from Five United Kingdom Birth Cohorts. *PLoS Medicine* 12(5), e1001828. www.ncbi.nlm.nih.gov/pmc/articles/PMC4437909/.

33. Murphy, S. L., J. Xu, K. D. Kochanek, and E. Arias (2018). Mortality in the United States, 2017. Centers for Disease Control and Prevention. NCHS date brief. November. www.cdc.gov/nchs/products/databriefs/db328.htm.

34. Office for National Statistics (2020). Life Expectancy at Birth and Selected Older Ages. www.ons.gov.uk/peoplepopulationandcommunity/birthsdeathsandmarriages/deaths /datasets/lifeexpectancyatbirthandselectedolderages.

35. Marmot, M., J. Allen, T. Boyce, P. Goldblatt, and J. Morrison (2020). *Health Equity in England: The Marmot Review 10 Years On.* London, Institute of Health Equity. www .instituteofhealthequity.org/resources-reports/marmot-review-10-years-on/the-marmot -review-10-years-on-full-report.pdf.

36. *Wired* (2016). Barack Obama: Now Is the Greatest Time to Be Alive. October 12. www.wired.com/2016/10/president-obama-guest-edits-wired-essay/.

37. Obama, B. (2016). Remarks by President Obama at Stavros Niarchos Foundation Cultural Center in Athens, Greece. November 16. https://obamawhite house.archives.gov/the-press-office/2016/11/16/remarks-president-obama-stavros -niarchos-foundation-cultural-center.

38. Office for National Statistics (n.d.). Births, Deaths and Marriages. www.ons .gov.uk/peoplepopulationandcommunity/birthsdeathsandmarriages/deaths/bulletins /deathsinvolvingcovid19bylocalareasanddeprivation/deathsoccurringbetween1march and17april.

## CHAPTER 6: THE SEX RECESSION, BABY BUST, AND DEATH OF MARRIAGE

1. Stephens-Davidowitz, S. (2017). *Everybody Lies.* New York, Harper Collins.

2. Cara, E. (2018). The Kids Are Boning Less. Gizmodo. January 5. gizmodo.com /the-kids-are-boning-less-1821823267.

3. Hirschlag, A. (2015). Millennials Are Killing Relationships and We Should Be Concerned. SheKnows. August 6. www.sheknows.com/health-and-wellness/articles/1091871 /millennial-daters-too-casual/.

4. Ramachandran, S. (2019). Let's Watch Netflix: Three Words Guaranteed to Kill a Romantic Mood. *Wall Street Journal.* April 21. www.wsj.com/articles/three-words-guaranteed -to-kill-a-romantic-mood-lets-watch-netflix-11555863428.

5. Original Boggart Blog (2010). Silver Shaggers Risk STDs. October 5. https:// originalboggartblog.wordpress.com/2010/10/05/silver-shaggers-risk-stds-9527525/; Pereto, A. (2018). Patients over 60? Screen for STIs. Athena Health. May 15. www .athenahealth.com/insight/over-60-stis-may-not-be-done-you; UK version: Forster, K.

(2016). More Elderly People Being Diagnosed with STIs Such as Chlamydia and Genital Warts. *Independent*. December 8. www.independent.co.uk/life-style/health-and-families /health-news/older-people-stis-sexually-transmitted-infections-50-to-70-chief-medical -officer-report-dame-sally-a7463861.html.

6. Abgarian, A. (2019). What's the Sexual Taboo That Will Define the Next Generation? *Metro*. May 29. https://metro.co.uk/2019/05/29/sexual-taboo-will-define -next-generation-9689501/.

7. Coontz, S. *The Way We Never Were: American Families and the Nostalgia Trap*. New York, Basic Books (1992).

8. K. Paul (2018). Millennials Are Killing Marriage—Here's Why That's a Good Thing. *MarketWatch*. February 16. www.marketwatch.com/story/millennials-are-killing -marriage-heres-why-thats-a-good-thing-2018-02-08.

9. Fearnow, B. (2018). Study: Millennials Waiting Much Longer to Have Sex, 1-in-8 Virgins at 26. *Newsweek*. May 6. www.newsweek.com/millennial-virginity-sex -intimacy-university-college-london-next-steps-project-912283.

10. Zaba, B., E. Pisani, E. Slaymaker, and J. T. Boerma (2004). Age at First Sex: Understanding Recent Trends in African Demographic Surveys. *Sexually Transmitted Infections* 80(suppl 2), ii28–ii35. https://sti.bmj.com/content/80/suppl_2/ii28.full.

11. Knapton, S. (2015). Couples Who Have Sex Just Once a Week Are Happiest. *Telegraph*. November 18. www.telegraph.co.uk/science/2016/03/12/couples-who-have-sex -just-once-a-week-are-happiest/.

12. Julian, K. (2018). Why Are Young People Having So Little Sex? *Atlantic*. December. www.theatlantic.com/magazine/archive/2018/12/the-sex-recession/573949/.

13. Twenge, J. M., R. A. Sherman, and B. E. Wells (2017). Declines in Sexual Frequency Among American Adults, 1989–2014. *Archives of Sexual Behavior* 46(8), 2389–2401. www .researchgate.net/publication/314273096_Declines_in_Sexual_Frequency_among _American_Adults_1989-2014.

14. Mitchell, K. R., C. H. Mercer, G. B. Ploubidis, K. G. Jones, J. Datta, N. Field, A. J. Copas, C. Tanton, C. Erens, and P. Sonnenberg (2013). Sexual Function in Britain: Findings from the Third National Survey of Sexual Attitudes and Lifestyles (Natsal-3). *Lancet* 382(9907), 1817–1829. www.thelancet.com/journals/lancet/article /PIIS0140-6736(13)62366-1/fulltext.

15. *Local* (2013). "Tired" Swedes Have Less Sex Than Ever: Study. May 24. www.the local.se/20130524/48104; Jackson-Webb, F. (2014). Australians Are Having Sex Less Often Than a Decade Ago. *Conversation*. November 7. https://theconversation.com/australians -are-having-sex-less-often-than-a-decade-ago-33935; Schifter, J. (2018). The End of Sex: The Frequency of Sexual Activity Has Decreased Significantly in the West of the World. *Wall Street International*. January 13. https://wsimag.com/culture/35096-the-end-of-sex; Wellings, K., M. J. Palmer, K. Machiyama, and E. Slaymaker (2019). Changes in, and Factors Associated with, Frequency of Sex in Britain: Evidence from Three National Surveys of Sexual Attitudes and Lifestyles (Natsal). *BMJ* 365. www.bmj.com/content/365/bmj.l1525.

16. Wellings et al. (2019).

17. University of Tokyo (2019). First National Estimates of Virginity Rates in Japan: One in Ten Adults in Their 30s Remains a Virgin, Heterosexual Inexperience Increasing. Press release. April 8. www.u-tokyo.ac.jp/focus/en/press/z0508_00035.html.

18. OECD (2019). *Age of Mothers at Childbirth and Age-Specific Fertility*. OECD Family Database. May 29. www.oecd.org/els/soc/SF_2_3_Age_mothers_childbirth.pdf.

19. Office for National Statistics (2017). Marriage and Divorce on the Rise at 65 and Over. July 18. www.ons.gov.uk/peoplepopulationandcommunity/birthsdeaths andmarriages/marriagecohabitationandcivilpartnerships/articles/marriageanddivorce ontheriseat65andover/2017-07-18.

20. Campbell, M. (2016). Forget Teen Pregnancies: Older Moms are the New Normal. *Maclean's*. August 30. www.macleans.ca/society/health/forget-teen-pregnancies -older-moms-new-normal/.

21. Picchi, A. (2015). Will Childless Millennials Turn America into Japan? CBS News. April 28. www.cbsnews.com/news/will-childless-millennials-turn-america-into-japan/.

22. Roser, M. (2017). Fertility Rate. Our World in Data. December 2. https://our worldindata.org/fertility-rate.

23. BBC News (2019). Birth Rate in England and Wales Hits Record Low. August 1. www.bbc.co.uk/news/health-49192445.

24. BBC News (2018). US Birth Rates Drop to Lowest Since 1987. May 17. www.bbc .co.uk/news/world-us-canada-44151642.

25. Office for National Statistics (2019). National Population Projections, Fertility Assumptions: 2018-Based. October 21. www.ons.gov.uk/peoplepopulationand community/populationandmigration/populationprojections/methodologies/national populationprojectionsfertilityassumptions2018based.

26. Mangan, D. (2015). Baby Bust! Millennials' Birth Rate Drop May Signal Historic Shift. CNBC. April 27. www.cnbc.com/2015/04/27/baby-bust-millenials-birth-rate-drop -may-signal-historic-shift.html.

27. Pew Research Center (2014). Chapter 4. Population Change in the U.S. and the World from 1950 to 2050. www.pewresearch.org/global/2014/01/30/chapter-4 -population-change-in-the-u-s-and-the-world-from-1950-to-2050/#:~:text=The%20old %2Dage%20dependency%20ratio,drop%2Doff%20in%20population%20growth.

28. Bakar, F. (2020). Are We Going to See a Coronavirus Baby Boom? *Metro*. March 31. https://metro.co.uk/2020/03/31/going-see-coronavirus-baby-boom-12484432/.

29. Udry, J. R. (1970). The Effect of the Great Blackout of 1965 on Births in New York City. *Demography* 7(3), 325–327. www.jstor.org/stable/2060151?seq= 2#metadata_info_tab_contents.

30. Kearney, M. S., and P. B. Levine (2020). Half a Million Fewer Children? The Coming COVID Baby Bust. Brookings. www.brookings.edu/research/half -a-million-fewer-children-the-coming-covid-baby-bust/.

31. Vilibert, D. (2009). Jessica Valenti Debunks the Purity Myth. *Marie Clare*. April 22. www.marieclaire.com/sex-love/a2975/jessica-valenti-purity-myth/.

32. Finer, L. B. (2007). Trends in Premarital Sex in the United States, 1954–2003. *Public Health Reports* 122(1), 73–78. www.ncbi.nlm.nih.gov/pmc/articles/PMC180 2108/.

33. Duffy, B. (2020). How Britain Became Socially Liberal. Policy Institute, King's College London. www.kcl.ac.uk/policy-institute/research-analysis/moral-attitudes.

34. United Nations Department of Economic and Social Affairs (2008). Singulate Mean Age at Marriage. www.un.org/en/development/desa/population/publications/dataset /marriage/age-marriage.asp.

35. Twenge, J. (2017). *iGen: Why Today's Super-Connected Kids Are Growing Up Less Rebellious, More Tolerant, Less Happy—and Completely Unprepared for Adulthood—and What That Means for the Rest of Us*. New York, Atria Books.

36. Cherlin, A. (2018). Marriage Has Become a Trophy. *Atlantic*. March 20. www .theatlantic.com/family/archive/2018/03/incredible-everlasting-institution-marriage /555320/.

37. Hymowitz, K. S. (2019). Alone—the Decline of the Family Has Unleashed an Epidemic of Loneliness. *City Journal*. Spring. www.city-journal.org/decline -of-family-loneliness-epidemic.

38. *Wikipedia* (2020). Rights and Responsibilities of Marriages in the United States. https://en.wikipedia.org/wiki/Rights_and_responsibilities_of_marriages_in_the_United _States.

39. Cloud, J. (2004). 1,138 Reasons Marriage Is Cool. *Time*. March 1. http://content .time.com/time/magazine/article/0,9171,596123,00.html.

40. Putnam, R. D. (2016). *Our Kids: The American Dream in Crisis*. New York, Simon and Schuster.

41. Brooks, D. (2020). Was the Nuclear Family a Mistake? *Atlantic*. February 10. https:// medium.com/the-atlantic/was-the-nuclear-family-a-mistake-f9fdddf8bde.

42. Musick, K., and A. Meier (2010). Are Both Parents Always Better Than One? Parental Conflict and Young Adult Well-Being. *Social Science Research* 39(5), 814–830. www.ncbi .nlm.nih.gov/pmc/articles/PMC2930824/.

43. Jeffreys, B. (2019). Do Children in Two-Parent Families Do Better? BBC News. February 5. www.bbc.co.uk/news/education-47057787; Reeves, R. V., and E. Krause (2017). Cohabiting Parents Differ from Married Ones in Three Big Ways. Brookings. April 5. www .brookings.edu/research/cohabiting-parents-differ-from-married-ones-in-three-big-ways/.

44. Harkness, S., P. Gregg, and M. Salgado (2016). *The Rise in Lone Mother Families and Children's Cognitive Development: Evidence from the 1958, 1970 and 2000 British Birth Cohorts*. Centre for Analysis of Social Policy, University of Bath. https://editorial express.com/cgi-bin/conference/download.cgi?db_name=SAEe2018&paper_id=127.

45. Cherlin, A. J. (2010). *The Marriage-Go-Round: The State of Marriage and the Family in America Today*. New York: Alfred A. Knopf.

46. Wilcox, W. B., and L. DeRose (2017). Ties That Bind Childrearing in the Age of Cohabitation. *Foreign Affairs*. February 14. www.foreignaffairs.com/articles/2017-02-14 /ties-bind.

47. McCathie, A. (2017). Marriages Prove Enduring in Germany as Divorce Rate Falls. DPA International. July 11. www.dpa-international.com/topic/marriages-prove -enduring-germany-divorce-rate-falls-urn%3Anewsml%3Adpa.com%3A20090101 %3A170711-99-199835.

48. Olito, F. (2019). How the Divorce Rate Has Changed over the Last 150 Years. *Insider*. January 30. www.insider.com/divorce-rate-changes-over-time-2019-1#since-the-turn-of-the -21st-century-the-divorce-rate-continues-to-decline-rapidly-13.

49. Wood, J. (2018). The United States Divorce Rate Is Dropping, Thanks to Millennials. World Economic Forum. October 5. www.weforum.org/agenda/2018/10 /divorce-united-states-dropping-because-millennials/.

50. Pinsker, J. (2018). The Not-So-Great Reason Divorce Rates Are Declining. *Atlantic*. September 25. www.theatlantic.com/family/archive/2018/09/millennials-divorce -baby-boomers/571282/.

51. Boyd, H. (2014). Silver Splicers Make Sixty the New Sexy. *Times* (London). June 15. www.thetimes.co.uk/article/silver-splicers-make-sixty-the-new-sexy-lh87snwhtxp.

52. Office for National Statistics (2017).

53. Office for National Statistics (2017).

54. Allred, C. (2019). Age Variation in the Divorce Rate, 1990 & 2017. Bowling Green State University. www.bgsu.edu/ncfmr/resources/data/family-profiles/allred-age-variation -div-rate-fp-19-13.html.

55. *Guardian* (2015). Meet the Silver Separators: Why Over-50s Top the Divorce Charts. November 24. www.theguardian.com/lifeandstyle/shortcuts/2015/nov/24 /silver-separators-over-50s-divorce-splitting-up-children.

56. Race, M. (2020). "Divorce Boom" Forecast as Lockdown Sees Advice Queries Rise. BBC News. September 13. www.bbc.co.uk/news/uk-england-54117821.

57. Eckholm, E. (2010). Saying No to "I Do," with the Economy in Mind. *New York Times*. September 28. www.nytimes.com/2010/09/29/us/29marriage.html?_r=2.

58. Wolfers, J. (2010). How Marriage Survives. *New York Times*. October 12. www .nytimes.com/2010/10/13/opinion/13wolfers.html.

59. Mr Skin (2019). Game of Nudes: 7 Seasons of Nudity from the HBO Series "Game of Thrones." www.mrskin.com/infographic/game-of-thrones-nudity-statistics.

60. Hald, G. M., L. Kuyper, P. C. Adam, and J. B. de Wit (2013). Does Viewing Explain Doing? Assessing the Association Between Sexually Explicit Materials Use and Sexual Behaviors in a Large Sample of Dutch Adolescents and Young Adults. *Journal of Sexual Medicine* 10(12), 2986–2995. www.jsm.jsexmed.org/article/S1743-6095(15)30225-3/fulltext.

61. University of Montreal (2009). Are the Effects of Pornography Negligible? Science Daily. December 1. www.sciencedaily.com/releases/2009/12/091201111202.htm.

62. Alexa (producer) (2020). Top Sites in GB. www.alexa.com/topsites/countries/GB.

63. Duffy et al. (2017).

64. Stephens-Davidowitz (2017).

65. Dubner, S. J. (2008). How to Think About Sex? A Freakonomics Quorum. *Freakonomics* (blog). September 12. https://freakonomics.com/2008/09/12/how-to -think-about-sex-a-freakonomics-quorum/.

66. Kushner, D. (2019). A Brief History of Porn on the Internet. *Wired*. April 9. www .wired.com/story/brief-history-porn-internet/.

67. Government Department for Digital Culture, Media & Sport (2018). *Age Verification for pornographic material online: Impact Assessment*. June 13. https://assets .publishing.service.gov.uk/government/uploads/system/uploads/attachment_data /file/747187/Impact_Assessment_Age_Verification_FINAL_20181009.pdf.

68. Bricker, D., and J. Ibbitson (2019). *Empty Planet: The Shock of Global Population Decline*. Signal.

69. Coontz, S. (2016). The Way We Never Were—for Much of the Century, Traditional "Family Values" Have Been More Myth Than Reality. *New Republic*. March 29. https:// newrepublic.com/article/132001/way-never.

70. Putnam (2016).

## CHAPTER 7: MANUFACTURING A GENERATIONAL CULTURE WAR

1. Bush, J. [@JebBush] (2018). Not cool, University of Manchester. Not cool. Twitter. October 2. https://twitter.com/JebBush/status/1047234246916677633.

2. CNN (2016). Jeb Bush to Audience: "Please Clap." Aired February 4, 2016. https:// www.youtube.com/watch?v=OUXvrWeQU0g.

3. Morgan, P. [@piersmorgan] (2018). Britain's losing its mind. Twitter. October 1. https://twitter.com/piersmorgan/status/1046996934496530432.

4. Furedi, F. (2019). Ban Applause? What Utter Claptrap! *Daily Mail*. October 27. www.dailymail.co.uk/debate/article-7619941/Professor-lashes-Oxford-latest-university -insist-jazz-hands-student-events.html.

5. Bacharach, J. (2019). Sometimes Inclusion Is Going to Be a Bit Embarrassing, but Disability—Invisible or Otherwise—Is a Working-Class Issue That the Left and Right Must Take Seriously. *Outline*. August 12. https://theoutline.com/post/7800/dsa -conference-2019-invisible-disability?zd=1&zi=dw23p6wl; Newshub (2016). Sydney School Disputes "Clapping Ban." July 21. www.newshub.co.nz/home/world/2016/07/sydney -school-disputes-clapping-ban.html.

6. Weale, S., and F. Perraudin. (2018). Jazz Hands at Manchester University: The Calm Behind the Storm. *Guardian*. October 5. www.theguardian.com/society/2018/oct/05 /jazz-hands-at-manchester-university-the-calm-behind-the-storm#maincontent.

7. Haidt, J. [@JonHaidt] (2019). If Oxford students replace clapping with "jazz hands" to protect some from anxiety, then those students will find clapping even more traumatizing after they leave Oxford. Safetyism backfires in the long run. Twitter. October 26. https:// twitter.com/jonhaidt/status/1188090469164765184?s=11.

8. Ryder, N. B. (1985). The Cohort as a Concept in the Study of Social Change. In *Cohort Analysis in Social Research*, 9–44. https://link.springer.com/chapter/10.1007 /978-1-4613-8536-3_2.

9. Ryder (1985).

10. Cision PR Newswire (2020). New Report Reveals Demographics of Black Lives Matter Protesters Shows Vast Majority Are White, Marched Within Their Own Cities. June 18. www.prnewswire.com/news-releases/new-report-reveals-demographics-of-black-lives -matter-protesters-shows-vast-majority-are-white-marched-within-their-own-cities -301079234.html.

11. Lewis, J. (1963). Speech at the March on Washington. August 28. Voices of Democracy. https://voicesofdemocracy.umd.edu/lewis-speech-at-the-march-on-washington-speech -text/.

12. Lewis, J. (2020). Together, You Can Redeem the Soul. *New York Times*. July 30. www .nytimes.com/2020/07/30/opinion/john-lewis-civil-rights-america.html.

13. Chivers, T. (2018). How Racist Is Britain? *UnHerd*. December 14. https://unherd .com/2018/12/how-racist-is-britain/.

14. Singal, J. (2017). Psychology's Favorite Tool for Measuring Racism Isn't Up to the Job. *Cut*. www.thecut.com/2017/01/psychologys-racism-measuring-tool-isnt-up-to-the-job .html.

15. Kelley, N., O. Khan, and S. Sharrock (2017). Racial Prejudice in Britain Today. London, NatCen Social Research and Runnymede Trust. September. http://natcen.ac.uk /media/1488132/racial-prejudice-report_v4.pdf.

16. Livingston, G., and A. Brown (2017). Trends and Patterns in Intermarriage. Pew Research Center. May 18. www.pewsocialtrends.org/2017/05/18/1-trends -and-patterns-in-intermarriage/.

17. Quillian, L., D. Pager, O. Hexel, and A. H. Midtbøen (2017). Meta-analysis of Field Experiments Shows No Change in Racial Discrimination in Hiring over Time.

*Proceedings of the National Academy of Sciences* 114(41), 10870–10875. www.pnas.org/content/early/2017/09/11/1706255114.

18. Putnam, R. D. (2020). *The Upswing: How America Came Together a Century Ago and How We Can Do It Again.* New York, Simon & Schuster.

19. Young, C., K. Ziemer, and C. Jackson (2019). Explaining Trump's Popular Support: Validation of a Nativism Index. *Social Science Quarterly* 100(2), 412–418. https://online library.wiley.com/doi/abs/10.1111/ssqu.12593; Goodwin, M., and C. Milazzo (2017). Taking Back Control? Investigating the Role of Immigration in the 2016 Vote for Brexit. *British Journal of Politics and International Relations* 19(3), 450–464. https://nottingham -repository.worktribe.com/preview/865063/Taking%20Back%20Control%20FINAL%20 SUBMISSION%2028%20April%202017.pdf; Davis, L., and S. S. Deole (2017). Immigration and the Rise of Far-Right Parties in Europe. *ifo DICE Report* 15(4), 10–15. www.ifo.de /DocDL/dice-report-2017-4-davis-deole-december.pdf.

20. Cliffe, J. (2015). *Britain's Cosmopolitan Future: How the Country Is Changing and Why Its Politicians Must Respond.* Policy Network. http://policynetwork.org/wp-content /uploads/2017/08/Britains-cosmopolitan-future.pdf.

21. Sosnik, D. (2015). America's Hinge Moment: Presidential Politics in 2016 Will Reflect the Shifting Reality of America. *Politico.* March 29. www.politico.com/magazine /story/2015/03/2016-predictions-americas-sosnik-clinton-116480.

22. Ipsos MORI (2017). Shifting Ground: 8 Key Findings from a Longitudinal Study on Attitudes Towards Immigration and Brexit. October 17. www.ipsos.com/ipsos-mori/en -uk/shifting-ground-attitudes-towards-immigration-and-brexit.

23. Chiripanhura, B., and N. Wolf (2019). Long-Term Trends in UK Employment: 1861 to 2018. Office for National Statistics. www.ons.gov.uk/economy/nationalaccounts /uksectoraccounts/compendium/economicreview/april2019/longtermtrendsinuk employment1861to2018#womens-labour-market-participation.

24. Goldin, C. (2014). A Grand Gender Convergence: Its Last Chapter. *American Economic Review* 104(4), 1091–1119. https://scholar.harvard.edu/files/goldin/files/goldin _aeapress_2014_1.pdf.

25. Faludi, S. (2010). American Electra: Feminism's Ritual Matricide. *Harpers.* October. https://harpers.org/archive/2010/10/american-electra/.

26. Eaves, K. L. (2008). Moms in the Middle: Parenting Magazines, Motherhood Texts and the "Mommy Wars." Wichita State University. Master's thesis. https://pdfs .semanticscholar.org/03df/007b8788ce3376096234e1e55f8d9a8e3317.pdf.

27. Duffy, B., K. Hewlett, J. McCrae, and J. Hall, J. (2019). *Divided Britain? Polarisation and Fragmentation Trends in the UK.* Policy Institute. September. www.kcl.ac.uk/policy -institute/assets/divided-britain.pdf.

28. Kliff, S. (2015). What Americans Think of Abortion. *Vox.* April 8. www .vox.com/2018/2/2/16965240/abortion-decision-statistics-opinions.

29. Center, P. R. (2013). The Global Divide on Homosexuality. Greater Acceptance in More Secular and Affluent Countries. Pew Research Center. June 4. www.pewresearch.org /global/2013/06/04/the-global-divide-on-homosexuality/.

30. NORC at University of Chicago (2020). GSS Data Explorer: Sexual Orientation. https://gssdataexplorer.norc.org/trends/Gender%20&%20Marriage?measure =sexornt.

31. Dahlgreen, W., and A.-E. Shakespeare (2015). 1 in 2 Young People Say They Are Not 100% Heterosexual. YouGov. August 16. https://yougov.co.uk/topics/lifestyle /articles-reports/2015/08/16/half-young-not-heterosexual.

32. Spencer, B. (2021). Only Half of Young Attracted Exclusively to Oppo- site Sex. *Times* (London). February 28. www.thetimes.co.uk/article/only-half -of-young-attracted-exclusively-to-opposite-sex-zbt9ckxwt.

33. Tsjeng, Z. (2016). Teens These Days Are Queer AF, New Study Says. *Vice*. March 10. www.vice.com/en_us/article/kb4dvz/teens-these-days-are-queer-af-new-study-says.

34. Kinsey, A. C., W. B. Pomeroy, C. E. Martin, and P. H. Gebhard (1948). *Sexual Behav- ior in the Human Male*. Philadelphia, W. B. Saunders.

35. Mitchell, K. R., C. H. Mercer, G. B. Ploubidis, K. G. Jones, J. Datta, N. Field, A. J. Copas, C. Tanton, C. Erens, and P. Sonnenberg (2013). Sexual Function in Brit- ain: Findings from the Third National Survey of Sexual Attitudes and Lifestyles (Natsal-3). *Lancet* 382(9907), 1817–1829. www.thelancet.com/journals/lancet/article /PIIS0140-6736(13)62366-1/fulltext.

36. The Pansexual Revolution: How Sexual Fluidity Became Mainstream. *Guard- ian*. February 14. www.theguardian.com/society/2019/feb/14/the-pansexual -revolution-how-sexual-fluidity-became-mainstream.

37. Steinmetz, K. (2014). The Transgender Tipping Point. *Time*. May 29. https://time .com/135480/transgender-tipping-point/.

38. Marsh, S. (2016). The Gender-Fluid Generation: Young People on Being Male, Fe- male or Non-binary. *Guardian*. March 23. www.theguardian.com/commentisfree/2016 /mar/23/gender-fluid-generation-young-people-male-female-trans.

39. Shrimpton, H. [@h_shrimpton] (2020). Could in part be driven by differences in fa- miliarity: 7 in 10 Baby Boomers have never met or encountered someone who uses gender neutral terms but 3 in 10 Gen Z has someone in their social circle who uses gender neutral terms. Twitter. July 15. https://twitter.com/h_shrimpton/status/1283394380850696192.

40. YouGov (2020). YouGov/PinkNews Survey Results: Do you think a person should or should not be able to self-identify as a gender different to the one they were born in? https:// docs.cdn.yougov.com/ogu5gtx9us/PinkNewsResults_200629_Education_Selfidentity .pdf.

41. Ipsos (2020). The Future of Gender Is Increasingly Nonbinary: New Report Explores Public Opinion, Marketing and Business in the Gender Spectrum. Press re- lease. January 7. www.ipsos.com/sites/default/files/ct/news/documents/2020-01/final _what_the_future_gender_pr.pdf.

42. Brown, A. (2017). Republicans, Democrats Have Starkly Different Views on Transgender Issues. Pew Research Center. November 8. www.pewresearch.org /fact-tank/2017/11/08/transgender-issues-divide-republicans-and-democrats/.

43. Stanley, T. (2017). The Gender Fad Will Pass, What's Important Is Getting Through It Without Permanent Damage. *Telegraph*. November 13. www.telegraph.co.uk /news/2017/11/13/gender-fad-will-pass-important-getting-without-permanent-damage/.

44. Neale, R. (1967). Working-Class Women and Women's Suffrage. *Labour History* (12), 16–34. www.jstor.org/stable/27507859?seq=1.

45. Allen, S. (2019). Over a Third of Generation Z Knows a Non-binary Per- son. *Daily Beast*. January 24. www.thedailybeast.com/over-a-third-of-generation-z -knows-a-non-binary-person.

46. Davie, G. (n.d.). Westminster Debates. http://faithdebates.org.uk/wp-content /uploads/2013/09/1335084386_Davie-Westminster-debates-copy.pdf.

47. Welby, J. (2019). Deo Gloria Trust Lecture on Evangelism and Other Faiths. March 14. www.archbishopofcanterbury.org/speaking-and-writing/speeches/archbishop -justin-welbys-deo-gloria-trust-lecture-evangelism-and.

48. Pew Research Center (2015). The Future of World Religions: Population Growth Projections, 2010–2050. www.pewforum.org/2015/04/02/religious-projections-2010-2050/.

49. Lippmann, W. (2015). *Drift and Mastery: An Attempt to Diagnose the Current Unrest.* Madison, University of Wisconsin Press.

50. Murray, D. (2019). *The Madness of Crowds: Gender, Race and Identity.* London, Bloomsbury.

51. Obama, B. (2020) *A Promised Land.* New York, Penguin Books.

## CHAPTER 8: CONSTANT CRISES

1. The reality is that Macmillan didn't say those words, and his actual, clunkier response was that he most feared "the opposition of events." The reworking didn't just make the saying more elegant, the quaint Edwardian phrasing has no doubt added to its popularity, giving a sense that the impact of the unforeseen is a historical constant of politics. *Evening Standard* (2006). Book Reveals the Famous One-Liners They Never Said. October 25. www .standard.co.uk/showbiz/book-reveals-the-famous-one-liners-they-never-said-7086553 .html.

2. Bochenski, N. (2012). Lying Is Easy: Turnbull Calls for Less Spin. *Sydney Morning Herald.* December 28. www.smh.com.au/politics/federal/lying-is-easy-turnbull-calls-for -less-spin-20121228-2bybw.html.

3. Grasso, M. T., S. Farrall, E. Gray, C. Hay, and W. Jennings (2019). Thatcher's Children, Blair's Babies, Political Socialisation and Trickle-Down Value-Change: An Age, Period and Cohort Analysis. *British Journal of Political Science* 49(1), 17–36. https://eprints.soton .ac.uk/390558/.

4. Desilver, D. (2014). The Politics of American Generations: How Age Affects Attitudes and Voting Behavior. Pew Research Center. July 9. www.pewresearch.org/fact-tank/2014/07/09 /the-politics-of-american-generations-how-age-affects-attitudes-and-voting-behavior/.

5. Thompson, D. (2019). The Millennials-Versus-Boomers Fight Divides the Democratic Party. *Atlantic.* December 10. www.theatlantic.com/ideas/archive/2019/12 /young-left-third-party/603232/.

6. OECD (n.d.). *Youth Stocktaking Report.* www.oecd.org/gov/youth-stocktaking-report .pdf; Philbrick, I. P. (2020). Why Does America Have Old Leaders? *New York Times.* July 16. www.nytimes.com/2020/07/16/opinion/america-presidents-old-age.html.

7. Matheson, A. (2019). There Are Almost Five Times as Many Millennials in the House Than Last Session. *Boston Globe.* January 5. www.bostonglobe.com/news/politics /2019/01/05/there-are-almost-five-times-many-millennials-house-than-last-session/un- 75ohNKZSQHEQGCHHw7dI/story.html; Filipovic, J. (2020). Why Is Congress So Old? *Gen.* December 10. https://gen.medium.com/why-is-congress-so-old-64f014a9d819.

8. Biden, J. (2020). Speech given in Miami, FL, October 6.

9. Van Bavel, J., and D. S. Reher (2013). The Baby Boom and Its Causes: What We Know and What We Need to Know. *Population and Development Review* 39(2), 257–288. https:// onlinelibrary.wiley.com/doi/epdf/10.1111/j.1728-4457.2013.00591.x?saml_referrer#.

10. Berry, C. (2012). *The Rise of Gerontocracy? Addressing the Intergenerational Democratic Deficit*. Intergenerational Foundation. May. www.if.org.uk/wp-content/uploads/2012/04/IF_Democratic_Deficit_final.pdf.

11. Gardiner, L. (2016). *Votey McVoteface: Understanding the Growing Turnout Gap Between the Generations. Resolution Foundation*. September 23. www.resolution foundation.org/publications/votey-mcvoteface-understanding-the-growing-turnout-gap-between-the-generations/.

12. Note that claimed turnout, where people self-report whether they voted, overstates actual turnout, either because the people responding to these sort of surveys are more interested in politics, because people misremember whether they voted, or they deliberately misrepresent themselves in a better light. There is no official record of the proportions of each age group that actually vote, but some survey studies do inspect the electoral register to check whether people who claimed they voted actually did, and these show that young people tend to overclaim *more* than older people. So, for our purposes, this confirms that generational gaps in turnout are real, and, if anything, probably bigger than shown here.

13. London School of Economics British Politics and Policy (2018). Why 2017 May Have Witnessed a Youthquake After All. LSE BPP (blog). https://blogs.lse.ac.uk/politicsandpolicy/was-there-a-youthquake-after-all/.

14. *Economist* (2017). Millennials Across the Rich World Are Failing to Vote. February 4. www.economist.com/international/2017/02/04/millennials-across-the-rich-world-are-failing-to-vote.

15. Burns, K. (2020). Democrats Are Coalescing Around Biden—Except for Young Voters. *Vox*. March 18. www.vox.com/policy-and-politics/2020/3/18/21184884/democrats-biden-young-voters-turnout-sanders.

16. Vinopal, C. (2020). Sanders Banked on Young Voters: Here's How the Numbers Have Played Out. *NewsHour*. March 11. www.pbs.org/newshour/politics/sanders-banked-on-young-voters-heres-how-the-numbers-have-played-out.

17. Broockman, D., and J. Kalla (2020). Bernie Sanders Looks Electable in Surveys—but It Could Be a Mirage. *Vox*. February 25. www.vox.com/policy-and-politics/2020/2/25/21152538/bernie-sanders-electability-president-moderates-data.

18. Walczak, A., W. Van der Brug, and C. E. De Vries (2012). Long- and Short-Term Determinants of Party Preferences: Inter-generational Differences in Western and East Central Europe. *Electoral Studies* 31(2), 273–284. www.sciencedirect.com/science/article/abs/pii/S0261379411001399?via%3Dihub.

19. *Economist* (2017). Millennials Across the Rich World Are Failing to Vote. February 4. www.economist.com/international/2017/02/04/millennials-across-the-rich-world-are-failing-to-vote.

20. Tilley, J., and G. Evans (2014). Ageing and Generational Effects on Vote Choice: Combining Cross-Sectional and Panel Data to Estimate APC Effects. *Electoral Studies* 33, 19–27. www.sciencedirect.com/science/article/abs/pii/S0261379413000875.

21. Ambinder, M. (2008). The GOP Generational Time Bomb. *Atlantic*. April 28. www.theatlantic.com/politics/archive/2008/04/the-gop-generational-time-bomb/52869/; Siegfried, E. (2017). Hey, GOP, Here's Why Millennials Hate Us. *Daily Beast*. June 26. www.thedailybeast.com/hey-gop-heres-why-millennials-hate-us; Larimore, R. (2019). Darwin Is Coming for the GOP. *Bulwark*. January 25. https://thebulwark.com/darwin-is-coming-for-the-gop/.

22. Ferguson, N., and E. Fraymann (2019). The Coming Generation War. *Atlantic*. May 6. www.theatlantic.com/ideas/archive/2019/05/coming-generation-war/588670/.

23. *Washington Post* (2020). Exit Poll Results and Analysis for the 2020 Presidential Election. December 14. www.washingtonpost.com/elections/interactive/2020/exit-polls /presidential-election-exit-polls/.

24. *Wall Street Journal* (2020). How the 2020 Presidential Election Divided Voters. November 4. www.wsj.com/articles/how-the-2020-presidential-election-divided-voters-11604 521705.

25. Muller, D. (2019). The 2019 Australian Election Study. Parliament of Australia. October 12. www.aph.gov.au/About_Parliament/Parliamentary_Departments /Parliamentary_Library/FlagPost/2019/December/The_2019_Australian_Election _Study.

26. Chan, G. (2019). From Tax to Climate: Five Factors that Could Swing 2019 Federal Election. *Guardian*. April 10. www.theguardian.com/australia-news/2019/apr/11 /from-tax-to-climate-five-factors-that-could-swing-2019-federal-election.

27. Edelman (2014). Trust in Government Plunges to Historic Low. January 19. www.edelman.com/news-awards/trust-government-plunges-historic-low; Edelman (2017). 2017 Edelman Trust Barometer Reveals Global Implosion of Trust. January 15. www.edelman.com/news-awards/2017-edelman-trust-barometer-reveals -global-implosion; Edelman (2018). 2018 Edelman Trust Barometer Reveals Record-Breaking Drop in Trust in the U.S. January 22. www.edelman.com/news-awards /2018-edelman-trust-barometer-reveals-record-breaking-drop-trust-in-the-us.

28. Prokop, A. (2014). Millennials Have Stopped Trusting the Government. *Vox*. May 5. www.vox.com/2014/5/5/5683176/millennials-have-stopped-trusting-the-government.

29. O'Neill, O. (2013). How to Trust Intelligently. *TED* Blog. September 25. https://blog.ted.com/how-to-trust-intelligently/#:~:text=Onora%20O'Neill%3A%20 What%20we,sensible%20simply%20wants%20more%20trust.&text=They%20want%20 well%2Ddirected%20trust,and%20honest%20%E2%80%94%20so%2C%20trustworthy.

30. Clarke, N., W. Jennings, J. Moss, and G. Stoker (2018). *The Good Politician: Folk Theories, Political Interaction, and the Rise of Anti-politics*. Cambridge, Cambridge University Press.

31. Taub, A. (2016). How Stable Are Democracies? Warning Signs Are Flashing Red. *New York Times*. November 29. www.nytimes.com/2016/11/29/world/americas /western-liberal-democracy.html.

32. *Economist* (2020). Global Democracy Has Another Bad Year. January 22. www .economist.com/graphic-detail/2020/01/22/global-democracy-has-another-bad-year ?gclsrc=aw.ds&gclid=EAIaIQobChMIy6erlvux6wIVFO3tCh1e6Q_XEAAYASAAEg J0RPD_BwE&gclsrc=aw.ds.

33. Saul, S. (2020). Watch Obama's Full Speech at the Democratic National Convention. *New York Times*. August 19. www.nytimes.com/2020/08/19/us/politics/obama-speech .html.

34. Mounk, Y., and R. S. Foa (2020). This Is How Democracy Dies. *Atlantic*. January 29. www.theatlantic.com/ideas/archive/2020/01/confidence-democracy-lowest -point-record/605686/.

35. Crozier, M., S. P. Huntington, and J. Watanuki (1975), *The Crisis of Democracy: Report on the Governability of Democracies to the Trilateral Commission*. New York, New York University Press.

36. Strauss, W., and N. Howe (1997). *The Fourth Turning: What the Cycles of History Tell Us About America's Next Rendezvous with Destiny*. New York, Bantam Press.

37. Ferguson and Fraymann (2019).

38. Gardiner, L., and T. Bell (2019). *My Generation, Baby: The Politics of Age in Brexit Britain. Resolution Foundation*. March 29. www.resolutionfoundation.org/comment/my-generation-baby-the-politics-of-age-in-brexit-britain/.

## CHAPTER 9: CONSUMING THE PLANET

1. Rahim, Z. (2019). Davos 2019: David Attenborough Issues Stark Warning About Future of Civilisation as He Demands "Practical Solutions" to Combat Climate Change. *Independent*. January 22. www.independent.co.uk/environment/david-attenborough-davos-2019-climate-change-switzerland-world-economic-forum-a8739656.html.

2. Krznaric, R. (2020). *The Good Ancestor: How to Think Long-Term in a Short-Term World*. New York, Random House.

3. Gilbert, D. (2009). *Stumbling on Happiness*. Toronto, Vintage Canada.

4. Krznaric (2020).

5. Skidelsky, R. (1992). *John Maynard Keynes: The Economist as Saviour 1920–1937*. New York, Macmillan.

6. Willetts, D. (2019). *The Pinch: How the Baby Boomers Took Their Children's Future—and Why They Should Give It Back*. London, Atlantic Books.

7. BBC News (2019). Extinction Rebellion: Climate Protesters "Making a Difference." www.bbc.co.uk/news/uk-england-london-48003955.

8. NASA (2019). Global Temperature. https://climate.nasa.gov/vital-signs/global-temperature/; Cook, J., N. Oreskes, P. T. Doran, W. R. L. Anderegg, B. Verheggen, E. W. Maibach, J. S. Carlton, S. Lewandowsky, A. G. Skuce, S. A. Green, et al. (2016). Consensus on Consensus: A Synthesis of Consensus Estimates on Human-Caused Global Warming. *Environmental Science Letters* 11(4). https://iopscience.iop.org/article/10.1088/1748-9326/11/4/048002/meta.

9. Kennedy, B., and C. Johnson (2020). More Americans See Climate Change as a Priority, but Democrats Are Much More Concerned Than Republicans. Pew Research Center. February 28. www.pewresearch.org/fact-tank/2020/02/28/more-americans-see-climate-change-as-a-priority-but-democrats-are-much-more-concerned-than-republicans/.

10. Cohen, S. (2019). The Age Gap in Environmental Politics. State of the Planet (blog). Earth Institute. February 4. https://blogs.ei.columbia.edu/2019/02/04/age-gap-environmental-politics/.

11. Becker, D., and J. Gerstenzang (2020). Millennials Reject Car Culture. *USA Today*. June 19. https://eu.usatoday.com/story/opinion/2013/06/19/millenials-car-culture-column/2435173/.

12. Wynes, S., and K. Nicholas (2017). The Climate Mitigation Gap: Education and Government Recommendations Miss the Most Effective Individual Actions. *Environmental Research Letters* 12(7). https://iopscience.iop.org/article/10.1088/1748-9326/aa7541.

13. Thompson, D., and J. Weissmann (2012). The Cheapest Generation. *Atlantic*. September. www.theatlantic.com/magazine/archive/2012/09/the-cheapest-generation/309060/.

14. Rosenthal, E. (2013). The End of Car Culture. *New York Times*. June 29. www.nytimes.com/2013/06/30/sunday-review/the-end-of-car-culture.html.

15. Delbosc, A., and K. Ralph (2017). A Tale of Two Millennials. *Journal of Transport and Land Use* 10(1), 903–910.

16. Thompson and Weissmann (2012); Thompson, D. (2012). Cars? Not For Us: The Cheapest Generation Explains "The Freedom of Not Owning." *Atlantic*. August 24. www.theatlantic.com/business/archive/2012/08/cars-not-for-us-the-cheapest -generation-explains-the-freedom-of-not-owning/261516/.

17. Knittel, C. R., and E. Murphy (2019). Generational Trends in Vehicle Ownership and Use: Are Millennials Any Different? National Bureau of Economic Research. March. www .nber.org/papers/w25674.

18. Oakil, A. T. M., D. Manting, and H. Nijland (2016). Determinants of Car Ownership Among Young Households in the Netherlands: The Role of Urbanization and Demographic and Economic Characteristics. *Journal of Transport Geography* 51, 229–235. https://pure .uva.nl/ws/files/2734560/177530_JTRG_Manuscript.pdf.

19. Vitale, J., K. Bowman, and R. Robinson (2020). How the Pandemic Is Changing the Future of Automotive. Deloitte. July 13. www2.deloitte.com/us/en/insights/industry /retail-distribution/consumer-behavior-trends-state-of-the-consumer-tracker/future -of-automotive-industry-pandemic.html?id=us:2el:3pr:4di6831:5awa:6di:071420:& pkid=1007226.

20. Campbell, P., J. Miller, C. Bushey, and K. Inagaki (2020). Time to Buy a Car? Industry Hopes for Coronavirus Silver Lining. *Financial Times*. May 19. www.ft.com /content/488d5886-c6af-4e80-a479-36aca26edd1d.

21. *Fortune* (2015). Why Ethical Brands Must Engage More: Millennials. October 6; Nielsen (2015). Green Generation: Millennials Say Sustainability Is a Shopping Priority. *Sustain*. www.sustainmag.ca/green-generation-millennial-say-sustainability-is-a-shopping -priority/.

22. Duffy, B., F. Thomas, H. Shrimpton, H. Whyte-Smith, M. Clemence, and T. Abboud (2018). *Beyond Binary: The Lives and Choices of Generation Z*. London. Ipsos MORI. July 4. 150. www.ipsos.com/ipsos-mori/en-uk/ipsos-thinks-beyond-binary -lives-and-choices-generation-z.

23. Ipsos MORI (n.d.). Key Influencer Tracking. www.ipsos-mori.com/researchs pecialisms/reputationresearch/whatwedo/kit/sustainablebusinessmonitor.aspx.

24. Kusek, K. (2016). The Death of Brand Loyalty: Cultural Shifts Mean It's Gone Forever. *Forbes*. July 25. www.forbes.com/sites/kathleenkusek/2016/07/25/the-death-of-brand -loyalty-cultural-shifts-mean-its-gone-forever/#30cca8526179; Retail Customer Experience (2016). Study: Brand Loyalty Not Such a Biggie for Millennials. June 24. www.retailcustomer experience.com/news/study-brand-loyalty-not-such-a-biggie-for-millennials/.

25. The Millennial Consumer Study (2015). Workplace Intelligence. millennialbranding .com/2015/millennial-consumer-study/.

26. Bazaar Voice (2012). *Talking to Strangers: Millennials Trust People over Brands*. media2.bazaarvoice.com/documents/Bazaarvoice_WP_Talking-to-Strangers.pdf; Yahoo Small Business (n.d.). How Millennials Are Changing the Face of Retail Shopping. https://smallbusiness.yahoo.com/advisor/resource-center/millennials-changing-face -retail-shopping-025220847/.

27. Barnes, N. G. (2015). Millennials Adept at Filtering Out Ads. eMarketer. April 10. www.emarketer.com/Article/Millennials-Adept-Filtering-Ads/1012335.

28. Damais, J.-F., and R. Sant (2016). *Healing the Pain: Responding to Bad Experiences to Boost Customer Loyalty*. Ipsos Loyalty. www.ipsos.com/sites/default/files /publication/1970-01/Ipsos-Loyalty-Healing-the-Pain.pdf.

29. Gore, A. (2013). *The Future*. New York, W. H. Allen.

30. Monbiot, G. (2019). My Generation Trashed the Planet: So I Salute the Children Striking Back. *Guardian*. February 15. www.theguardian.com/commentisfree/2019/feb/15 /planet-children-protest-climate-change-speech.

31. Karpf, A. (2020). Don't Let Prejudice Against Older People Contaminate the Climate Movement. *Guardian*. January 18. www.theguardian.com/commentisfree/2020/jan/18 /ageism-climate-movement-generation-stereotypes.

32. Frumkin, H., L. Fried, and R. Moody (2012). Aging, Climate Change, and Legacy Thinking. *American Journal of Public Health* 102(8), 1434–1438. www.ncbi.nlm.nih.gov/pmc /articles/PMC3464837/.

33. McGrath, M. (2020). UN Report: Covid Crisis Does Little to Slow Climate Change. BBC News. September 9. www.bbc.co.uk/news/science-environment-54074733.

34. Gates, B. (2020). COVID-19 Is Awful: Climate Change Could Be Worse. Gates-Notes. August 4. www.gatesnotes.com/Energy/Climate-and-COVID-19.

35. Davies, P., and M. Green (2020). The EU Recovery Fund: "Building Back Better" in a Post-COVID-19 World. Latham & Watkins. May 29. www.globalelr.com/2020/05 /the-eu-recovery-fund-building-back-better-in-a-post-covid-19-world/.

36. *Financial Times* (2020). Covid-19 and the Generational Divide. March 16. www .ft.com/content/6a880416-66fa-11ea-800d-da70cff6e4d3.

## CHAPTER 10: US AND THEM

1. Massis quoted in Hentea, M. (2013). The Problem of Literary Generations: Origins and Limitations. *Comparative Literature Studies* 50(4), 567–588.

2. Dylan Thomas, quote taken from biography of Wilfred Owen (n.d.). Wilfred Owen Association. www.wilfredowen.org.uk/wilfred-owen/biography#:~:text=Wilfred%20 Owen's%20Draft%20Preface&text=Nor%20is%20it%20about%20deeds,Poetry%20is %20in%20the%20pity.

3. Biography of Wilfred Owen (n.d.).

4. Hentea (2013).

5. Turner, B. S. (1998). Ageing and Generational Conflicts: A Reply to Sarah Irwin. *British Journal of Sociology* 49(2), 299–304.

6. Bristow, J. (2019). *Stop Mugging Grandma: The "Generation Wars" and Why Boomer Blaming Won't Solve Anything*. New Haven, CT, Yale University Press.

7. Ipsos MORI (2014). *BBC Identity Polling*. April 4. www.ipsos.com/sites/default/files /migrations/en-uk/files/Assets/Docs/Polls/ipsos-mori-bbc-identity-poll-2014-tables.pdf.

8. Ipsos MORI (2019). Ok, Boomer! Baby Boomers and the Consumption of the Future. November 8. www.ipsos.com/en-us/knowledge/overview/ok-boomer.

9. Lloyd Jones, J. (1969). The Worst-Raised Generation in History. *Muscatine Journal* (IA). May 7.

10. Martin, C. (2018). One in 10 Millennials Would Rather Lose a Finger Than Give Up Their Smartphone: Survey. MediaPost. July 25. www.mediapost.com/publications /article/322677/one-in-10-millennials-would-rather-lose-a-finger-t.html.

11. Cooper, G. F. (2020). Fur Real: 40 Percent of People Would Give Up Dog to Keep Smartphone. *CNET*. September 23. www.cnet.com/news/survey-says-40-percent-of -people-would-give-up-dog-to-keep-smartphone/; Chansanchai, A. (2011). Survey: One-Third Would Rather Give Up Sex Than Phone. NBC News. August 4. www.nbcnews.com /news/world/survey-one-third-would-rather-give-sex-phone-flna121757; Telenav (2011).

Survey Finds One-Third of Americans More Willing to Give Up Sex Than Their Mobile Phones. August 3. http://investor.telenav.com/news-releases/news-release-details/survey -finds-one-third-americans-more-willing-give-sex-their; Bates, D. (2013). Truth About Women's Relationship with Technology: Half Would Rather Go Without Sex Than Give Up a Smart Phone. *Daily Mail*. December 10. www.dailymail.co.uk/news/article-2521626 /Half-women-sex-smart-phone.html.

12. Ballard, J. (2018). Over Half of Millennials Say They Waste Too Much Time on Smartphones. YouGov. June 25. https://today.yougov.com/topics/technology /articles-reports/2018/06/25/smartphone-habits-millennials-boomers-gen-x.

13. Digital Day Research (2016). www.digitaldayresearch.co.uk/.

14. Comunello, F., M. F. Ardevol, S. Mulargia, and F. Belotti (2016). Women, Youth, and Everything Else: Age-Based and Gendered Stereotypes in Relation to Digital Technology Among Elderly Italian Mobile Phone Users. *Media, Culture & Society* 39(6), 798–815. https://doi.org/10.1177/0163443716674363.

15. Sweney, M. (2018). Is Facebook for Old People? Over-55s Flock in as the Young Leave. *Guardian*. February 12. www.theguardian.com/technology/2018/feb/12/is -facebook-for-old-people-over-55s-flock-in-as-the-young-leave; Cuthbertson, A. (2018). Facebook Is Officially for Old People. *Newsweek*. February 12. www.newsweek.com /facebook-officially-old-people-803196.

16. A Group Where We All Pretend to Be Boomers (n.d.). Facebook. www.facebook .com/groups/1288197298014311/?ref=group_header.

17. Whalen, A. (2020). What Is "Boomer Remover" and Why Is It Making People So Angry? *Newsweek*. March 13. www.newsweek.com/boomer-remover-meme-trends -virus-coronavirus-social-media-covid-19-baby-boomers-1492190.

18. The Irish Times [@IrishTimes]. More than half of young people who worked before pandemic now claiming support. Twitter. May 4. https://twitter.com/irishtimes /status/1257320516144074752?s=21.

19. BBC News (2020). "Generation Covid" Hit Hard by the Pandemic, Research Reveals. October 26. www.bbc.co.uk/news/uk-54662485.

20. Robertson, H. (2020). Young People Face Economic "Scarring" from Covid, Says Top Think Tank. City A.M. July 3. www.cityam.com/young-people-face-economic-scarring -from-covid-says-top-think-tank.

21. Bell, J. [@jamesrbuk] (2020). Millennials and Gen Z are supportive of lockdown largely to protect others. Twitter. May 18. https://twitter.com/jamesrbuk/status /1262325042525941762?s=12.

22. Byrne, D. (2020). As an Isolated Older Person, I've Been Deeply Moved by the Sacrifices of Others. *Guardian*. March 31. www.theguardian.com/commentisfree/2020/mar /31/isolated-older-person-underlying-conditions-coronavirus-crisis.

23. Evans, A. (2020). COVID-19 and the Intergenerational Covenant. Global Dashboard. March 31. www.globaldashboard.org/2020/03/31/covid19-and-the -intergenerational-covenant/.

24. Rudolph, C. W., and H. Zacher (2020). "The COVID-19 Generation": A Cautionary Note. *Work, Aging and Retirement*. www.ncbi.nlm.nih.gov/pmc/articles/PMC7184414/.

25. Goff, N. [@nickgoff79]. I would open pubs for 35-45 year olds exclusively first. Twitter. April 28. https://twitter.com/nickgoff79/status/1255103061841842 177?s=21.

26. Gray, P. (2011). The Special Value of Children's Age-Mixed Play. *American Journal of Play* 3(4), 500–522. www.psychologytoday.com/files/attachments/1195/ajp-age-mixing -published.pdf.

27. McLeod, S. (2018). Erik Erikson's Stages of Psychosocial Development. *Simply Psychology*. www.simplypsychology.org/Erik-Erikson.html.

28. Brooks, D. (2015). The Moral Bucket List. *New York Times*. April 11. www.nytimes .com/2015/04/12/opinion/sunday/david-brooks-the-moral-bucket-list.html.

29. Nesterly (n.d.). www.nesterly.io/.

30. Hentea (2013).

31. Bristow, J. (2016). *The Sociology of Generations: New Directions and Challenges*. New York, Palgrave Macmillan.

32. Annan, N. (1980). Grand Disillusions. *New York Review*. April 3. www.nybooks.com /articles/1980/04/03/grand-disillusions/?lp_txn_id=991894.

33. Lambert, T. A. (1972). Generations and Change: Toward a Theory of Generations as a Force in Historical Process. *Youth & Society* 4(1), 21–45. https://journals.sagepub.com /doi/pdf/10.1177/0044118X7200400103.

34. Delaney, K. J. (2017). The Robot That Takes Your Job Should Pay Taxes, Says Bill Gates. *Quartz*. February 17. https://qz.com/911968/bill-gates-the-robot-that-takes -your-job-should-pay-taxes/.

## CHAPTER 11: THE END OF THE LINE?

1. United Nations (n.d.). Ending Poverty. www.un.org/en/global-issues/ending-poverty.

2. Queen's broadcast to the UK and the Commonwealth (2020). Royal household. April 5. www.royal.uk/queens-broadcast-uk-and-commonwealth.

3. Comte, A. (1869). *Cours de philosophie positive*. 3rd ed. 6 vols. Paris, J. B. Baillière. 4: 450–451.

4. Singapore Ministerial Committee on Ageing (2016). *I Feel Young in My Singapore: Action Plan for Successful Ageing*. https://sustainabledevelopment.un.org/content /documents/1525Action_Plan_for_Successful_Aging.pdf.

5. Discussion between Professor Sakura Osamu and Professor Saijo Tatsuyoshi (2019). Discuss Japan. January 9. www.japanpolicyforum.jp/society/pt20190109210522.html.

6. Mulgan, G. (2020). Social Sciences and Social Imagination. Campaign for Social Science. May 12. https://campaignforsocialscience.org.uk/news/social-sciences -and-social-imagination/.

7. Mazzucato, M. (2021). *Mission Economy: A Moonshot Guide to Changing Capitalism*. London, Allen Lane.

8. Robinson, K. S. (2020). *The Ministry for the Future*. London, Orbit.

9. Encyclical Letter "Laudato Si" of the Holy Father Francis on Care for Our Common Home (2015). Vatican. www.vatican.va/content/francesco/en/encyclicals/documents /papa-francesco_20150524_enciclica-laudato-si.html.

10. Fisher, R. (2019). The Perils of Short-Termism: Civilisation's Greatest Threat. BBC. January 9. www.bbc.com/future/article/20190109-the-perils-of-short-termism -civilisations-greatest-threat.

11. Robinson, J. (2020). *#Futuregen: Lessons from a Small Country*. White River Junction, VT, Chelsea Green.

# INDEX

*Page numbers in italics refer to figures and tables.*

**Bobby Duffy**, one of the UK's most respected social researchers, is professor of public policy and director of the Policy Institute at King's College London. Duffy previously directed public affairs and global research at Ipsos MORI and the Ipsos Social Research Institute, which, among other initiatives, ran the world's largest study of public misperceptions. He is the author of *The Perils of Perception*, which was published as *Why We're Wrong About Nearly Everything* in the United States. His research has been covered in the *Washington Post, Economist, Financial Times, Wall Street Journal,* the *Guardian,* CNN, PBS, NBC, BBC, and elsewhere. He lives in London.